2

CW00832849

26/11

THE ATTACK ON MUMBAI

PENGUIN BOOKS

 Hindustan Times

PENGUIN BOOKS
Published by the Penguin Group
Penguin Books India Pvt. Ltd, 11 Community Centre, Panchsheel Park,
New Delhi 110 017, India
Penguin Group (USA) Inc., 375 Hudson Street, New York, New York 10014, USA
Penguin Group (Canada), 90 Eglinton Avenue East, Suite 700, Toronto,
Ontario, M4P 2Y3, Canada (a division of Pearson Penguin Canada Inc.)
Penguin Books Ltd, 80 Strand, London WC2R 0RL, England
Penguin Ireland, 25 St Stephen's Green, Dublin 2, Ireland
(a division of Penguin Books Ltd)
Penguin Group (Australia), 250 Camberwell Road, Camberwell,
Victoria 3124, Australia (a division of Pearson Australia Group Pty Ltd)
Penguin Group (NZ), 67 Apollo Drive, Rosedale, North Shore 0632,
New Zealand (a division of Pearson New Zealand Ltd)
Penguin Group (South Africa) (Pty) Ltd, 24 Sturdee Avenue, Rosebank,
Johannesburg 2196, South Africa

Penguin Books Ltd, Registered Offices: 80 Strand, London WC2R 0RL, England

First published by Penguin Books India 2009

Copyright © *Hindustan Times* 2009

10 9 8 7 6 5 4 3 2 1

The views and opinions expressed in this book are the contributors' own and the facts
are as reported by them which have been verified to the extent possible, and the
publishers are not in any way liable for the same.

ISBN 9780143067054

Typeset in Adobe Garamond by SÜRYA, New Delhi
Printed at De Unique, New Delhi

INTRODUCTION
Vir Sanghvi

SOMETIMES CRISES TELL us more about the victims than they do about the perpetrators. So it has been with the Bombay attacks of 26 November 2008. We know now that they were carried out by *jihadis* who were trained in Pakistan, possibly by official agencies. That is politically significant—at least in terms of international relations—but it is hardly a surprise. The same was true of the attack on Parliament a few years ago and of many other terrorist incidents. But the real lessons of the Bombay attacks emerge out of the Indian response. The way we have reacted holds up a mirror to our society and tells us something about our country and how it responds to hostility, aggression and pressure.

The Bombay incidents have caused so many debates within Indian society that it is hard to think of a contemporary parallel that has so provoked the Indian intelligentsia. There has been an outpouring of anger against the political establishment, a radicalisation—no matter how temporary—of the upper middle class, a rethinking of the we-all-want-peace attitude that characterised the educated Indian's response to Pakistan, a debate on the role of the media in times of crisis and the apparent sensationalism of television news, and a recognition of how vulnerable India and its civilians are to terrorist attacks.

In a sense it is surprising that the incidents in Bombay should have had such far-reaching consequences. India is no stranger to terrorist attacks. Nearly every month, bombs go off in some Indian town or the other. The predictability of the attacks has brutalised most of us. We are shocked for the first fifteen minutes after we hear of the bombings and then it is back to business as usual.

Even the attack on Parliament did not have the same impact on debate and discourse. The government of India, recognising that the intention of the terrorists had been to take the Cabinet hostage, reacted with anger and aggression. Thousands of troops were moved to the Pakistan border, war seemed imminent and, for the several months that Operation Parakram lasted, India spent crores of rupees hoping that Pakistan would blink. But neither did Pakistan blink—the confrontation just sort of faded away over time—nor did the Indian intelligentsia respond with the sort of outrage and soul-searching that resulted from the Bombay attacks.

■

Most nations react to terrorist attacks in a sadly predictable manner. Israel invades the West Bank. The United States threatens to get the perpetrators of the attack 'dead or alive'. The general wisdom is that the best way to take revenge on the terrorists and to reclaim national honour is to launch an attack using conventional forces and conventional weapons against the States that have either armed or harboured the terrorists. The US response to 9/11 was to launch an attack on Afghanistan in the hope of apprehending Osama bin Laden and effecting a regime change that unseated the barbaric Taliban government. The Indian response to the Parliament attack was to threaten Pakistan with war.

The interesting thing about the Bombay attacks is that in their immediate aftermath Indians seemed less interested in taking revenge on the terrorists or in going to war than in blaming ourselves, our government and our politicians. I can think of few societies where an attack—clearly planned and launched by a hostile neighbour—should not result in a desire for war. Instead, India spent its time working out what went wrong and in looking for those who failed in their duty to protect our cities and our civilians.

Some of this took the foreign press by surprise and perhaps it astonished foreign governments as well. If you go over the coverage of the attacks in British and American newspapers you will find that all the articles focussed on the imminent India–Pakistan war and, then, on the almost certain Hindu backlash that would lead to the targeting of local Muslims.

In fact, neither of these predictions came to pass. There was hardly any desire to 'punish' Pakistan—except perhaps for a few bimbos who were invited to TV studios—and few people saw

Indian Muslims as being associated with the terrorists or responsible in any way for the attacks.

What accounts for the uniqueness of the Indian response?

Everybody will have his or her own explanation. This is mine: Indians are used to terrorism. It no longer shocks us as it once did. Nor are we startled by the recognition that Pakistan might be involved. We have come to accept this as a part of our lives.

We are not like the United States before 9/11, secure in some cocoon, believing that nobody can touch us. We know that we are vulnerable. And we know that we have enemies who hate us with a mindless intensity. So we had none of the knee-jerk responses that Westerners have to terrorist incidents. We did not react with anger against the terrorists or seek to make scapegoats of Indian Muslims.

Instead, we asked a deeper question: if all of us already know that India is a prime terrorist target, then why, in God's name, did our government not make more of an effort to protect India's greatest city?

As it rapidly became clear that there was no good answer to this question, the anger grew and the debates raged.

■

The debate about governmental inaction still continues at some level. We know now that the Research and Analysis Wing (R&AW), India's external intelligence agency had intercepted communications from known terrorist leaders that hinted at an attack on Bombay. Some of the intercepts were even more specific. They talked about an attack on a hotel at a street where the Taj was the only major hotel. They talked about seaside targets. And, most damning of all, they even had an intercept from the terrorists on their boat as they sped towards Bombay.

This intelligence was buried somewhere within the bowels of the Indian intelligence system. It was not analysed in time and the warnings were not passed on. Had India's intelligence czars acted in time, the attacks could have been averted.

In any other country, heads would have rolled for such a lapse.

In India, on the other hand, no accountability has been fixed. Not one intelligence officer was sacked. And there has been no public apology for this glaring failure. There are problems with the chain of command as well. One of the most infuriating aspects of the way in which the authorities coped with the attack was how, for nearly ten hours, they did not cope at all.

When the terrorists first attacked the Taj Mahal hotel, the Bombay Police were informed. They concluded that the hotel was the centre of a gang war and entered its precincts with their weapons drawn. Shortly afterwards, they realised that they had got it badly wrong and withdrew. After that they refused to enter the hotel claiming that they were ill-equipped to take on terrorists armed with assault rifles and grenades. So, four terrorists who had taken no hostages wandered cheerfully around the Taj while the entire police force of Bombay skulked outside.

Desperate, some officials suggested that the armed forces be brought in. The army arrived in strength but its troops did no more than ring the Taj and the Oberoi hotels. They too lacked the expertise to fight terrorists. Eventually, somebody thought of the Indian navy's commandos.

The commandos arrived at the Taj but declared, in the finest traditions of Indian bureaucracy, that they would not enter the hotel unless they received a written request from the Maharashtra government.

While all this was going on, the fire brigade stood by arguing that it had no mandate to rescue people. The management of the Taj begged the firemen to rescue guests on the sixth floor, including the family of the Taj's general manager. The fire brigade shrugged its shoulders. It had to be given permission, it said.

But who would give it permission? The police, who had abdicated responsibility? The army, which was not fully in charge? Or the navy, whose commandos were waiting for their invitation in triplicate?

By the time this was sorted out and the fire brigade moved in, the guests on the sixth floor—including the Taj's manager's wife and young children—were dead.

The story of ineptitude and confusion does not end there. It is still not clear whether the navy's commandos engaged the terrorists at all. They certainly did not manage to wound a single one of them at the Taj. At the Oberoi, it now seems, the terrorists commandeered a room and slept the night in a comfortable bed knowing they were in no danger.

It was only when the National Security Guards (NSG) arrived from Delhi the following morning that the operation began in earnest. By then the terrorists were fully in control.

And even then the confusion on the ground continued. Various army generals continued to address the press, sometimes providing information that was simply wrong ('there's only one terrorist and he's wounded'—actually there were three firing at the NSG) or, at other times, acting as though they were in charge which they were not.

Most shameful of all was the role of the navy. Even while the operation was in progress and NSG officers were fighting for their lives, the navy's commandos—an allegedly secret force—held a bizarre televised press conference in which they bragged about non-existent achievements and provided lots of misinformation (the terrorists have ID cards from Mauritius, etc.).

In the circumstances, can it be a surprise that it took so long to clear the Taj and the Oberoi of a relatively small number of terrorists?

Of course there were individual acts of bravery. An inspector of the Gamdevi police station pounced on Ajmal Kasab, one of the terrorists, and would not let go even though six bullets were shot into his body. The inspector died, but his sacrifice ensured that Kasab was captured alive and the plot behind the attacks unravelled.

■

All this is reason enough to be angry. But public anger was not directed towards the intelligence officials and armed forces' chiefs who were responsible for so many of the screw-ups. Instead, the Bombay middle class went for the politicians.

It was all the fault of India's corrupt politicians, we were told again and again. They should all resign. They should apologise. They should eat dirt. And so on.

Some of the anger was justified. As the crisis unfolded, the politicians were hardly reassuring and few of them seemed in control. Many were also responsible for the misjudgements that led to the crisis. Why should the NSG be based only in Delhi? Why shouldn't the force have a designated plane? Why should it take so long to send commandos to India's premier city? Why were the local police so badly equipped? Why had nobody provided funds for better bullet-proof vests and assault rifles? Why had the police force been systematically weakened through political interference and favouritism?

And yet it is hard to deny that some of the anger was also unjustified. Politicians make for easy targets when the middle class is doing the shooting. In Bombay, the upper middle class is well off and generally contemptuous of politicians who do not speak good English or do not belong to India's cities. This class finds it much easier to identify with the armed forces and the bureaucracy. The generals speak good English. Top policemen have been to the best colleges. India's spymasters have travelled the world and can parley on equal terms with Bombay's sophisticates.

Plus there's the whole issue of universal franchise. Among the uglier moments on the sidelines of the crisis was when assorted Bombay socialites went on TV to declare how unfair it was that they should be subjected to terrorist attacks when they paid so much in taxes. Surely, that entitled them to something better?

From that basic grudge, there flowed a litany of idiotic suggestions. The people of Bombay should stop paying taxes. India should be handed over to the army. We should recall our politicians. Democracy had failed. The police force should be privatised.

It was the anger of disenfranchised affluence. South Bombay may well be India's Manhattan as some of its socialites claim. But when it comes to democracy, all of the beautiful people in Bombay cannot swing the mandate in a single Assembly seat.

So the anger against politicians was born out of frustration, out of a sense of having no control. And the reason why the policemen, officials and officers got off so easy was because they were, at the end of the day, people like us.

∎

Have we learnt anything from the Bombay crisis? In some ways, I think we have. Perhaps for the first time in the history of independent India, politicians were sacked in response to public anger. The chief minister and deputy chief minister of Maharashtra were driven from office. The home minister of India was forced to put in his papers.

I am not sure that this means that Bombay is much safer now but it does demonstrate that the political system is responsive to public anger. At least some of the criticisms of the anti-terrorist response have had some effect. The NSG now has a designated plane. The government has announced plans to increase the strength of the NSG and to establish centres in major Indian cities. There is some talk of a new intelligence body that will coordinate and analyse all the information that has been gathered.

As significant has been the change in public attitudes to Pakistan. In the week before the Bombay attacks, Indians had been encouraged by the new Pakistan President Asif Zardari's claim that he desired good relations with India and that he acknowledged our shared heritage. Few Indians take Zardari seriously any longer. Even if he was sincere it is clear that civilian governments count for nothing in Pakistan. It is the army and the *jihadi*s who call the shots. And as long as they are in charge India will always be under threat.

But there's something encouraging about the absence of public anger. The Parliament attack was followed by sabre-rattling and troop movements. Even then, despite the threat of war, Pakistan refused to acknowledge that the attack had been planned on its soil. This time around, the government of India forced Pakistan to acknowledge the role of its citizens without moving a single Indian soldier or firing a single bullet. Sometimes a cool head achieves more than the marching of many battalions.

There have been other positive effects. The public backlash against the television channels over their coverage of the crisis has led to a great deal of soul-searching within the media. The threat of governmental regulation (since dropped) has caused the channels to evolve their own internal code of conduct.

■

And yet, I wonder how much things have really changed. The radicalisation of the Bombay middle class has disappeared almost as quickly as it began. Public anger has not led to very many other long-term positive consequences. Nor did it help that the debate was conducted at the level of 'we hate these bloody politicians anyway' on most TV channels. Nor am I at all convinced that the structural weaknesses that were exposed by the crisis have been attended to. The intelligence agencies are in as much of a mess as they were last year. R&AW is demoralised and the Intelligence Bureau is politicised and divided.

The NSG is the one force which emerged with credit from the crisis. But nothing has changed with the police, and nor can it as long as the present system continues. Since the attacks, the director general of the Maharashtra Police at the time of the terrorist incidents has been forced to step down by the courts because a colleague filed a petition alleging favouritism in promotion. This kind of jostling, accompanied by needless sucking up to politicians, continues to characterise the force. This hardly makes for a crack anti-terrorist outfit.

Nor is it clear that the armed forces have understood how the chain of command works. Chastened by the reprimands delivered by the Defence Ministry over his commandos and their lust for publicity, the naval chief has become an unguided missile attacking everybody else and accepting no responsibility. Even the army is reluctant to work under the command of an NSG officer.

So yes, if terrorists try and attack Bombay again, they won't find it that easy. But my guess is that they won't find it that difficult either.

THE ATTACK

DAY 1

In flames and fighting
Team *HT*

Mumbai, November 27: INDIA ON THURSDAY woke up to its bloodiest *fidayeen* (suicide squad) attack. The series of attacks in south Mumbai late on Wednesday unfolded into a hostage crisis on Thursday as militants holed up at two iconic hotels—the Trident and the Taj—and at Nariman House, a building on Colaba Causeway that houses a few Jewish families, dug their heels in for a 24-hour standoff. As the army, navy and National Security Guards engaged the militants in a day-long gunbattle, the death count rose to 127 and the number of injured to 327. Victims included seven foreigners and 14 policemen. At the time of going of press at midnight, security forces were locked in fierce battles with the terrorists at all three spots. By evening, 12 militants had been shot dead, officials said. Three were arrested, among them one identified only as 'Ismail' from Faridkot in Pakistan. Chief Minister Vilasrao Deshmukh said: 'We think 20 to 25 terrorists are involved in the operation.' Officials could not say if any of the militants had got away. Following the discovery of two boats at Cuffe Parade and Sassoon Dock, two ships, *MV Alpha* and *Al Kabir*, were intercepted. 'Navy personnel are questioning the crew and verifying their documents,' a Defence Ministry spokesperson said. *MV Alpha* is registered in Panama and arrived in Mumbai from Karachi. The Mumbai Police can begin investigation only after all hostages are freed. So far, 242 people have been able to come out of the three sites. 'We can start the probe once the National Security Guards completes its operation,' Patil said. 'The Anti-terrorism Squad will then start investigations.' Deshmukh said: 'We still don't know which group—international or otherwise—is behind this, or the terrorists' nationality. Our priority is to rescue people from these three sites.' Major General R.K. Hooda, General Officer Commanding (Maharashtra, Gujarat and Goa), said: 'The language spoken by terrorists (during their phone call to a TV channel) is similar to Punjabi. Involvement from across the border cannot be ruled out.' Pakistan has denied any involvement in the attacks.

As the battles raged in south Mumbai, the city—shocked and scared—stayed in. Stock markets and educational institutions were shut and many companies declared a holiday. In the evening, PM Manmohan Singh and Congress chief Sonia Gandhi visited JJ Hospital. Later, US President George W. Bush called Singh to offer support. An upset Ratan Tata, chairman of the Tata group, which owns the Taj, criticised the government: 'We had a bomb blast some years ago. We should have learnt to get a crisis infrastructure in place that could snap to attention as soon as something happened.' The Board of Control for Cricket in India called off the remaining two one-day matches between India and England.■

When terror walked into CST
Rajendra Aklekar

Mumbai, November 27: IT TOOK TWO armed terrorists to belie the tall claims made by the Railways and their security agencies. Over 109 security personnel were stationed at Chhatrapati Shivaji Terminus (CST) on Wednesday night when two terrorists entered the station premises, firing and lobbing hand grenades indiscriminately. The security personnel were from the Railway Protection Force (RPF), Government Railway Police, Railway Protection Special Force and Home Guards.

'The Railways security cannot open fire indiscriminately, as it could hit passengers,' said Central Railways Chief Public Relations Officer S.C. Mudgerikar. Images of the terrorists were captured on the 30 closed circuit television cameras installed at CST. The footage has not been opened. It will now be sealed by the Railways administration. 'The tapes will be handed over to the Anti-terrorism Squad (ATS),' said a top Railways official. In the melée, three security officials lost their lives. Five Railways employees died and seven others were injured. Mukesh Agrawal, an employee of a food outlet at CST, tried calling up his friends as an unexploded grenade landed near his stall. 'Nobody could come to his rescue,' said director of the food stall, Pankaj Goel. Agrawal has been admitted to Bombay Hospital.

Railways announcer V.D. Zende could see the drama unfold from his strategic position, though he was out of everyone's sight. Without waiting for orders, Zende made announcements asking the public from trains pulling into CST, telling them not to get down. 'He ended up saving many lives,' said Mudgerikar. The terrorists did shoot in his direction, but he escaped unhurt.

The terrorists lobbed three hand grenades in the outstation terminus lobby, two of which were rendered ineffective by the bomb disposal squad, said a Railways security official.

'Nobody knows exactly how many died at CST though 56 people were injured at CST,' said another official. On Thursday, train services returned to normal. Meanwhile, CST, a UNESCO-listed World Heritage site is now riddled with bullet marks. Curious onlookers and commuters were seen taking pictures of the bullet holes on their cell phone cameras—a mute remembrance of a terror-filled night.■

Taxi with bomb jumped signal, saving many lives
Debasish Panigrahi

Mumbai, November 27: AN OLD HABIT taxi drivers in the city find difficult to kill, jumping signals, saved hundreds of lives on the Western Express Highway on Wednesday. Around 10 p.m. on that day a bomb in a taxi turned the car into a fireball, but only after the driver had begun moving at a red light a few seconds before it would have turned green, a traffic constable said on Thursday.

Posted at the signal immediately after the under-construction airport flyover in Vile Parle, the traffic policeman saw the blast that was part of the string of terror strikes in the city just yards from where it happened. 'Had the explosion occurred in the stationary taxi, hundreds would have been killed,' said the constable, who did not wish to be named while the operations against terrorists holed up in other places were still on. The intensity of the blast can be gauged from the fact that the taxi was twisted into a mangled heap of metal and the driver, identified as Mohammad Umer, had his head blown off at least 100 metres away from the spot. Umer had halted the vehicle near the signal when it was red.

'The road was choc-a-bloc with vehicles,' the constable said. 'Hundreds of pedestrians were crossing the road as the walker signal was on. Seconds before the signal turned green, the taxi driver accelerated the vehicle. Then the bomb went off, but the trailing vehicles were at least 15–20 metres behind. This is why there were no casualties, other than the taxi driver and the passenger inside.' The blast shattered the windshields of several vehicles coming from the opposite direction and created a deep crater in the multi-layer, steel-strengthened asphalt road. ■

Battle rages at Taj, hostages still trapped in scarred hotel
Stavan Desai

Mumbai, November 27: INDIAN COMMANDOS CONTINUED to fight four terrorists inside the Taj Mahal Palace & Tower, a full 24 hours after the terrorists stormed the luxury hotel, located just a 100 metres away from the iconic Gateway of India in south Mumbai. Although Maharashtra Director General of Police A.N. Roy told reporters that by late Thursday afternoon everyone trapped inside the hotel had been evacuated, including people taken hostage by the four militants. But a highly placed security source told *Hindustan Times* (*HT*) that hostages remained inside. 'About 50 people are still under the control of the militants,' said the source, who declined to be identified.

The militants entered the hotel at 9.30 p.m. on Wednesday and opened fire on the ground floor, inaugurating a night of terror for the at least 250 people that security officials estimated were trapped inside the hotel. They included tens of foreigners. Through the night, the militants wreaked havoc on the beautiful hotel, setting fire to three places, periodically setting off explosions and firing their weapons.

The Taj was just one of several high-profile locations in south Mumbai that the *fidayeen* (suicide squad) attacked on Wednesday night in the worst terror strike this city has seen. They seem to have deliberately targeted places with high concentrations of Westerners. About eight to ten people died in the Taj attack, according to Ravindra Singh, a chef at the hotel who had left early that day. 'We were all taking it pretty easy until the dome exploded,' said Bhisham Mansukhani, 31, a journalist who was attending a friend's reception in the hotel when the terrorists attacked. 'We were packed in a narrow passageway and the slightest panic could have created a stampede,' he said. 'The closest I came to the attackers was when this man running ahead of me was shot. I thought we were gone.' Mansukhani was evacuated at 9 a.m. on Thursday. 'None of us were convinced we were safe until we had reached the police station,' he said.

The National Security Guards (NSG) and naval commandos stormed the hotel at 6.30 a.m. on Thursday. At 3.30 a.m., there was a huge explosion at the dome, shattering window panes and setting fire to the topmost, fifth floor. According to the police, the serial attacks began with firing at Leopold Café at 9.15 p.m. About 15 minutes later, four *fidayeen* stormed into the Taj, opened fire in the Shamiana café on the ground floor, then went to the swimming pool area and threw a hand grenade. From there, they went up to the rooms and started locking people in.■

'Nothing to worry about. The first bullet will go through me'

Parizaad Khan

THE EVENING STARTED rather innocuously at the Taj Mahal Palace & Tower's Crystal Room, with a glass of juice. We got there at 9.30 p.m., for the wedding reception of a friend. At the Crystal Room in the old wing, we met friends and got our drinks. We hadn't been there 15 minutes when we heard sounds we dismissed as construction work or crackers. When the boom-boom went on and got nearer, it was apparent they were neither. The staff had secured the doors by now. We were planning our next move when a window shattered, and shots rang through. Instinctively, we ducked and crouching, made our way to the service door, which led to an alcove. Then we were ushered by the staff through corridors, kitchens and other areas till we reached Chambers, an elite club.

The staff kept ushering new refugees in, and soon the place was full—there were probably 300 people there. The doors were locked and the staircase and elevator secured, we were told. By then we'd stopped hearing gunfire and felt safer. Phone calls coming in confirmed many places in the city had been similarly targeted.

That's when the Taj staff kicked in. Crates of water bottles came in, followed by tins of potato chips and trays of sandwiches and canapés. Soon, we had towels and crisp sheets. Though we were frightened—by now we'd heard a few blasts and rumours that the heritage dome had exploded—we weren't really in fear of our lives. The cops and special forces had come to the building, we were told, and everything would be cleaned up soon. At no point did we see the gunmen. We soon heard whispers that we were going to be evacuated. Media friends on the outside started sending messages that the ATS had arrived, the army had arrived. It was probably 3 a.m. when we gathered at the service door and were asked to be silent. It was a crush as everyone wanted to be first to

8

be out, but it was also orderly and people didn't panic. I was probably in the fourth or fifth bunch of people to be evacuated. About ten of us were led into a narrow corridor. That's when it got chaotic. In the corridor, we were fired at. We couldn't tell where the shots came from, but they were close. We turned and ran back inside. There was almost a stampede situation.

After half an hour, we heard gunfire from the corridor outside. Everyone flattened themselves to the ground. The floor was a tangle of bodies and limbs. The lights were off. We stayed that way till morning. Dawn broke but still no word. We heard from phone calls that the rest of the building had been evacuated. At 8.30 a.m., a commando rushed in. We were asked to line up. Just then, some commotion caused us to panic—I can't remember if it was more shots but someone shouted get down, and we all dived. 'I want you all to stay calm. Listen to me, there is nothing to worry about. The first bullet will go through me, I'm leading you out,' the commando said. We got back up and stepped out into a corridor. We walked down a flight of stairs and through corridors, into the lobby and were finally led out into the sunshine on the porch.

But it wasn't over yet. As a cop van and BEST bus pulled up and people started getting in, shots rang out at the vehicles from the hotel. Some gunmen were still inside. We all ran back to the lobby doors, but there was not much fear; the presence of the commandos and other personnel gave us courage. My friend and I were soon put into a BEST bus. Some of us didn't lift our heads till we got to Azad Maidan police station. We heard later that many police personnel and hotel staff had lost their lives. We're probably alive because of them.■

It's gunshots and grenades at Oberoi
Presley Thomas & Gigil Varghese (Inputs from Barney Henderson, Riddhi Shah & Manish Pachouly)

Mumbai, November 27: THE OBEROI TRIDENT hotel witnessed a fierce gun battle for over three hours on Thursday evening as

National Security Guards, army personnel and police commandos tried to flush out the terrorists and rescue hostages. Around 9.15 p.m., the marine commandos pulled out of Oberoi. Defence spokesperson Captain M. Nambiar said the NSG could handle the rest of the operations. The exchange of fire left at least one person and two marine commandos injured. One of them is critical but out of danger, said defence spokesperson Captain M. Nambiar. According to an ATS officer, two NSG commandos and 25 army personnel were injured. Thirty-nine people were rescued on Thursday evening. The security personnel cleared one floor after the other. Twenty-seven cabin crew members of Lufthansa airlines trapped in the hotel since Wednesday also had a narrow escape though one of them suffered injuries. Major General R.K. Hooda, GOC, Maharashtra, Gujarat and Goa area, said there were 10 to 12 terrorists—five or six at the Taj, two or three at Nariman House and the remaining at the Oberoi. 'We suspect there were two militants in the room where hand grenades were lobbed and a fire broke out,' said Hooda. 'However, this can be confirmed only after operation is over.' Actor Ashish Chowdhary was waiting outside the Oberoi since his sister (he did not wish to reveal her name) was trapped inside since Wednesday night. Activity at the Oberoi started at 6 a.m. on Thursday with nearly 300 NSG commandos entering the building. Security personnel, gauging that the terrorists were trying to buy time, were rescuing hostages on one hand and engaging terrorists in exchange of fire on the other to exhaust their ammunition. Outside, crowds gathered to witness the battle, cheered marine commandos entering the hotel with chants of '*Vande Mataram*', '*Ganpati Bappa Morya*' and '*Jai Hind*'. Around 2.50 p.m., four hand grenades were lobbed inside the hotel and the NSG and terrorists exchanged fire behind the Oberoi. NSG personnel checked each room and opened windows to signal to their colleagues below that the room was sanitised. At around 3.35, security forces zeroed in on the terrorists' location. They were hiding in the corner most room on the last but third floor of the building. Nearly 28 rounds were fired in a span of 45 minutes.■

Jewish centre under siege

Sayli Udas Mankikar & Kanchan Chaudhari

Mumbai, November 27: A FULL 24 hours after terrorists seized Nariman House in Colaba, several police personnel and over 100 commandos were preparing to strike to rescue the captives. Nariman House is the headquarters of the orthodox Jewish outreach group, Chabad-Lubavitch, in Mumbai. Eight Israelis were taken hostage, said the group's spokesman Moni Ender from Israel. Three were later released. Security personnel said there were five terrorists in the house who had killed five people. An eerie silence prevailed in the evening after intermittent rounds of firing till 5.30 p.m. Police sources said that a Jewish priest, Rabbi Gavriel Holtzberg, his wife Rivka and three guests were held captive. In the morning, terrorists had let the priest's one-year-old son and maid and a 16-year-old boy leave.

Hanif Shaikh, a resident of a nearby building, said that around 9.20 p.m. on Wednesday four men hurled a grenade at a nearby petrol pump, before running into Nariman House at around 10 p.m. Before that they killed two members of a Muslim family in the nearby 'Colaba Court' building. After remaining silent through the night, the terrorists surfaced again at around 7 a.m. in the morning and held people hostage. One of the terrorists, 25-year-old Imran Babar, within the house had called up a news channel. He said that the Indian army should withdraw from Kashmir and let the Shariah prevail in the Muslim-dominated region. 'The Israelis too have hurt Muslims. We will release the hostages. Ask the government to talk to us,' he said. 'And convey what we have told you to your government, our government and the Israeli government,' he added.

The world seemed to be coming together to help the people being held hostage in Nariman House. An official statement in a Jewish journal says: 'Chabad-Lubavitch representatives in New York and Israel are working alongside the Israeli Foreign Ministry, the US Consulate in Mumbai and a volunteer team of local residents to ascertain the well being of the Holtzbergs and other Jews in the area.'∎

Terrorists in for the long haul: Cops
HT Correspondent (Inputs from Vijaita Singh)

Mumbai, November 27: DEPUTY CHIEF MINISTER R.R. Patil, who also heads the Home department, said the Anti-terrorism Squad would investigate the multiple terror attacks once the National Security Guards completed operations at the Taj and Oberoi Trident hotels and Nariman House. K.P. Raghuvanshi, current Director General of Police (Railways), will temporarily head the ATS, Patil said.

Central security officials said the tactic used by the terrorists at the Taj and Oberoi was an old modus operandi. After security forces storm the area, the terrorists buy time and wait for nightfall. During the day, they stand the chance of revealing themselves. Since Wednesday night, they have set fire to the hotel thrice to divert the attention of security forces, officials added. 'This is going to be a long night,' an official admitted. The terrorists were prepared for a long haul, said a senior intelligence official. The official said the police had recovered bags of dry fruits from the terrorists killed at the Trident, enough to last them a few days, besides AK-47 and AK-56 assault rifles, hand grenades and several hundred rounds of ammunition. This isn't the first time that terrorists have been found with dry fruits. Terrorists who had stormed into Parliament on December 13, 2001 also carried dry fruits in their 'survival kit'. Meanwhile, Chief Minister Deshmukh said that in the face of such unprecedented attacks, the government was looking at setting up a separate mechanism for tackling terror with special commandos, coastal security and intelligence officers. The special cell of the Delhi Police is providing vital inputs to the Mumbai Police, sources said. 'The terrorists (in the two hotels) were in touch with each other through phones and we got valuable information about their next move,' said a senior Delhi Police officer. 'We are sharing minute-to-minute details with the Mumbai Police,' said Karnal Singh, Joint Commissioner of Police (Northern Range).■

Lashkar is the prime suspect

Stavan Desai, Aloke Tikku, Aurangzeb Naqshbandi & Chetan Chauhan

Mumbai/New Delhi, November 27: THE TERROR ATTACKS in Mumbai bear all the hallmarks of the Lashkar-e-Tayyeba (LeT). They were similar to the attack on the Akshardham temple on September 24, 2002, the one in Ayodhya on July 5, 2005, and the one at the RSS headquarters in Nagpur on June 2, 2006—all handiwork of the Lashkar, which has been inspired by al-Qaeda. All the attacks were carried out by highly motivated, trained men in the 20- to 25-year age group. The attackers in all the cases were armed with Kalashnikov assault rifles and grenades. Security personnel said the militants were eating little, consuming mainly almonds, dates and chocolates—as in the previous attacks. These are all typical of the Lashkar, which carried out the hijacking of Indian Airlines flight IC 814 from Kathmandu to Kandahar.

In Delhi, leaders of India's security establishment too insisted the terrorists in Mumbai were Lashkar members operating out of Pakistan. There were intelligence inputs that about a dozen terrorists travelled by sea to Gujarat two days ago and used a fishing vessel to get close to Mumbai. 'They then took a motor boat to reach Colaba,' a senior Home Ministry official said. Special Secretary at the Home Ministry M.L. Kumawat said the terrorists passed through a fishing colony before going to south Mumbai. 'This is not a splinter group like the Indian Mujahideen or one which calls itself Deccan Mujahideen. Given how they targeted Britons and Americans, it seems to be a Qaeda-inspired affair,' an Intelligence official said. Navy officers too said this. 'A mother ship or a dhow appears to have ferried them to a point from where they boarded inflatable boats that can carry about ten people and run on petrol,' a naval officer said. The Lashkar denied involvement. Spokesman Abdullah Gaznavi said the Lashkar didn't operate outside Kashmir.■

Hospitals no sanctuary in time of terror
Team *HT* (Reporting by Neha Bhayana, Alifiya Khan & Chitrangada Choudhury)

Mumbai, November 27: THE STREETS WERE silent and shops shut, but while the city holed up at home, victims and their relatives poured into major city hospitals, especially in south Mumbai. JJ Hospital was the busiest, with a death count of 17 and 127 injured. At every hospital, the scene was morbidly similar. Frantic people searching for loved ones, harried doctors who hadn't slept a wink since the attack, queues outside operation theatres and that quiet corner where a family was told its son, daughter or father was no more.

At Gokuldas Tejpal Hospital at Dhobi Talao, victims of firing, dead and injured, were brought in all night. These included victims from Colaba, the Taj hotel's staff and policemen in the line of duty. Policemen watched in tears as the bodies of their colleagues in blood-splattered uniforms were brought in. These included the bodies of Vijay Salaskar, his driver Constable Arun Chitte, Constable Vijay Khandekar and Police Sub-Inspector Pradip More. Hospital staff said most of these officers were brought in dead.

Three staff of GT Hospital were also killed by gunmen who opened fire indiscriminately at the staff quarters. The dead included Thakur Wagle (31), a support staff member posted at the OPD who was on night shift on Wednesday night and had gone to the staff quarters. 'We were all eating and talking in groups on the pavement around 10.30 p.m. when two gunmen dressed in blue and black with jackets and big guns burst onto the scene and began firing,' said Thakur's younger brother Bharat, outside the hospital's morgue. 'We rushed into our homes and bolted the doors, and some minutes later my brother's son came rushing to say his father has been shot badly. We ran and brought his bloodied body here, but he was already dead.'

14

At St. George Hospital, close to several shooting sites, many casualties were reported. Police Constable N.B. Gawane (58) was on his usual patrolling duty near the Taj hotel on Wednesday night. After he got an anonymous call on his wireless saying gunshots had been heard near Leopold Café in Colaba, he rushed to the spot. 'I got shot several times in my leg. I am lucky to have survived as two bullets got stuck in the metal badge of my belt,' said Gawane, who is currently recuperating at JJ Hospital.

A taxi driver and a passenger lost their lives and two passersby suffered injuries when terrorists blew up a taxi on the Western Expressway in Vile Parle on Wednesday night. The injured identified as Bal Krishna Bare (40) and Shyamsunder Chaudhary (40) were admitted to Cooper Hospital with severe injuries on the shoulder and face.■

Pain echoes across Mumbai, hospitals grapple with crisis
Alifiya Khan & Chitrangada Choudhury

Mumbai, November 27: THE HOSPITALS OF south Mumbai reverberated through Wednesday night and Thursday morning with the anguished cries of devastated relatives of those killed in the city's worst terrorist attack. St. George Hospital, near the Chhatrapati Shivaji Terminus, where terrorists opened fire at random on Wednesday night, saw the largest number of casualties—officials said that about 78 dead bodies and 103 injured had been brought there. The bodies have been shifted to JJ, KEM and Nair hospitals for conducting post mortems, and some injured were also shifted to these hospitals. 'Most of the injured who have shifted to JJ Hospital have head injuries, bullet wounds and amputations,' said Sudesh Stalian, medical officer of St. George. 'We did not have the capacity to treat them.' Out of the total dead, there were four foreigners, including one Australian identified as Brad Wilberd Taylor (49) and Tim Murphy, a UK citizen. The dead included at least two children.

A taxi driver Mohammed Israel Ansari was making rounds of

the JJ Hospital to locate his 17-year-old son, who has been missing since last night. Ansari, a resident of Tardeo, said that he had gone to leave his family of ten at the station to catch a train to Bihar. 'After I left them I went to the parking area. I then heard bullet sounds. I ducked, but when I ran to locate my family I saw six of them dead and two with bullet wounds, but since last night I have not been able to locate Murtuza,' said Ansari, weeping for his son.

Janardan Chitekar, a migrant labourer, lost his daughter Deepali and son Rajesh in the attack. Chitekar, a native of Buldhana in Maharashtra, had called his children to the city for the first time as they were having Diwali vacations. 'After leaving them at the station with their uncle to go back, I heard gunshots. When I rushed inside I could not find them. After I located my brother-in-law and enquired about my children, I saw my son's dead body lying on the St. George Hospital floor. But I had no time to look at him as I am still trying to locate my daughter,' he said.∎

Email warns of more strikes
Abhishek Sharan

New Delhi, November 27: *'CHETAWANI NAHIN, HAQIQAT* [Not (just) a warning, but reality]'—this was the title of the two-page terror email that has been sent to the media by a group calling itself Deccan Mujahideen. The email was sent a few hours after the terror attacks began in Mumbai on Wednesday night.

The email, of which *Hindustan Times* has a copy, has been composed in flawed Hindi (liberally interspersed with chaste Urdu and Punjabi words) and makes disparaging remarks on India, and Hindus in particular. Flaunting rhetorical flourish, the email warns of continuous terror attacks till 'we show the Hindus their (actual) *auqaat* (status) . . . Till Muslims in India get to live according to Quran Hadith (Quran's principles) [in] a free Islamic State . . . Till we avenge each atrocity (perpetrated on Muslims) and each drop (of blood shed by Muslims)'. Intelligence Bureau (IB) officials said the name of the group seemed 'fake', though they were taking its content 'seriously'. 'We suspect with the kind of Hindi they have used, and the mindset of the email, that it shows a Pakistani, Punjabi or Pashtu linkage. But we are inspecting if the language is akin to the kind spoken in Kashmir.' Issuing a dire warning to the 'Indian government', the terror document read: 'We today warn the Indian government that it should end its series of atrocities on Muslims, it should return to them their states . . . We know Hindus belong to a race of *baniya*s (shopkeepers) who only take (what is owed to them), but never give back. 'But the Hindu *baniya* should know that we are a *qaum* (community) that never forgets its history and in fact repeats its history.' It warns India against ignoring its warnings, saying 'our warnings prove correct, you have seen a live example in Mumbai'.

The email also swears of incessant terror attacks in the name of a few of its role models who do not seem to be Indians—like 'Ummer Farokh Raji', 'Abu Baqar Siddiq Raji', 'Usman Raji' and 'Khalid Bin Walid Raji'.

Excerpts from the email

Today, we alert the Indian government with a warning that it should stop its atrocities perpetrated on the Muslims. It should return to the Muslims the states that were snatched from the community. It should pay, with interest, the cost of atrocities. We know that the Hindu race is of the baniya (shopkeepers), which only takes accounts (of what may be owed to them) but never gives accounts (of what it may owe to others). But the Hindu baniya should know that we are a community that never forgets its history; it repeats its history . . . Recent proof are in Iraq, Afghanistan, . . . and Kashmir. You've done what you could; we tolerated what we had to because of our inactive leaders and clergy. But now it's our chance. We'll play this innings in a manner in which Allah has instructed us.■

Police ignored warnings on threats of terror from the sea
Abhishek Sharan

New Delhi, November 27: WEDNESDAY'S DEADLY ATTACK in Mumbai has demonstrated the shoddiness of the country's existing coastal security framework despite repeated threats of terror from the sea. The latest terror attack on Mumbai has left officials of the central Intelligence Bureau fuming. Despite the IB repeatedly warning the Maharashtra Police and the ATS over the past few years to prepare against terror from the sea, there is little on the ground to indicate any effective coastal patrolling, claimed a senior IB officer. The state police still depend on a few boats to patrol the shore sometimes, he pointed out.

In January 2007, *Hindustan Times* was the first to report an IB alert sent to the Maharashtra Police, about Lashkar-e-Tayyeba's plan to send its operatives to Mumbai via the sea using 'fishing boats/dhows'. Pakistan's ISI had allegedly trained the operatives, along with the Pakistani navy, to carry out terror attacks in 'Mumbai and Delhi, aiming at securing the forcible release of Afzal Guru, accused in the 2001 Parliament attack case'. Only four weeks later, the eight-man team arrived in Mumbai from Karachi. Three of them—Mohammed Zameer, Mohammed Zuber and Abdul Majid—were arrested in Kashmir. They had allegedly claimed before Maharashtra ATS interrogators that they had bribed a coast guard patrol vessel's ship's captain, who intercepted them, to reach Mumbai. The then Maharashtra Director General of Police P.S. Pasricha, when asked, had, however, said the 'bribery' allegations were probed but could not be verified.■

Attack a failure of customs, coast guard
Manish Pachouly

Mumbai, November 27: THE TERROR ATTACKS across Mumbai are being considered a joint failure of the customs, coast guard and police. The three agencies have been jointly patrolling the seas after the 1993 serial blasts in Mumbai. But the terrorists managed to enter with heavy arms and ammunition. Police officials said that about 20 terrorists came through the sea route in boats. They entered the city from the shores at Sassoon Dock (in Colaba) and Badhwar Park (near Cuffe Parade) on Wednesday. Officials added that the terrorists came from the direction of Gujarat. Indian agencies were on Thursday questioning crew members of merchant vessel *Alfa* and another vessel, *Matara*, both reported to have come from Karachi. The terrorists disembarked from the vessel mid-sea and entered Mumbai in boats. Senior customs officials were in closed-door meetings on Thursday following the failure to trace the terrorists while they were entering the city. Attempts to contact Customs Commissioner (Preventive) Shobha Ram were futile. Questions are now being raised as to why the vessel carrying terrorists was not tracked as it entered Indian territory.■

We'll go after them . . . make sure they pay a price: PM
Nandini R. Iyer

New Delhi, November 27: IN AN EXTRAORDINARILY harsh stance, Prime Minister Manmohan Singh in an address to the nation made it clear that neighbouring nations would have to face a 'cost' if they allowed their territory to be used to launch attacks on India. Singh, who has been moderate in his speeches so far, said: 'We will take up strongly with our neighbours that the use of their territory for launching attacks on us will not be tolerated, and that there would be a cost if suitable measures are not taken by them.'

Asserting that India would not countenance such attacks, the prime minister said the government would 'restrict entry of suspects into the country'. 'We will go after these individuals and organisations and make sure that every perpetrator, organiser and supporter of terror, whatever his affiliation or religion may be, pays a heavy price,' he said. The prime minister announced that the government would immediately set up a Federal Investigation

Agency to look into terrorist crimes. 'Instruments like the National Security Act will be employed to deal with situations of this kind and existing laws will be tightened to ensure that there are no loopholes available to terrorists to escape the clutches of the law.' Describing the attacks as 'well-planned and well-orchestrated, probably with external linkages', Singh said, 'It is evident that the group which carried out these attacks, based outside the country, had come with single-minded determination to create havoc in the commercial capital.' Promising that his government would 'attend in an urgent and serious manner to police reform', the prime minister said India would not countenance a situation in which the safety and security of citizens could be violated with impunity by terrorists. 'We are determined to take whatever measures are necessary to ensure the safety and security of our citizens.'■

When politics took a backseat, foes joined hands
Shekhar Iyer & Saroj Nagi

New Delhi, November 27: FOR ONCE, POLITICS took a backseat as the government and the party in opposition, BJP, spoke along the same lines, sending out messages of unity and resolving to combat terrorism in the wake of the Mumbai attacks. 'No politics and no blame game for now' was their response on Thursday to the events in Mumbai, described as India's worst terror attack. Prime Minister Manmohan Singh and leader of opposition L.K. Advani spoke at least thrice since Wednesday night, when the first reports of the attacks came in. BJP president Rajnath Singh said his party was with the government 'at this hour' on the challenge posed by the terrorists. Party leader Arun Jaitley said, 'We think the government knows best how to handle the crisis now.'

For her part, Congress chief Sonia Gandhi said the terror attacks in Mumbai would be met with 'resolutely' and the country would defeat the threat posed by the enemies of the nation. Since the party had been under opposition fire until now—in the run up to the assembly elections in six states—for soft-pedalling the terror issue, Congress sources spoke of using the Parliament session starting December 10 to convey the country's resolve to unitedly fight terror. The session could also be used to make a case for a federal anti-terror agency and strengthen anti-terror laws, a major demand of the opposition parties. In the morning, Advani accepted the PM's invitation to join him for a visit to Mumbai. Later, when he was told Singh might not travel immediately, Advani informed him that he and Jaswant Singh would go ahead and visit the wounded and families of those killed in Mumbai. In the evening, Singh flew down separately with Sonia and SP's Amar Singh.

'I am traumatised by the events in Mumbai since last night,' Advani said. 'The terrorists have declared a full-scale war on India and seek to sever the country's economic nerve with their meticulously planned carnage across the metropolis.' He emphasised that the entire country should stay united and calm. Advani paid tributes to ATS chief Hemant Karkare and other police officers who lost their lives. RSS chief K. Sudarshan too praised Karkare and appealed for calm and unity. Sonia sent out a message of reassurance while underlining that the centre and the Maharashtra government assess the security scenario and take immediate steps to boost security. 'We will rest only after eliminating terrorism,' she said. There was a sense of unease in some sections of the party that the Mumbai attacks could mar the Congress's prospects in the ongoing assembly elections.■

Patil under fire, from all sides
Nagendar Sharma

New Delhi, November 27: UNION HOME MINISTER Shivraj Patil and intelligence agencies came under fire over the Mumbai terror strikes in a series of cabinet meetings on Thursday. 'The home minister and Intelligence Bureau chief P.C. Haldar, called to brief about the situation, were both at a loss for words when asked whose work it might be,' a person in the know said, requesting anonymity. Some ministers wanted to know the outcome of the two-day meet of the top cops held over the weekend. 'It was perhaps a day of the longest meetings during this government's tenure,' a senior UPA minister, who didn't wish to be identified for reasons of protocol, said.

Prime Minister Manmohan Singh and cabinet colleagues went into a huddle early in the day. The Cabinet Committee on Security was the first to meet. It reviewed the security situation after Patil, back from a Mumbai visit, briefed his colleagues. Real drama followed. At the Cabinet Committee on Political Affairs meeting, Railways Minister Lalu Prasad reportedly slammed Patil and intelligence agencies for 'repeated failures'. He was said to have remarked that newspapers and television had given them much more information than the briefing did. The PM reportedly listened to his colleagues and spoke only when it became 'necessary to intervene'. Patil termed the attacks 'very disturbing' in an interaction with media. 'Before I could reach there, the terrorists who had attacked . . . the Cama Hospital had left and those who attacked the railway station had also left,' he said. Patil refused to talk about the terrorists' identity. 'We have certain information but it's premature,' he said. 'It'll not be proper to share premature information.'

A Congress minister, also requesting anonymity, said the PM was likely to consult UPA allies on counter-terrorism measures. 'We don't want to target any particular community, but the situation can't be allowed to spiral out of control,' he said. The CPI demanded Patil's resignation. The CPM, however, was restrained. 'We don't think it's fair to make political comments now. We should wait for the operation . . . to get over,' Politburo member Sitaram Yechury told *HT*.■

Scared fliers skip flights to Mumbai
Soubhik Mitra

Mumbai, November 27: SEVERAL FEAR-STRUCK FLIERS in Mumbai stayed home on Thursday morning, forcing domestic carriers to cancel several flights and club others during peak departure hours. Ten domestic flights flying out of the city were cancelled in the first half of the day. 'Kingfisher, Jet Airways, Indigo and Air India (Indian) cancelled flights because of low passenger turnout,' said the spokesperson for Mumbai International Airport Ltd. Arrival of flights was also affected. Jet and Kingfisher, which hold 60 per cent of the domestic market share, also cancelled a few flights coming to Mumbai. The low passenger turnout also forced some airlines to club flights. Delhi-bound Air India flight IC-601, scheduled for departure at 6 a.m., was combined with IC-806 and left an hour later. Earlier in the wee hours of Thursday, Lufthansa, Air France and North West cancelled flights because the crew could not reach the airport.

The construction work at the airport has been stalled for a couple of days as a security measure. 'Hundreds of casual labourers work inside the airport, including the sensitive parts of the airfield. The measure has been taken to restrict their entry,' said the airport spokesperson. Further, airlines conducted physical frisking of passengers before they climbed the aircraft ladder. Every 15 minutes, dustbins inside the airports were checked by a dog squad. Airlines have advised passengers to reach the airport early with valid photo-identification.∎

Theatres shut, film shootings cancelled
Vajir Singh

Mumbai, November 27: DUE TO THE ongoing terror attacks in Mumbai since Wednesday night, the state government ordered all cinema houses in the city to shut down for a day, on Thursday. Bhumika Tewari, AVP Programming, Fun Cinemas, confirming the news said: 'The decision was left to us. For precautionary sake,

23

we decided to call it off for a day.' Tewari said, there won't be any morning shows on Friday. For the noon and evening shows, a decision will be taken later. 'We've got orders from the state government for Thursday but so far we haven't been informed what to do on Friday,' Manoj Desai, executive director of Maratha Mandir and Bandra's G-7 complex, said.

Two Hindi films—*Sorry Bhai!* and *Oye Lucky! Lucky Oye!*, which were scheduled to release on Friday—have been pushed to Saturday.

According to Desai, till Thursday evening, these two new films weren't supposed to release on Friday but after a meeting post-evening, there's a possibility they might. Actor Sanjay Suri, co-producer of *Sorry Bhai!* said, Movie Mantra, the company releasing the film, would take the final call in the night. But Ram Mirchandani, senior VP—Creative and Projects, UTV, who is producing *Oye Lucky! Lucky Oye!* said, the movie would be released on Friday as scheduled.

Even shootings were cancelled on Thursday. Ajay Devgan decided take a day's break from the shoot for his home production *Toonpoor Ka Superhero* to be held at Chembur. Leena Yadav, too, decided to call it off for a day for her film *Teen Patti*. The shooting was supposed to be held in Centaur, Juhu.■

Spirit of Mumbai shines through tragedy
Neha Dara

Mumbai, November 27: AT 10 P.M., NITIN Maheshwari was just finishing dinner at Henry Tham's restaurant in Colaba when he got a call from a friend asking if he was safe. A few calls and a word with the management later, he realised the police had asked the restaurant to put out the outside lights and down shutters, keeping all patrons safely inside while they pursued the terrorists holed up in the Taj hotel nearby.

Henry Tham's is one of a string of popular nightspots on the street leading up to the Taj. The back entrances of the restaurants open into a common courtyard, which is where most of the customers made their way as news of the attacks around the city poured in, sharing bits of information and trying to make sense of the little they knew. A young girl, frantic to get back to her home in Navy Nagar, where her worried family was waiting, was reassured by other guests that she was safer where she was. Another guest, enlisted to help by a guard who couldn't speak English, explained the situation to a worried foreigner. As shots broke out nearby, the staff ushered patrons back in, bending the no-smoking rule to keep smokers inside.

At Gordon House, Amit Varma and his friends were waiting outside to get a table at the hotel's restaurant. They were quickly guided inside as the first shots rang out. With a pregnant woman in their midst, they quickly decided to rent rooms at the hotel and stay put for the night. 'In the morning, they refused to accept payment for the room, insisting that it was their duty,' Varma told *HT*. Down the same lane, at Indigo, Gayatri Rangachari of *Hello* magazine was at a team dinner. 'The restaurant seemed like a bomb shelter, we all huddled and listened to the explosions at the Taj. A girl who was shot on the street was brought in. The staff tended to her and made sure she got to a hospital.'

At Inox, Nariman Point, the management directed patrons into an auditorium. Akshaye Rathi, who was at the theatre, describes the experience on his blog: 'Coffee and snacks were passed around . . . they even brought and cooked some rice and *dal* for people who may not have had their dinner.'■

OBITUARIES: Three officers, three gentlemen

Hemant Karkare (54), Inspector General of Police
Hemant Karkare, head of the ATS, was known as a gentleman. An engineer who graduated from Nagpur's prestigious Visvesvaraya College of Regional Engineering, Karkare spent a brief stint with a private company before joining the IPS in 1982.

Karkare, eldest among three brothers and a sister, was born in a lower middle-class family at Nagpur and did his schooling at the local New English High School in Congress Nagar. His mother was a primary school teacher at the local Bengali School while his father was a class III employee with the Central Railways. He then spent more than ten years in Mumbai, before being sent on a diplomatic mission to Geneva by the Research and Analysis Wing.

A no-nonsense, soft-spoken policeman, he was a tight-lipped intelligence man who was secular to the core and was known to have no enemies. That was partly why he was considered the best man for the tough task of heading the ATS. He served as superintendent of police in Chandrapur district in Vidarbha region for two years, and was later an assistant commissioner of police in his hometown.

Vijay Salaskar (48), Police Inspector

Inspector Vijay Salaskar is best known for gunning down 70 top gangsters over his 20-year career and breaking the backbone of the powerful Mumbai underworld, with help from fellow batchmates Pradeep Sharma and Praful Bhosale. But among the gangsters that remained loyal informants throughout his career, he was also known as a sensitive, benevolent man. Legend has it he once passed around a collection plate after he found out that the thief he had just arrested was stealing to pay his daughter's school fees.

Salaskar was serving on the Anti-extortion Cell of the Mumbai Crime Branch when he was gunned down outside Metro Cinema in south Mumbai early on Thursday. He had spent most of his career in the Crime Branch, developing a wide network of sources and informers that had made him very popular with his bosses.

A teetotaller who did not smoke, Salaskar was known as a tough but well-mannered man, always chivalrous. He is survived by his wife and daughter.

Ashok Kamte (42), Additional Commissioner of Police

Ashok Kamte was an alumnus of St. Stephen's College, New Delhi. A national power-lifting champion, Kamte hailed from a family of policemen and armymen. He had an encyclopaedic knowledge of weapons, explosives and unarmed combat. Kamte was summoned late on Wednesday night to deal with terrorists holed up near Metro Cinema, where he was gunned down. 'We have lost the bravest officer in the entire Maharashtra police force,' said Additional Director General of Police Arup Patnaik.

Kamte, a 1989 batch IPS officer, was one of the brightest. Twice, he was sent on UN peacekeeping missions in Bosnia for a year (1998–99) and later in Somalia. An *HT* correspondent spoke to him on his return from Bosnia. Kamte said he was thrilled to meet policemen from other countries but said it was not as exciting being a 'soldier without an enemy' as a peacekeeper.

'I want to be in real combat situations,' he said. The much-loved former police commissioner of Solapur also served as superintendent of police in Naxal-infested Gadchiroli. There are ten pages set up by fans on Orkut, with comments from over 400 people, most of them ruing the fact that he could not continue as their police chief forever.■

An emotional farewell by friends, admirers
Satyajit Joshi

Pune, November 27: IT WAS AN emotional day for many friends and admirers as they came to see off the officer who was known for handling hostage situations. One such situation claimed Ashok Kamte's life on Wednesday as he died fighting the terrorists at Girgaum Chowpatty. Kamte was especially called on Wednesday night due to his reputation. 'This is one of the most unfortunate days in my life. Kamte and (ATS chief) Hemant Karkare were my roommates at the police training centre in Hyderabad,' said an emotional Vikram Bokey, a former IPS officer who knew Kamte since his early days.■

Amidst death, a new life
Alifiya Khan

Mumbai, November 27: CROUCHED IN THE labour ward on the second floor of Cama Albess Hospital for Women and Children, Dr Priti Acharya (name changed) delivered a baby girl as terrorists fired just two floors above her. After hearing the gunshots, she and her colleagues rushed first to ensure the safety of the patients. Acharya had to steady her trembling fingers and concentrate on the crying woman before her when she heard the building's watchman scream when the terrorists shot him. The woman was already in labour, but her labour worsened as the terrorists rushed into the hospital. 'In about ten minutes we heard firing from the lane right behind the hospital. We informed the patients to move into the adjoining operation theatre and they locked themselves in,' she said. 'One woman was in labour on the second floor so all doctors in the ward rushed there and we locked ourselves in. We heard those people coming up the steps and going to the upper floor.'■

DAY 2

Waiting to cope with tragedy, exhausted Mumbai celebrates a Commando triumph. A war lies ahead.
Team *HT*

Mumbai, November 28: AFTER 48 NERVE-WRACKING hours, Mumbai watched as security forces shot down terrorists at the Trident hotel in Nariman Point and the Nariman House in Colaba on Friday evening. At the time of going to press at midnight, the National Security Guards were still reportedly trying to hunt down remaining terrorists at the Taj hotel's old building. This battle, with 155 killed, might be all but over, but it has made evident how India is the new territory for global *jihad*—and how vulnerable it is. Union Minister of State for Home Shriprakash Jaiswal said: 'This is a work of an international terror group. Among them are some Pakistanis.' Jaiswal said the government had come to this conclusion based on the interrogation of an arrested terrorist.

Official sources said 11 terrorists have so far been killed. The number is likely to go up once the operation at Taj comes to an end. Government spokesperson Bhushan Gagrani said: 'Around 350 people have been rescued from Taj and 138 from Oberoi.' As security forces overpowered the attackers and cleared both sites, the official death count rose to 155—34 bodies were found at the Trident and five hostages were found dead at the Jewish housing complex. The number of injured is 238. Among the dead: Yes Bank chairman Ashok Kapur and actor Ashish Chaudhary's sister and her husband at the Trident. For the first time in a rescue operation in the city, helicopters air-dropped NSG commandos on the Nariman House roof. The building turned into a battleground as the firing and explosions blew apart its walls. The bystanders didn't make operations any easier. Rabbi Gavriel Holtzberg and his wife Rivka were among the five hostages found dead. Two terrorists were killed. Earlier, at the Trident, the operation ended around 3 p.m. 'Both terrorists have been killed,' DG of NSG Jyoti Krishan Dutt said. 'Two AK-47 rifles, one pistol and Chinese-made grenades were recovered.' At the Taj, there was firing through the day. Action intensified in the evening and a bystander and a videographer were injured.■

Commandos kill 2 terrorists, marathon battle at Trident ends

Presley Thomas & Megha Sood (Inputs from Vignesh Iyer)

Mumbai, November 28: INDIAN SECURITY FORCES killed two heavily armed militants in the Trident hotel in Nariman Point and freed at least 121 people inside, thus ending a 40-hour siege. The two militants stormed the hotel on Wednesday night, indiscriminately firing and killing at least 30 people and injuring tens of others, the police said. 'Both the terrorists have been killed,' said Jyoti Krishan Dutt, director general of the National Security Guards who led the onslaught. 'We have recovered two assault Kalashnikov (AK-47) rifles, one pistol and Chinese-made hand grenades from them.' The operation, carried out by the NSG, army and police, ended at about 3 p.m. on Friday. The forces combed the hotel, floor by floor, twice over. They escorted the captives, most of them shell-shocked foreigners, to the nearby Air India building for first aid and counselling. The injured were sent to Breach Candy Hospital. The NSG had an able ally in the Mumbai Police, one of whose officers climbed to the 11th floor of an apartment adjacent to the hotel and waved at the terrorists, who were on the 16th floor. Almost immediately, the terrorists directed their guns to the apartment from where the officer waved, and this seemed to have given their location away, enabling the Guards inside the hotel to locate them. Among those dead were Rita and Sanjay Agarwal of Napean Sea Road. 'They were newly married and had come to Trident for dinner,' said Pramila, their aunt. Among those who were injured and rushed to Breach Candy was Apoorva Parekh.

Several staff members of the hotel were also killed, including an intern and a lobby manager. 'We were working on the tenth floor, when we heard gunshots,' said Jason Mascarenhas, an employee.■

Horror in the heritage wing
Urvi Mahajani & Presley Thomas

Mumbai, November 28: THE GUNBATTLE AT the landmark Taj hotel continued for the second day as the National Security Guards commandos tried to pin down terrorists using hostages for cover. Six persons, including two US citizens, Nationalist Congress Party Member of Parliament Jaisingrao Gaikwad-Patil and Bharatiya Janata Party MP Lalmani Chaube, were rescued on Friday. Four bodies were taken out but there was no information on their identities. Security forces and the terrorists were engaged in intermittent exchange of fire through the day. The action was mostly concentrated in the Gateway-facing area of the hotel. Grenades were lobbed at regular intervals. A bystander, identified only as Dilip, and a videographer with news agency AFP received shrapnel injuries.

British food entrepreneur of Indian origin Ghulam Noon was rescued from the hotel on Thursday morning. 'As a Mumbaiite I feel sad about what is happening,' said Noon. 'If they don't have any demands why kill innocents?' The day was tense for all those conducting and witnessing the operations at the Taj. At one point, forces spotted a suspicious bag and sniffer dogs were called in. Earlier, General Commanding Officer in Chief N. Thamburaj said it seemed like terrorists had taken a family hostage and were using them as cover. 'We don't want to do anything hasty. We are moving slow but steady.'

The Marine Commando (MARCOS), who led the contingent that entered the Taj, said militants lobbed grenades and disappeared. 'The militants were very familiar with the layout of the hotel. And knew precisely the entry and exit points,' he said. The MARCOS team leader said they had seen at least 12 to 15 bodies and many others seriously injured within the first two floors of Taj hotel. The MARCOS who were the first to fight the militants at the Taj on Wednesday midnight recovered a rucksack with dry fruits, seven filled magazines of AK-47, 400 rounds of ammunition, four Chinese-made grenades, seven credit cards and a national ID card of Mauritius. The seven credit cards were procured with the same Malaysian address.■

Peaceful home for Jews from around the world
Barney Henderson

Mumbai, November 28: A PEACE-LOVING CENTRE for Jews from around the world to take rest, pray and learn about the religion is how Nariman House has been described by leading Jews in the city. Mumbai's Jewish community united in prayer for Rabbi Gavriel Holtzberg, his wife Rivka—they were among those killed by the terrorists—and other Jews held hostage inside the House. Nariman House, also Chabad House, is the headquarters of the ultra-orthodox Chabad-Lubavitch movement of Hasidic Jews. It has been housing Jewish travellers in Mumbai since 2003. Many residents of Nariman House are Israelis travelling in India. It provides fully kosher food.

In an interview to an Israeli newspaper, Rabbi Holtzberg, who grew up in New York, had earlier said the centre helped many young Jews who 'need relief' from their time in the army. The Consul General of Israel in Mumbai, Orna Sagiv, said: 'It functions as a social group and many Jews from Mumbai go there on Fridays. The Jews staying there are either backpacking travellers or businessmen. Nariman House is a nice place for them to go to and be with people from their own community,' Sagiv told *Hindustan Times* before receiving news of their deaths. 'I know Rabbi Holtzberg well and his lovely wife and their child. They are nice people. It is a very worrying time and we are just waiting and praying.' The chairman of a Jewish charitable trust, who knew Rabbi Holtzberg well, said the entire Jewish community here—

about 5,000—was praying. 'He was one of the finest human beings I knew,' said chairman of Sir Jacob Sassoon Charity Trust based in Warren Road and city's leading Jewish community figure Solomon Sophar. 'The Rabbi gave Jews coming from Israel and elsewhere a place to stay and, importantly, a place to be able to pray. He was doing his duty to God and to man. He was not preaching to outsiders and, as our religion states, did not try to convert others from outside the religion.'∎

Nariman House turns battleground
Kiran Wadhwa & Kanchan Chaudhari
(Inputs from Vignesh Iyer & Shahkar Abidi)

Mumbai, November 28: HOURS BEFORE HE could turn two, baby Moshe lost his parents in the Nariman House terror attack. The bodies of his parents, Rabbi Gavreil Holtzberg and wife Rivka, were among the five pulled out of the building at the end of Operation Black Tornado on Friday evening. 'Rabbi Gavriel and Rivka Holtzberg, directors of Chabad-Lubavitch of Mumbai, were killed during one of the worst terrorist attacks to strike India in recent memory,' the Jewish site chabad.org said.

The Nariman House encounter ended around 9 p.m. on Friday—48 hours after terrorists took Jewish people hostage—leaving five hostages, two terrorists and one NSG commando Gajendra Singh dead. 'We have captured Nariman House. We had to tread carefully as it was a populated area,' said J.K. Dutta, director general, NSG. Three bodies of the hostages were found on the second floor and the two terrorists were shot on the fourth floor, where bodies of two more hostages were found. The façade had changed dramatically in 12 hours. From a simple, white building housing Jewish families in a narrow bylane, the building turned into a battleground with walls blown apart and shattered windows. The Rabbi, his wife and six other Jews, including Holtzberg's two-year-old boy Moshe, were held captive by the militants. Two, however, were rescued with Moshe on Thursday.

33

'I kept dialling their cellphone every second since the moment I heard of them being kept hostage,' said Shnior Kup, a family friend of the Rabbi. Kup, who is in his mid-twenties, did not know whether the Rabbi was alive when he spoke to *HT* on Friday. 'The baby is under my care.' Kup said that it is Moshe's second birthday on Saturday. 'He is crying for his mother. I don't know how to console him.'

There were tense moments prior to the official end of the encounter when crowds gathered around the building stormed into the cordoned area assuming that the operation was over as some saw commandos emerge from the building and thought it was the end of the 48-hour ordeal. The security forces had to lathi charge the surging crowd chanting slogans like *Bharat Mata ki jai* to disperse them. Announcements were made that the NSG was still to gain control of the last floor of the building. Action at Nariman House began at 7.30 a.m. after 23 NSG commandos were air-dropped by a helicopter. Keeping in mind the possibility of the terrorists possessing sophisticated weapons, the commandos entered the building from the fifth floor. They had to carry out their operation cautiously as there was a petrol pump nearby and any wrong move could have proven hazardous. Both sides were engaged in a gun and grenade battle. The NSG, deployed in six buildings surrounding Nariman House, also attempted to enter. Terrorists, hiding behind heavy orange curtains, were lobbing grenades from an apartment on one of the higher floors of the building. Frugal with their use of ammunition, they hurled hand grenades only when commandos got too close. After a brief break between 12.32 p.m. and 3 p.m., the action resumed even as onlookers thronged the bylanes leading to the building. Gopinath Rao, a technician, had come from Parel to watch the operation. 'I have never seen a commando and a friend who lives close by asked me to come over and watch the action,' he said. Around 4.40 p.m., as commandos reached the fourth floor, there followed at least six explosions. An hour later, sources said, they placed an explosive on the fourth floor and carried out a controlled explosion.

The intensity of the explosion was so strong that it blew apart the entire floor. Nariman House, which houses the Chabad House, is inhabited by Israelis and Jews. Chabad is a network of such places operated by a Jewish organization, which provides shelter to Jewish and Israeli travellers.■

Police depend on commandos when the going gets tough
Stavan Desai

Mumbai, November 28: ILL-FITTING BULLETPROOF VESTS, riot helmets, .303 Enfield rifles, World War II carbine sub-machine guns, bulky self-loading rifles and vehicles that cannot speed over 50 kmph—this is the ammunition the Mumbai Police has to counter a terror attack of the magnitude of the one Mumbai has battled for over 48 hours. The terrorists, armed with sophisticated weapons such as AK-47s and hand grenades, left the Mumbai Police weak and exposed their ill preparedness. Without a match for the terrorists' ammunition and losing some top officers to their bullets, the police had no option but to wait for the NSG commandos to arrive. The NSG are not only armed to the teeth but are also well trained to deal with such situations.

This is not the first time that a city's police force has shown helpless dependence on the NSG. On September 24, 2002, when young, armed militants attacked the world acclaimed Swaminarayan Temple at Akshardham, the Gujarat Police faced a similar problem. For lack of enough equipment or expertise, they were forced to wait for the NSG to arrive from Delhi. The Mumbai Police have tried to create a similar set-up here with the recent formation of the 'Quick Reaction Teams' (QRT). The idea of the QRT is to deal with such emergencies and the police had planned to give them equipment and training on the lines of the NSG. The project, however, has hit bureaucratic roadblocks. The Mumbai Police, in fact, do not even have enough cartridges to provide members of the QRT routine training. Police officials refuse to say anything on record but off-the-record admit that no police force in any city in India is equipped or trained to handle an attack as well planned and intensive as the one Mumbai is facing now. 'Right now the NSG is our only hope and option,' said a top policeman. ∎

'We thought we were fighting commandos'
Haidar Naqvi

Kanpur, November 28: THE MEN THEY took on at the two besieged Mumbai hotels—the Taj and the Trident—weren't just terrorists, they fought like army regulars and even trained commandos, said some of the people involved in the operations at the luxury hotels. They told the *Hindustan Times* over the phone that they had a strong feeling they were up against very well-trained men, adept at warfare tactics and movements. 'Their training is excellent; they were behaving the way Indian commandos would have, if they were playing terrorists in Pakistan,' they said over the telephone. These people can't be identified as they aren't authorised to speak to the media. 'At times, we found them matching us in combat and movement; it was their high degree of training which was prolonging the operation every hour. They're either army regulars or have done a long stint of commando training,' they said. A little hesitant in labelling them 'militants', the sources said the men knew the Taj like the back of their hand. They had taken positions at strategic places when the hotel was stormed, even succeeded in hitting and injuring two commandos and 'didn't allow the teams to move for two to three hours, using grenades in best possible fashion at around 6.30 a.m. on Thursday'. The teams retaliated, pushing them back to take upper floors. First they entered the kitchen where they saw bodies. 'There were around 50 bodies, almost heaped over each other; there were no survivors,' they said. The forces then shifted focus to the close circuit television monitor room to ascertain the positions of hostage-takers. The move, however, had been pre-empted—the room had been burnt down.

The security teams then slowly moved to Chamber Hall on the second floor and found nearly 200 people held hostage. There were three armed men pacing the floor, with exit points under their control. Soon, a fierce battle started. After four–five hours of exchange of fire, the terrorists made a hasty retreat through a hidden door, which the security teams didn't even know existed. Of the 200 hostages, 125 were foreigners who just couldn't stop thanking the forces. It was in this hall that the credit cards, AK-47 magazines, an identity card issued in Mauritius and some China-made grenades were recovered. The terrorists had a distinct advantage 'because of their better knowledge of the topography', the sources said.■

News channels blocked, cell networks jammed
HT Business Bureau

Mumbai, November 28: NEWS CHANNELS WERE blocked for two to three hours on Friday, after the police issued a directive to network operators saying news updates on the ongoing terror attacks were impeding operations against the terrorists. 'The authorities personally came and asked us to stop telecast of news channels, including DD News, across Mumbai,' an official source with a cable network said. Cellphone networks were also jammed from time to time in south Mumbai on Friday. The directive to black out channels was probably triggered by rumours on firing at CST spread due to unconfirmed reports on television channels. According to a reliable source, there are around 5.5 lakh cable homes in south Mumbai and 28 lakh cable homes in the whole of Mumbai. An order issued by DCP (Enforcement) Sheela Sail to InCable—one of the multi-system-operators in Mumbai—on Thursday read: 'transmission of various clippings/live relay/coverage of the action being taken by the police against the terrorists in south Mumbai is causing impediment in the police action.' It also stated how the transmissions by television channels were causing operational difficulties in police action against the terrorists, thereby endangering the lives of the personnel and hostages.■

Commandos from South Africa save lives at Taj

Mumbai, November 28: SIX SOUTH AFRICAN commandos who were having dinner at the Souk restaurant at the Taj hotel during Wednesday night's terror attacks, saved scores of lives. The commandos accompanying the South African cricket team, who had come to participate in the now-cancelled Champions League, quickly escorted all the 150 diners through the fire exit gate. 'We realised that the area is not secured. We imagined there is a good possibility that the terrorists may make their way to the top of the building where we are,' Bob Nichols, member, said.■

How the terror machine worked

WHO: LeT, al-Qaeda and Global Terror Inc join hands
Pramit Pal Chaudhuri & Haider Naqvi

New Delhi, November 28: US PRESIDENT-ELECT BARACK Obama's main advisor on South Asian terror says he believes that the Mumbai attack is a combined operation of al-Qaeda and Lashkar-e-Tayyeba. Terrorism experts say this would explain the non-Indian focus of some of the terrorist teams who attacked the city. 'This has the hallmarks of al-Qaeda: a very sophisticated attack at multiple targets. The US, the UK and Israel are global jihadist targets, not Indian Mujahideen targets,' said Bruce Riedel of the Brookings Institute and author of *The Search for Al Qaeda*. 'Thorough casing is an al-Qaeda trademark. My suspicion is a joint al-Qaeda–Lashkar project. If it also creates an India–Pakistan crisis or worse, all the better for the masterminds,' added Riedel, an advisor to Obama's transition team. This would explain the dichotomy in the choice of targets by the terrorists. One team of terrorists indiscriminately killed Indian civilians at Victoria Terminus and Cama Hospital. They did not seek places frequented by foreigners. That, as well as the Pakistani-Punjabi origin of the terrorists, points to Lashkar involvement. Three other terrorist teams attacked Leopold Café, the Oberoi and Taj, and a Jewish guesthouse. These teams made the killing of Americans, Britons and Israelis priority. This reflects al-Qaeda thinking. Osama bin Laden, said G. Parthasarathy, former high commissioner to Pakistan, 'has long said he wishes to plant the flag of Islam in Delhi, Tel Aviv and Washington.' Al-Qaeda working alongside a local *jihadi* group is a growing norm in Islamic terrorism. Hyderabadi Muslim Abu Abdel Aziz 'Barbaros' is cited by Indian officials as the militant who helped forge ties between Qaeda and Lashkar. The FBI has shared details of interrogation of Qaeda operatives which cited Barbaros's work in hitching Lashkar to Osama bin Laden's international *jihad*. 'The ties started in early '90s have grown. Thanks to Barbaros, the Lashkar for eight years has had unhindered access to Qaeda's training facilities,' said a source. 'Lashkar could be carrying out attacks on Indian soil on behalf of Qaeda.' Qaeda no longer has a sizeable body of fighters. It provides ideological guidance and training to groups like Lashkar. This is especially important if al-Qaeda is beginning to wean itself off its trademark suicide bombings. The use of suicide fighters, as in Mumbai, requires personnel-heavy groups like Lashkar. Mumbai has shown how lethal the mix is. 'This is a new horrible milestone in the global *jihad*,' says Riedel.■

WHEN: **Six days ago they took rooms at Taj, stocked up**
Abhishek Sharan

New Delhi, November 28: TWO PAKISTANI SUICIDE attackers, part of a group of 20–25 alleged Lashkar-e-Tayyeba operatives that launched a deadly attack in Mumbai on Wednesday night, had checked into the Taj hotel four days earlier. This is what two of the apprehended terrorists now in Mumbai Police's custody told Intelligence Bureau officials. 'One of the two terrorists who had checked into the Taj hotel on November 22 was Ajmal Amir, a resident of Faridkot, Multan. The other could have been shot dead in operations,' a senior IB officer told *HT* after the suspects' debriefing. 'The two used false identities and checked into room number 630,' he added. 'The duo received several visitors between

Saturday, November 22 and Wednesday, when the attacks began. These visitors carried bags probably filled with weapons and explosives.' The officer said Manjar, who was also held by police, told interrogators the group was in telephonic contact with mentors in Karachi throughout the attacks. The suspects allegedly revealed the plan to attack Mumbai was formulated by the LeT brass a year back. They also claimed the group of men 'specialised in terror training at Muzaffarabad in PoK and naval training in Karachi' from Laskhar trainers, another interrogator said. An IB alert issued last January had claimed that an LeT terror team had been assigned to strike Mumbai from the sea.■

HOW: Terrorists used our thirst for 24/7 news to succeed
Chetan Chauhan & Poonam Saxena

New Delhi, November 28: ON FRIDAY, THE entire nation saw dramatic visuals of masked commandos descending from helicopters and dropping down on the roof of Nariman House—just one frame of an Indian fascination for 24/7 news that the terrorists had banked on. Create mayhem, make it last. And leave the rest to the power of television news. Vikram Sood, former chief of India's Research and Analysis Wing (R&AW), said lots needed to be self-censored. 'It was horrific,' he said. 'The terrorists would have got to know exactly what was happening.' The visuals were shown despite a Thursday night advisory from the Ministry of Information and Broadcasting asking news channels not to report on operational details. The advisory was issued after Home Ministry officials complained that channels were indirectly helping militants keep tabs on the security forces' operation. Government officials said that the militants in the Taj and Oberoi hotels were getting details of the movement of security forces around the hotels on Wednesday night from Pakistan through satellite phones and laptops, even though cable television lines were snapped in the hotels on Wednesday night itself. 'The satellite phone intercepts indicated that television was being used to provide information to militants inside the hotels till Thursday evening when the government issued an advisory,' said an I&B Ministry official. Added an official: 'The militants knew from where the security forces were zeroing in.' That could have slowed down the operation. News channels were also advised not to show the bodies of victims till the operation was over as it could give a boost to the morale of the militants inside the hotels. 'We also asked the channels not to show the burning hotel rooms repeatedly. If they were shown, then the logo of repeat telecast should be clearly mentioned,' an official said. Though senior ministry officials described the TV coverage overall as restrained and much better than in earlier times, there were lapses. A channel actually broadcast a live interview with an alleged terrorist. Said Star Network CEO Uday Shankar, who has in the past run the 24-hour Star News channel, 'There has to be a consensus that you don't give that kind of platform to such terrorists. Even if a channel does get such an interview, it should be recorded and gone over carefully before airing, if at all.' On Friday, many news channels also put out unconfirmed 'news' that there had been firing at Chhatrapati Shivaji Terminus, creating panic and fear among Mumbai's citizens. Later the 'news' turned out to be inaccurate. Soon after, cable channels went off the air in Mumbai, though they were restored after a while. 'Terrorists want to create fear. Anything that generates fear is in their interest. News channels must guard against that,' added Sood. But the former RAW chief was in favour of media briefings by the authorities in question. 'That's important so that there's no panic. Every impression should be given that the authorities are in control, even if that may not be a hundred per cent true.' Shankar says anchors play a critical role in maintaining balance in the midst of live coverage. 'Unfortunately, many channels have people of poor intellectual calibre and maturity as anchors. And this is across English and Hindi news channels,' he said. 'We also need to find more dignified ways of approaching victims who've just emerged from a traumatic experience rather than thrusting mikes in their faces as if they have just come out of a matinee show.' Not surprisingly, the television rating points of news channels increased four to five times in the last two days as against normal news days, Audience Measurement and Analytics, a company measuring television viewing, said on Friday. The increase was witnessed more for Hindi news channels than English news channels.■

Never before

Amit Baruah (Inputs from Aloke Tikku, Nandini R. Iyer & Zia Haq)

New Delhi, November 28: IS THE UNTHINKABLE going to happen in India–Pakistan relations? Reversing decades of policy, Pakistan's civilian government announced on Friday afternoon that it would send Inter-Services Intelligence (ISI) chief, Lt. Gen. Ahmed Shuja Pasha, to India to help with the investigations into the terrorist strikes in Mumbai. But, like everything else in India–Pakistan relations, there's a twist in the tale. Late on Friday night, Pakistan's military spokesman, Major-General Athar Abbas, said no decision had been taken to send the ISI chief to New Delhi. Abbas said the military would await a written letter from the civilian government, spelling out the exact scope and jurisdiction of the ISI chief's visit. There have been tensions in the past between the civilian government and the army on who controls the ISI.

As Pakistan dilly-dallied, the *Haaretz* daily reported that Israel had sent a number of intelligence agents to India on Thursday to 'assist in analyzing' the attacks. 'This is going to be a case which will need close coordination with all countries concerned,' an official, who preferred anonymity, said, recalling how Indian sleuths had coordinated investigations into the hijacking of IC-814 aircraft in 1999 with the FBI. 'There has been no specific request yet to collaborate on the Mumbai attacks (from India), but the FBI is open to any support India might want,' an official at the US mission in Delhi said. 'He (Pasha) will be travelling to India soon. The decision to send him was taken following a request made by

PM Manmohan Singh to PM Yousaf Raza Gilani,' a Pakistani official said by telephone from Islamabad. Zahid Bashir, Gilani's spokesman, said: 'This is a very positive development. My PM has directed me to make this statement to the press.' A South Block official concurred: 'This is a big development. Whether he is coming in response to an invitation or a summons is not important.'

In Mumbai, investigating agencies have extracted considerable information from one of the detained terrorists, Ajmal Mohammed, said to be a Pakistani national from Faridkot. Singh told Gilani preliminary reports 'point towards Karachi' and called for 'increased intelligence sharing and cooperation'. Earlier, External Affairs Minister Pranab Mukherjee suggested 'some elements' in Pakistan were responsible for the terror strikes. Speaking in Jodhpur, he said Pakistan had to live up to promises made to India in 2004 and 2008 that it wouldn't allow terrorists to use its soil for terrorist activities. He also called on Pakistan to dismantle the terror infrastructure. He argued that 'outrages' like Mumbai and the attack on the Indian embassy in Kabul make advances in India–Pakistan relations 'impossible'.■

'Terror global, not local'
Renuka Narayanan

New Delhi, November 28: INDIA SHOULD HAVE 'pondered more' before coming to a conclusion on elements in Pakistan being responsible for the 26/11 terrorist attacks in Mumbai, Foreign Minister Shah Mehmood Qureshi said on Friday. Condemning the attacks in Mumbai, the Pakistani minister said: 'I understand the pain and anger. We have to rise above politics and I'm sure the leadership in India is very mature and responsible.' He said he had 'seen death very closely, I was on the truck with Benazir Bhutto on October 18; my son was injured.' He said there was 'institutional consensus' in Pakistani society now for the first time and that 'the military and intelligence are taking orders from the elected political leadership.' On why Lashkar-e-Tayyeba and Jaish-e-Mohammed leaders were not arrested, Qureshi said: 'Terrorism is not local or regional, but global,' and that Pakistan 'has banned the LeT and frozen its assets'. 'Pakistan is ready to cooperate with India at all levels,' he said, adding that he could not give a definite answer on when the ISI chief would arrive in New Delhi.■

Victims' families grieve

'Mother is dead; they killed her'
Bhavika Jain

THE CHATTERJEES WERE planning to start a new life in their hometown Kolkata. That plan is still on, but with a tragic twist. George Chatterjee (50), who had retired three months ago from his job at a courier firm in Goregaon, lost his mother to terrorists' bullets. The family was to leave for Kolkata by the Geetanjali Express at 6 a.m. from CST. Chatterjee, his mother Meera and wife Shobha reached the station 12 hours in advance at 6 p.m. on Wednesday from their Nalasopara residence. Since they were leaving the city forever, they had a lot of luggage; so after dropping his wife and mother at the station, Chatterjee left for home to get the remaining luggage. 'At 9.50 p.m. when I was returning, I called my wife, but she didn't answer the phone. After ten minutes she called back but her voice became unclear with every word she spoke,' said Chatterjee. 'All I could hear was: "Mother has been killed; they killed her".' A stunned Chatterjee rushed to the station—and then St. George Hospital. 'My mother was shot in her back and neck by the terrorists,' he said, dissolving into tears. 'I feel I have been deserted to face life on my own.'■

She was meeting chat buddy
Sayli Udas Mankikar

TWENTY-SIX-YEAR-OLD MEETU ASRANI, a resident of Charkop, set out excitedly on Wednesday evening to meet an American 'chat' buddy she had met on a social networking site. She never returned. She was among the first victims of the terror attack at Leopold Café. 'She was friends with this 45-year-old woman, Lean, who had come to Mumbai for a holiday,' said Sunita Chauhan, a close friend who studied with Asrani at Jai Hind College. 'They had decided to meet at Leopold Café where Meetu was helping Lean plan her holiday in India.' Sounds of sobbing filled the Asrani household at Sector 3 in Charkop on Friday. Her father Arjun and brother Sunil had left with the body for the funeral at 11.30 p.m. Before she left for what would be her last trip, Asrani had spent most of her day watching a movie on television. She was expected to be back home for dinner. Instead, her body was claimed from Sion Hospital, her relative Anurag Gupta said. 'She was extremely creative and Balaji Telefilms had taken her on as a creative associate, a post she was yet to assume,' Chauhan said. 'She was very happy and excited that she finally found a job she was looking for.' For Asrani's kin and friends, intense grief is mixed with anger. 'We expect the government to do something to prevent such young promising lives to be finished this way,' said Kranti Gupta, a relative.■

A guiding star fades
Bhavika Jain

MOHIT BAHTIA AND his classmates can barely believe that their beloved biology teacher Roopinder Randhawa (54) will never teach them again. Randhawa, a senior teacher at Cuffe Parade's B.D. Somani International High School, was shot dead by terrorists inside the Taj hotel on Thursday morning. 'She was our guiding star,' said Bhatia. 'We will always remember her smile that we would call the "evil" smile as it would get bigger before announcing a test in class.' Randhawa, a resident of Cuffe Parade, had gone for dinner with her husband to Shamiana, a restaurant in the Taj. 'While they were having dinner, they heard gunshots followed by a loud bang. The hotel management asked them to crouch and hide behind the furniture,' a neighbour said, requesting that her name be withheld. 'At 5.30 in the morning when somebody said it was safe, she got up but was shot by a terrorist.' Randhawa is survived by her husband and two daughters who are settled in the US. Her students remember her as a dedicated teacher. 'Her enthusiasm and dedication towards her work was something I have imbibed from her,' said her former student Radhika Sheth of Cathedral School where Randhawa earlier taught. 'I don't remember a single day when she had declined any student's request.'■

SBI employee dies in Leopold firing

P.K. GOPALKRISHNAN, A 52-YEAR-OLD manager with the State Bank of India's Nariman Point office, was shot dead in the firing at Leopold Café on Wednesday night. Gopalkrishnan was having dinner with friends at the Colaba cafe when he was killed by the terrorists. He had been posted in Mumbai four years ago, and is survived by his wife, a son and a daughter.■

Wife of Ispat exec dies in Oberoi shooting

UMA GARG, WIFE of executive director (commercial) of Ispat Industries, Vinod Garg, is believed to have been shot dead by terrorists. Garg was with her family at the Oberoi hotel, when terrorists struck. The Ispat executive, however, managed to escape alive from the hotel on Thursday.■

Bank official hit by bullet, recuperating

C.M. PURI, DIRECTOR, Central Bank of India who was at the Oberoi Trident on Wednesday night decided to go to the hotel's coffee shop for dinner at 8 p.m. He heard gunshots while in the elevator. It was pitch dark outside and Puri was hit by a bullet the minute he stepped out of the elevator. He fell to the ground and was lying there. 'Just then, a hotel staff dragged me to the back office which had an exit point. We left the hotel and I was rushed to a hospital. Life has changed for me now,' he said.■

YES Bank chairman dead

YES BANK'S CHAIRMAN, Ashok Kapur, who had gone for dinner at the Oberoi, the day the terrorists seized it, is still missing. A Yes Bank official said that Kapur had gone to the hotel for dinner on Wednesday night, and has since been missing. 'We don't have any news about him since then. We are all praying for him and hoping for the best,' he said.■

Iconic Taj chef mourns lost 'family'
Aditya Ghosh

Mumbai, November 28: HEMANT OBEROI, CORPORATE executive chef at the Taj Group, is disconsolate. 'I have lost half my family,' he said, breaking down. Six of his colleagues, all star chefs, lost their lives in the terrorist attack on the Taj Mahal Palace & Tower in Mumbai. Kaizad Kamdin (27), one of the best young chefs in the country, was extremely enthusiastic about his profession. 'He wanted to become the best chef in the hotel. It (his death) feels like losing a family member,' said Oberoi. Kamdin's childhood friend Sheroy Raj, a Dubai-based airline executive, told *HT* over the phone: 'He emailed me recently saying he was tasting success professionally.' Kamdin helped everyone out from the kitchen, but lost his life in the bargain. If Kaizad was one of the best budding chefs in the country, 42-year-old Vijay Banja was already getting there. 'He was a talent to reckon with,' said Rajiv Gujral, Vice President, Indian Hotels Ltd, which owns the Taj brand. Banja lived in Colaba along with some of his colleagues in a family suite of the Taj. On Friday evening, the residents of the building were in mourning. 'He would go for morning walks every day and buy stuff from my shop,' said a local shopkeeper. Faustin Martis (50) was another Taj employee who was unlucky to be in the wrong place at the wrong time.■

MPs pulled out of Taj after 42 hours
Zia Haq

New Delhi, November 28: TWO MEMBERS OF Parliament hiding in their rooms in the terrorist-besieged Taj hotel were pulled out by commandos as evening approached on Friday.

MPs Lal Mani Prasad from Uttar Pradesh and B.G. Patil from Maharashtra were whisked out of their third-floor rooms and the hotel around 3 p.m., ending 42 hours of anxiety. The two were part of a four-member lawmaker team that had checked in some time before the terrorists took the hotel on Wednesday, of which two managed to escape. Krishnadas, MP from Palghat in Kerala, and Godhra MP B.P. Solanki were down for dinner at the Shamiana restaurant when the bloodshed began at the Taj, and just about got out. Prasad and Patil could not, and shut themselves up on specific instructions passed on to them by the National Security Guards via Krishnadas. 'After escaping, I knew I had to do everything possible for the other two MPs,' Krishnadas said. 'I was working closely with the NSG since yesterday. I was constantly updating them (the MPs). This kept their morale high. It was important to not let them suffer a breakdown.' Krishnadas became a two-way crisis centre of sorts with his mobile phone as his tool, helping provide details about the holed-up MPs to the NSG and passing on NSG instructions to the MPs. 'After I gave the room details of the two MPs, the NSG said they should lock themselves up and stay that way,' he added. 'The NSG said they would be rescued only when it was best to do so.' Solanki also did his bit, helping rescuers cart off a group of foreigners, including a bullet-riddled man, a woman with morbid obesity and children unable to walk because of shock. 'I was wondering what to order when we heard a blast,' Solanki said. 'I thought a gang-war had broken out.' Two gunshots later, he found himself walking over shards of glass through an exit leading to a corner of the Taj swimming pool. In the dark—the pool lights had gone off—Solanki called for help; a police van was on its way. 'In one corner, I saw a group of foreigners, one of whom had a bullet in his leg,' Solanki said. 'I carried him to the police van that came looking for me.' Krishnadas heads the Parliament's subordinate legislation committee that had checked in for a series of meetings spread over November 28–29; MP Giridhar Gomango was to have joined them on Thursday.■

Survivor tales
Vijay Dutt & IANS

London, November 28: TWO BRITISH TYCOONS were caught in the terror strike at Mumbai's Taj Mahal hotel. One, Mumbai-born Sir Gulam Noon lived to tell the tale. Yacht tycoon Andreas Liveras, 73, did not. Liveras was the only Briton to die in the attack.

Also known as Curry King, Noon had booked a table for four— his brother and two businessmen were the guests—at one of the hotel's restaurants, but decided to have the meal in his hotel room because he felt unwell. That decision saved his life as the restaurant was among the first places to be attacked by the terrorists. This is the second time that Noon had a tryst with terror in Mumbai and had a miraculous escape. He was staying at the Taj hotel during the 1993 bomb blasts but was not hurt.

Noon sounded shaken when he spoke to *HT* from Mumbai as he stood outside the building. 'I was locked up in my room from 9 p.m. to 6 a.m., without electricity, water or food.' He was asked to barricade himself in his room until help reached him and he did so. 'I heard footsteps in the corridor and occasional shots being fired. I had intended to dine in the restaurant but felt a bit unwell and ordered food from the Room Service. It saved my life.'

Sir Noon, who always stays at the Taj whenever he goes to Mumbai, told *HT*, 'I have been shifted to Taj President and have said on television that India's Home Minister must resign. This is done everywhere, ministers take responsibility for security failures and go.' He, however, refuses to give up on Mumbai. 'Of course, I will be back. Mumbai and India are my home. If I do not come home, these terrorists would win. We can't allow that.' On the effect of the terror on the economy, he said: 'It will take time. But we all are resilient and will help restore the economy to health.' He said efforts should be made from now to restore the confidence of investors. Unlike the Curry King, multi-millionaire Liveras was not lucky. He had gone to the Taj for dinner on Wednesday night because he heard they served the best food in the city and was among the first few to fall to the gunmen's bullets. But Liveras had spoken to a BBC journalist shortly before he died. He had said: 'We hid ourselves under the table and then they switched all the lights off. But the machine guns kept going, and they took us into the kitchen, and from there into a basement, before we came up into a salon where we are now. There must be more than 1,000 people here. There are residents and tourists and locals. We are not hiding, we are locked in here—nobody tells us anything, the doors are locked and we are inside. All we know is that the bombs are next door and the hotel is shaking every time a bomb goes off. Everybody is just living on their nerves.'

Liveras was pronounced dead on arrival at St. George Hospital at 9.30 p.m. on Wednesday.■

Terrorist acts and your investments
Arnav Pandya

New Delhi, November 28: TERROR STRIKES HAVE hit India quite a few times in different ways and with varying impacts. The impact of such strikes is felt on the value of various investments, especially on share prices. To get a good overall picture, an investor needs to take a careful look at the entire situation and the manner in which this turns out. It is important to get a good overview of the expected impact that can be broken up into several parts.

Overall impact: Terror strikes like the one witnessed in Mumbai have a direct impact on market sentiments and lead to movement in markets. Often such strikes have an immediate negative impact because of worries of economic fallout. At the same time there can also be a feeling of resistance to not bow to such situations and this can often lead to a sharp bounce back in prices, as there is some level of overall buying. The important point is not the short-term impact, which can go either way, but the long-term impact, which for a country like India is not very high. This will be a reassuring sign for investors.

Sector impact: While the overall sentiment might return to normal in a short period of time, there can be specific sector impact due to the terror strikes. For example, the tourism industry can take a hit as tourists might tend to stay away for some time. This will impact all the sectors associated with tourism, which include airlines, hotels, tour operators and even local entities. As long as such incidents are not repeated, even this impact wears out after some period of time and things start returning to normal. This kind of sector impact can be specific to each position and hence has to be watched carefully.

Company impact: There is also likely to be specific impact on companies that are directly affected by the terrorist strikes. The impact is on account of two factors. One is the loss that has occurred because of the specific hit that has been taken. So in case of the five star hotels there will be a cost involved in restoring the damaged parts. At the same time there is also the question of loss of potential and future business that takes place due to the event. This has to be estimated and will result in the actual change witnessed in the share price of the company over a period of time.

Points to ponder

- Terror strikes leave a trail of impact that is felt in various areas
- There is the overall impact that often dips immediately after a strike
- For a country like India, the long-term impact is usually very low
- Specific sectors may feel the heat due to these events
- The share price of the individual companies that suffer also changes in proportion to the impact.■

DAY 3

Mumbai's nightmare ends, finally

Team *HT* (Inputs from Ketaki Ghoge, Aloke Tikku & Nandini R. Iyer)

Mumbai, November 29: MUMBAI'S 59-HOUR ORDEAL of terror ended on Saturday morning when security forces announced that the Taj Mahal Palace & Tower was free of terrorists. National Security Guards commandos completed the anti-terror operations that began late on the night of November 26. The attack left 173 dead and 239 injured. The victims include 20 dead and 23 injured foreigners. Till Saturday evening, officials said nine terrorists had been killed, while one had been captured.

The Crime Branch has begun investigations into the attack under the leadership of Joint Commissioner of Police Rakesh Maria. The police are piecing together a picture of the terror operation, thanks to information provided by Mohammed Ajmal Amir Kasav, who was captured at Girgaum on Wednesday night.

Deputy Chief Minister R.R. Patil said the terrorists' plan was to kill at least 5,000 people and that they had enough ammunition for this. 'There were ten terrorists and they came from Karachi by sea,' said Patil. Besides, they made calls from their satellite phones to Pakistan during the attacks. The government did not explain how the bombs in a taxi at Vile Parle and at Mazgaon were set off. Chief Minister Vilasrao Deshmukh said there was no proof that any of the terrorists was a British national. The state is planning to set up a unit of commandos, to be called the Maharashtra Security Guards (MSG), along the lines of the NSG. The state unit will function under the director general of police but will be trained separately and called in only during emergencies.∎

How the Trident battle was won
Rahul Singh

New Delhi, November 29: PEERING INTO THE dark hallway, the two commandos of the National Security Guards saw a silhouetted figure walking towards them. He looked like one of them, but he soon opened fire with his Kalashnikov. 'Hey, it's us,' shouted an NSG commando, 'It's us.' The silhouette let go of another burst.

The Black Cats, as NSG commandos are also called, retaliated. One of the two buddies—they always work in pairs—who had taken position at the entrance swung around his Kalashnikov and shot the terrorist in the legs. He collapsed to the ground, but quickly dragged himself away. That was the first firefight with the terrorists who had taken over the Oberoi Trident hotel Wednesday night, details of which were exclusively shared with *Hindustan Times*. A group of 50 Black Cats had made it to the top of the 21-floor hotel around noon on Thursday. Operational details such as how they managed it—airdropped or scaled up—were not disclosed. 'The commandos saw six bodies on the 21st floor,' said a source close to the Trident operation. They had walked straight into a situation. They started climbing down, painstakingly securing every room on every floor. The 20th was safe, so was the 19th. Then, they reached the 18th. There were two terrorists holed up in a room. They knew the commandos had arrived. Their room, however, caught fire soon because of a hand grenade tossed in their direction by the Black Cats. One of the two terrorists caught the full force of the grenade and died. The other one tried to slip out, to escape the fire, but he walked into the commandos. 'The commandos thought he was one of them,' said the source, adding, 'he was dressed in similar combat fatigues. Or so it seemed to them in the dark.' He then started shooting. Shot in the legs, the man crawled behind something that couldn't be seen very clearly in the dark. But he wasn't shooting back any more. He was trying, instead, to rile the Black Cats into making a mistake. Abusing them in Hindi, the terrorist shouted, '*Dam hai to samne aakar maro* (If you have the guts come out and kill me).' A commando shouted back: 'Coward, you have been hiding like a rat all this while. Why don't you show some courage and step out.' Neither took the bait.

The commandos decided to wait until first light. But they kept firing short bursts in that direction to make sure the terrorist stayed down, if alive. When day broke, the structure behind which the terrorist had taken cover became visible. The Black Cats shot it up. And kept shooting till they were sure no one could survive that kind assault. The terrorist didn't survive it. The raiders quickly secured the floor and declared it sanitized. And then began moving down the building, securing the remaining floors.

They were not to encounter any more terrorists, but they didn't know that then. Securing every room and then the floor was a painfully slow process. The guests had locked themselves inside their rooms and refused to open up even when they were told that it was the commandos. 'Every time a room wouldn't open, we would suspect there were terrorists inside. We were following one simple rule: there could be a terrorist in every room. But we knew there were guests in most rooms. It was Russian Roulette of sorts,' said a commando who took part in the operation. Breaking into a room followed simple procedures: the locks were opened with a master key, adequate warnings were given and then the storming. 'The intention was minimize collateral damage.' They managed zero collateral damage. At the end of the 30-hour operation, the Black Cats had freed over 160 hostages, among them four Israelis and other foreign tourists. The commandos walked out of the building on Saturday evening to thunderous applause from a crowd of onlookers. But they didn't stop to enjoy the moment. It was just one more job done, and done well.∎

Most deaths happened in first hour
Riddhi Shah & Gigil Varghese

Mumbai, November 29: MOST OF THE deaths at the Oberoi Trident happened within the first hour—the most in Tiffin restaurant, then Kandahar and then the lobby, P.S. Oberoi, chairman of the Oberoi group of hotels said on Saturday. After a 48-hour-long operation, security forces rescued 250 people. But 32 people died, including ten staffers and four foreigners—Japanese, Americans and a Singaporean. AK-47 rifles, eight magazines and two pistols were found. Of two groups taken hostage, one was taken to the 19th floor, the other to the 21st and all the people were shot. Yes Bank Chairman Ashok Kapur, real estate developer Sunil Parekh and Solicitor Anand Bhatt were among those killed. When asked about possible security measures that the hotel would take, Oberoi said that they were considering hiring a security expert to help them understand what needed to be done. 'I would like to have armed guards for both hotels, but I suspect that it will take a long time for the government to agree. I also think it's necessary for us to have cameras not just in the hotel, but also on the road outside,' he said. The other possible option is to start scanning each guest's luggage. 'The problem with many of these measures is that security and hospitality don't go hand in hand,' he said.■

Hotel or terror museum?
Sweta Ramanujan-Dixit & Urvi Mahajani

Mumbai, November 29: AFTER BATTLING FOUR terrorists for 60 excruciating hours, security forces finally killed them and rescued the last of those trapped inside the ravaged Taj Mahal Palace & Tower. But the toll was heavy, with at least 22 people killed in the attack.

The bodies of three terrorists were found in the morning while the fourth was recovered in the afternoon with an AK-47, when commandos were sanitising the hotel and looking for booby traps. The Guards tried their best to capture the terrorists alive but the intensity of the gun battle left them with no option but to finish them. 'We gave them a chance to surrender,' said J.K. Dutt, director general, NSG, on Saturday evening, about the four terrorists killed at the hotel. 'If they had a commitment our commandos also had a noble cause.' Dutt said the process of declaring the premises safe, i.e. checking each room for explosives or suspicious objects, would be completed late in the night after which the hotel would be handed over to the state government authorities. One hotel employee was rescued on Saturday morning and 22 bodies were recovered until the end of the day. Seven to eight NSG commandos were injured. 'It looked like they had been killed much earlier. We are still checking all the rooms,' said Dutt. 'We do not know, yet, if there more bodies.'

After the siege ended at 7.30 a.m., the commandos tried to catch their breath, but people mobbed them to shake hands, say thank you and ask for autographs. Many wanted photographs with the commandos and the latter, though weary, happily obliged. Among them was Eijaz Qureishi, who does not remember when he last visited the Gateway of India or even noticed the Taj Mahal Palace & Tower. But on Saturday, the Kurla-resident and a friend paid a visit to see what the 60-hour gun battle between terrorists and security forces had done to the city's landmark building. Instead of the fluttering of pigeons, a common site outside Taj, there were dead birds and shards of glass strewn all over. The magnificent heritage structure was charred beyond recognition at several places.

Many people wanted to take pictures of the hotel from every angle and were looking for any sign of the ordeal that they could capture. Among the favourites were the charred windows of the ballroom on the first floor and the long rope made from bed sheets hanging from a window by the poolside, indicating it was used to escape. The poolside clock, though, had survived the carnage. It showed the time accurately.■

Mumbai cops fight back

THE MUMBAI POLICE were not as tardy as is now believed, according to Mohammed Ajmal Amir Kasab, who told interrogators that he and his comrade—told to stay at CST and keep killing people—

were forced out by retaliatory firing by policemen. They stole through the bylanes, reaching the nearby Cama Hospital where they ambushed three officers: ATS chief Hemant Karkare, Additional Commissioner Ashok Kamte and Inspector Vijay Salaskar. Salaskar shot Kasab through the hand with his service revolver before the terrorist killed them with indiscriminate fire from his AK-56. He and his unidentified comrade then hijacked the officers' Qualis.■

Fourth-class pass to deadly terrorist
Presley Thomas, Abhishek Sharan & Nandini R. Iyer

Mumbai/New Delhi, November 29: IT TOOK 62 hours and India's best commandos to subdue ten terrorists by Saturday—but not before the killers had shot 173 people, ravaged Mumbai and shaken India. As he lies in an unidentified safe-house in Mumbai, with multiple gunshot injuries, Mohammed Ajmal Amir Kasab has—in five-minute spurts of conversations allowed by doctors trying to save his life—told interrogators of the meticulous, rigorous training in arms, navigation and communication that allowed a fourth-standard pass like him to become a deadly terrorist.

On Saturday, the Mumbai Police were given custody of Kasab by an unidentified local judge, who went to the safe-house. It was Kasab, compact and cleanshaven, wearing cargo pants and a t-shirt with 'Versace' emblazoned on it, an AK-56 with multiple magazines strapped together, whose face became the face of India's deadliest urban terror attack.

From Faridkot in Pakistani Punjab, Kasab and his comrades (aged between 18 and 28), nine of them now dead, were trained in close combat, hostage-taking, explosives handling, using satellite navigation, and swimming, a senior police officer said in Delhi, requesting anonymity since he is not authorised to talk about the interrogation. The officer said 'of what he [Kasab] told us, we've been able to confirm that the terrorists whose bodies were found were all from Pakistan'. He did not disclose what evidence corroborated that. Asked about reports about terrorists from various countries, the officer said: 'It does not matter which nation they held passports from—the men whose bodies we found were Pakistanis'.

According to accounts from various interrogators pieced together by *Hindustan Times*, the terrorists, all belonging to the Lashkar-e-Tayyeba (Army of the Pure), were trained at Karachi, Muzaffarabad (in Pakistani Kashmir) and at a dam on the Jhelum river. Banned in Pakistan, the Lashkar has denied its involvement. Kasab and his comrades watched video recordings of their targets and studied south Mumbai topography, an interrogator said. This information was provided either by a recce team that supposedly came four months ago or by what an Intelligence Bureau official called 'local logistics providers', perhaps men from underworld don Dawood Ibrahim's gang, now reportedly holed up in Karachi.

'These are trained terrorists who came from Karachi via the sea route,' said Mumbai's crime chief, Joint Commissioner of Police Rakesh Maria. They boarded either a merchant vessel or fishing trawler—two interrogators differ on this—on November 15, nervously watching Indian coast guard and naval ships near Indian territorial waters. But the patrols never checked them, Kasab reportedly said. They then hijacked the *MV Kuber* near Porbandar, Gujarat, killed three crew, dumped their bodies into the sea, and forced the captain to guide them to Mumbai. 'At around 3 nautical miles from Mumbai, they killed the man [captain] and coast guards found his body in the boat,' said Maria. Kasab told interrogators that the ten terrorists got into their inflatable raft: Six got off at Badhwar Park, about 3 kilometres from CST, and the other four—who engaged commandos in a fierce gun battle at the Taj hotel till they were killed on Saturday morning—came ashore at Sassoon Docks, less than a kilometre away.

The pack of six split into groups of two, with each sub-group given a task kept hidden from the others.■

Working against time to save lives
Team *HT*

Mumbai, November 29: IT WAS EMERGENCY duty that never seemed to end. As the full horror of Wednesday night's massacres at south Mumbai filled television screens and clogged mobile phone inboxes, the area's colonial-era civic hospitals were the first to deal with the bloody onslaught, with medical staff working around the clock to treat the unconscious and extricate bullets from the injured.

Doctors and support staff worked for over 48 hours—and the results show. More than 90 per cent of the injured have been saved. 'We always have an emergency unit of senior and junior doctors of all disciplines ready, and they were fully equipped to handle the cases as soon as we received the news,' said Dr Ashok Borisa of the general surgery department of JJ Hospital. 'There was no shortage of blood and the para-medical staff was plenty.' He has been working non-stop since Wednesday night. 'We are tired but we can't leave our patients.' Most patients had received multiple bullet injuries, he said. 'All patients are stable except one [who died].'

At Cama Hospital, itself a target of terror, most patients were discharged against medical advice. There was the added responsibility of filling discharge forms and taking care of those who decided to stay on, a young gynaecologist who had not returned to the doctors' quarters for over 36 hours, said. 'We can't leave patients in the lurch. I am very scared. I was in the hospital when they attacked. I heard the firing and grenade blasts but can't shun my duty,' said the doctor.

Private hospitals chipped in too. 'We have over 142 resident doctors on call and all senior consultants are available on a 24x7 basis,' said Col (Retd) Bhim Khemani, executive director at Jaslok. At Bombay Hospital in Marine Lines, which has admitted 76 terror victims, off-duty doctors were called back. 'When the first lot of patients was brought in at 11.30 p.m. on Wednesday, many stretchers had been brought down and lined up in the compound,' said spokesperson Dr Ashish Tiwari.

Dr Santosh Goyal, a retired trauma specialist who runs two private hospital, rushed with her staff and ambulance to various civic hospitals. She helped ferry over 30 patients from GT Hospital and St. George Hospital to the better-equipped JJ and Bombay hospitals through Wednesday night.■

Counter-insurgency school changes course
Rahul Karmakar

Vairangte (Mizoram), November 29: THE BLUEPRINT FOR India's answer to terror post Mumbai's 26/11 nightmare is being drawn up in Mizoram, 3,200 kilometres away. When the Counter-Insurgency and Jungle Warfare School (CIJSW) here, some 130 kilometres from state capital Aizawl, was set up in 1970, the credo was: 'Fight a guerrilla like a guerrilla.' The guerrilla, who followed certain 'ethics of bush war', is an endangered species today, having evolved into terrorists and shifted from the jungles to the urban landscape. CIJWS has evolved too in the last couple of months.

'Our regular job is to train the armed forces in India and abroad to beat guerrillas in their own game,' CIJWS commandant Brigadier Anil K. Ram told *Hindustan Times*. 'But we have been updating ourselves to deal with the changing face of extremism, tailoring special courses for the police, who would be manning the battlefields of the future—thickly populated urban centres.'

Accordingly, CIJWS has devoted three of its 13 training ranges to hostage intervention. Simulated urban conditions mark the hostage intervention ranges. New 'kill houses'—many-roomed buildings with mannequins and moving targets—turn into concrete jungle war zones. 'With raptor sights and paintball guns, trainees are divided into terrorists and counter-terrorists, each encouraged to outwit the other in innovate ways,' Brigadier Ram said.■

Terror strikes at cricket's financial muscle

Pradeep Magazine

New Delhi, November 28: TO TALK ABOUT cricket or its financial health in the immediate aftermath of the Mumbai tragedy may sound insensitive, but life has to go on.

Sport, for many, symbolises the coming together of various nationalities, races and religious identities, in conflict with each other. In this war minus the shooting, the conqueror and the vanquished share a drink together once the battle is over. And given the financial health of cricket, especially in India, it is also a sport now which is making the players and the boards of various countries richer by the day. Even after the chilling terrorist strikes in Mumbai, aimed among many things, to maim its economic stability, India may still not be seen as vulnerable to terror as Pakistan in the eyes of the world. The world of cricket refuses to travel to Pakistan, citing threat to life as the reason. The Australians, Kiwis and West Indians have cancelled their tours to Pakistan and now even the Indians are threatening to do so. India, so far, despite also being ravaged by bomb blasts, was not seen by the players and the boards as an 'untouchable'.

During the IPL, the bomb blasts in Bangalore and Jaipur did not deter players from Australia and South Africa from playing in our country. They did not see India as a country where terrorists could strike at will and with impunity. A withdrawal would have also meant considerable loss of earnings from the IPL for the players. The brave decision of the players could be seen as much as an affirmation of sports triumphing over the politics of hate and divide, as the lure of money being stronger than a threat to one's life. It is understandable why no one has raised an eyebrow when the England team withdrew from the one-day series after what happened in Mumbai. Even the Indian players were too traumatised to think of playing. The Indian Board readily decided to cancel the rest of the two matches but have managed to persuade the English Board to send its team back for the two-match Test series. It may be difficult for the England authorities to allay the fear of the players who are reluctant to return for the Tests but it is not an impossible situation.

The stakes are high, not just for England or India but the very survival of the game could be threatened if India as a venue gets excluded from international cricket. Unlike Pakistan, India is the hub of cricket, both in terms of its popularity and its financial health. If the game's revenues have grown manifold and the players are earning more, it has a lot to do with India and its growing economic clout. Already the postponement of the Champions League is having a negative impact on state teams from Australia and South Africa. They and even their boards were hoping to make huge financial gains from the League, which is supposed to impact the future of cricket in a major way. If India loses its primacy in cricket's pecking order due to the fear of terrorist strikes and if the economic meltdown further erodes the investments in the game, then cricket could be in serious danger of losing the kind of mind-boggling revenues it had started generating of late. It is because of these very reasons that foreign teams will think ten times before refusing to come and play here. India is not Pakistan, at least not yet.■

Frontline faces
As Mumbai suffered, these young TV journalists became familiar faces in viewers' homes. They speak of those hours.

George Koshy, 28,
Principal Correspondent, Business, CNN-IBN
Damini Purkayastha

'I WAS AT CST when the firing started, and I tried to get inside when a cop came up to me yelling that it was not safe to go in. Just as I turned, he was shot dead . . . I was at the Taj for 48 hours and though I have reported on tragic events like bird flu deaths, this is something else altogether. I haven't been afraid, no, but there's a fine line between fear and getting facts right. A friend called me and said that his friend was stuck inside the Taj, and though the NSG had come into his room, he was afraid they were terrorists and did not come out. So he was stuck inside for another 27 hours. Our Delhi office sent his location to the NSG DG and in 15 minutes he was rescued. After about 18 hours outside the Taj we went looking for some tea, and there was a guy sitting with tea and biscuits who refused to take any money from us. He said he was doing it in the name of Babulnath. Such touching stories really make the spirit of Mumbaikars real.'∎

Rohan Singh, 23, Reporter, DD News
Himadree

'THIS IS MY first real assignment. I've never experienced such a panicky situation in my life. I flew down to Mumbai on Thursday at 10 a.m., and since noon I've been reporting non-stop. I don't remember the last time I had a nap. But it doesn't matter. I wasn't afraid even when the terrorists fired straight at the media people, but I was shaken for a moment when this girl standing just next to me was shot. I don't know where she is now. It was my choice to take up this assignment. The final assault was what I'll always remember. Saturday morning at six, after a long lull, the NSG suddenly sprang into action. Watching them, we were all just rooted to the ground. I felt exhausted, but not for a moment did I regret coming. I am in the same clothes, same spot, and I've been running endlessly from one spot to another, gathering news. My mom has called several times to keep a check on me. While it's a great loss for humanity, I'm really proud of what I've done.'∎

Manish Prasad, 24, Senior Correspondent, India TV
Namya Sinha

'I'M A CRIME reporter and I knew I'd be sent to Mumbai once the news broke. I reached at 6.30 a.m. on Thursday and headed for Nariman House. We could feel the impact and the splinters of the blasts whenever the terrorists threw grenades. More than fear, I think all of us could feel the adrenaline rush. My cameraman and I went to a building behind Nariman House, from where we had a better view. Though we couldn't see the terrorists, we could see movements and saw someone waving a white hanky. Before we knew it, they were shooting at us, My mother was terrified for me and angry that I was being a daredevil.■

Abhishek Bhalla, 26, Correspondent, Headlines Today
Kirti Mehta

'I HAVE BEEN on my toes since 10 p.m. on Wednesday, the time when the news broke. I first went to the PM's residence for a reaction, and then flew down to Mumbai at 6 a.m. Thursday. Since then it has been almost non-stop on-site reporting. On Thursday, I had to live on chai from a Colaba tea stall, and on Friday, we got some food from the office. I have seen encounters and attacks, but nothing like this. This is one of the biggest terror attacks after 9/11. There seems to be no end to these attacks. But I don't feel the fear; it is basically work for me. I am also most impressed by the police and the commandos.'■

Ishan Choudhary, 24, Senior Correspondent, NewsX
Garima Sharma

'I BEGAN REPORTING from the Taj at 10 pm on November 26. Bodies were then being wheeled away from the hotel. We were not sure if this was a terrorist attack or some psycho's handiwork. It was only when the army came in that the truth sank in. At first, when I started reporting, I was plagued by fear. Soon, the fear was buried in a sense of duty and urgency. Two moments define these attacks for me—when a taxi driver trying to get an elderly couple out of harm's way was shot, the couple covered him and took him to the nearest hospital; the other was when a senior police official died protecting a press photographer. During this ordeal, my mother sent me an SMS every hour. I am quite tough when it comes to death. But the deaths of Hemant Karkare, Ashok Kamte and Vijay Salaskar were a huge shock. It is hard to believe that people you spoke to in the morning are just not there anymore.'■

Toral Varia, 27, Senior Special Correspondent, CNN-IBN
Damini Purkayastha

ABOUT 9.30 P.M. on Wednesday, I got a call from Leopold Café [in Colaba] and thought it was a random firing, but then colleagues on the way home from CST started calling and said something huge had happened. I knew then it was a terrorist attack. I was at the Metro Junction when the terrorists drove past in the police Qualis, opening fire. One guy from our team was hurt and someone lost his life. I've covered crime for nine years, I've seen death and blasts, but in the face of this hugely coordinated, bizarre attack, the media, the police were all stumped. I knew the ATS chief personally; his death was shocking. I was outside the Oberoi Trident the whole time and the locals gave us water, tea and samosa and Marine Plaza across the road allowed me to use their premises to send my news. I went home for a nap on Friday night and I kept hearing gun shots . . . I had been hearing the sounds of gunfire for so many hours that I was imagining them even at home.■

Unknown heroes: Ordinary folk, extraordinary moments

'I crossed my fingers and decided to take a chance':
Dr Tilu Mangeshikar
Mini Pant Zachariah

WHEN TERRORISTS OPENED fire, Dr Tilu Mangeshikar, along with daughter Kalindi and her doctor husband Prashant, was attending a wedding reception in the Taj hotel. 'I remember wondering why they were bursting loud crackers now when the baraat was already here,' says Mangeshikar. Within seconds, the hotel staff confirmed gunshots, shut the doors to the Crystal Room and told the guests to duck. Mangeshikar, along with the other guests, crawled to the Taj Chambers where they were holed up for four hours.

'Around 2 a.m., we were evacuated. Three men in khakhi escorted us through a narrow corridor when suddenly bullets rained at us from the front. We stumbled back into the room that had been our refuge and barricaded the door with tables and chairs,' she recalls. Mangeshikar then realised one of the hotel employees had been hit. 'The bullet entered Rajan's back and had come out from the front, through the abdomen. His intestines had popped out.' With no sanitised gloves in sight, Mangeshikar grabbed the hotel serviettes and pushed back the intestines into the wounded man.

'The bleeding was controlled but Rajan was writhing in pain. We did not know how long the ordeal would last and I had to do something.' Fortunately, one of the foreigners had some painkillers. 'I just had to take a call. I had to take a chance and cross my fingers Rajan would make it,' she says. The painkillers worked. The injured man calmed down. When help finally came at 8 a.m. on Thursday, Rajan was rushed to Bombay Hospital for immediate medical care. He was reported to have survived, thanks in no small way to Dr Mangeshikar. ■

'I wasn't afraid. I just wanted to ensure they got out safe': Abhijit Dalvi
G. Mohiuddin Jeddy

LITTLE DID 26-YEAR-OLD Italian Consulate employee Abhijit Dalvi know that heavily armed terrorists would play party pooper at the end of the Festa Italiana 2008 held at the Oberoi on the evening of November 26. What he did know, however, was his duty—to help evacuate 13 Italian delegates who were caught in the death trap that was the luxury hotel. The Mumbai resident had just returned home when he received calls from Italian delegates informing him of the firing at the hotel. Accompanied by his boss Salvatore Ianniello, Dalvi rushed out in his motorbike.

He recalls, 'While parking my bike, I saw a speeding police jeep pass by escorting a Skoda car. The car changed its route; the police opened fire and there was an exchange of fire.' Despite witnessing the shootout, Dalvi went on to help rescue 13 Italian delegates hiding in the kitchen's basement along with other guests. 'No one was allowed near the hotel. But the guests were being let out in batches of ten and the last of my delegates came out by midnight,' says Dalvi.

The delegates, 12 of whom were women, were in a state of shock, says Dalvi, who heard their accounts first hand. 'They saw the terrorists barge into the hotel and fire indiscriminately and said that around 50 bodies were lying in the lobby,' he narrates.

Until morning, Dalvi and his troupe of 13 hid in the parking lot of the INOX cinema hall nearby. 'When I learnt of a Lufthansa bus leaving the area, I sent the delegates in it to the Italian Consulate on Peddar road.' He also arranged vehicles for some foreigners who were hiding.

Recounting the horror of the delegates and the volatility of the situation, Dalvi admits that it was a very dangerous situation as the terrorists could have attacked anytime. 'I wasn't really scared. I just wanted to ensure that the delegates got out safe.'■

'I told my family this was more important': Sanjay Sawant
Riddhi Shah

ON WEDNESDAY NIGHT, 39-year-old Sanjay Sawant was taking an unwell friend to GT Hospital. And then the terrorists struck. 'We heard gunshots,' says Sawant. 'The cops told me that they couldn't do much. They were completely unprepared to deal with the terrorists who were so heavily armed,' he says.

His family was calling every five minutes, begging him to come home but, Sawant says 'injured people and bodies were pouring into the hospital' and the staff couldn't handle everything. So after calling fellow Shiv Sainiks from the shakha nearby, he got some injured back by ambulance and helped load dead bodies into the cars. He got home at 3.30 a.m., only to return in four hours. 'We then started helping the patients out. 'Some needed blood. We donated. Others needed to get in touch with family. We organised that,' he says. At 9 p.m., Sawant headed to Colaba, close to

Nariman House. 'The restaurants in the area were shut. People in neighbouring buildings didn't have much to eat. We got a restaurant opened up, and gave food and water to several residents,' he says. The police were focussed on the Taj and the Oberoi operations. Every time guns went off near Nariman House, Sawant's heart jumped. 'But by then, I'd dealt with the fear. If I have to die, I'd rather die while helping others.'■

'I was scared but my voice didn't fumble': Vishnu Zende
Rajendra Aklekar

THIS MAN SAVED three trainloads of passengers. Thirty-seven-year-old Vishnu Dattatram Zende, a Railways employee for the last 18 years had been posted at CST for the last five years. As an announcer, he was at a vantage point above the stationmaster's office. He could see the terrorists calmly firing indiscriminately and lobbing hand grenades at innocent passengers while they couldn't spot him. 'Two gunmen entered the waiting hall of CST for the long-distance trains. I heard an explosion and immediately thought there had been a blast. I made announcements asking the Railway Protection Force and Government Railway Police staff to rush to the station for emergency help,' Zende told *HT*. His first instinct was fear, but he decided to use the public address system to alert the police and the general public. 'In an aggressive tone I began alerting passengers that they should exit the station from the rear gate on platform one and not attempt to come to the CST front entrance and lobby since there was a problem,' Zende says. He never let on that terrorists were in the station. 'I was scared, but my voice did not fumble. I do not know how many lives I saved, but I was just doing my job.'■

One battle won, another lost
Kiran Wadhwa (Inputs from Urvi Mahajani & Presley Thomas)

Mumbai, November 29: THE BATTLE AT Nariman House has been won, but not far away from the five-storeyed building another was lost. On Saturday, the Gohils finally mourned for their son Harish (25), who died on Wednesday in terrorist fire. The call-centre employee mistook the gunfire as firecrackers being burst to celebrate India's victory against England and went out, but never returned.

'We still can't believe that we lost our innocent brother in such a gruesome way,' said Reena (23). 'We did not even have a chance to mourn or have a decent funeral until today.' A few feet away, at Nariman House, the police combed the ruined building for evidence. 'Security forces recovered two AK-47 rifles, nine magazines, two pistols and mobile phones,' said an official. A commando, who was part of the operation, said that terrorists had tied the hands of hostages and seem to have shot them one at a time.

The national security forces on Saturday defused explosives that terrorists had placed below the three hostages' bodies. Had the bodies been lifted, the explosives would have gone off, killing everybody. 'The attack has shocked the world. We are viewing it as India's 9/11,' said Raz Haiabenharosh, an Israeli journalist.■

OBITUARY: Sabina Sehgal Saikia
Vir Sanghvi

THE LAST TIME I saw Sabina Sehgal Saikia, she held my hand for the TV cameras, led me past platters laden with rice dishes, told me that rice was Indian Viagra and reached for a drink. That single image sums up my view of Sabina: irrepressible, extroverted and blessed with the ability to add life and laughter to the world around her.

Of course there was much more to Sabina than that single image. She could be as brutal as she could be funny. For over a decade she was Delhi's—no, India's—leading restaurant critic and her scorn was widely feared in the food business. She could make restaurants with a single review. She could destroy them with a few well-chosen words of derision. (Just ask the folks at Veda which she stripped of all its trendy pretensions and which now survives as a better-looking Kwality's almost entirely because Sabina destroyed it in the first week.) Restaurateurs never understood that no matter how much Sabina laughed or drank with them, her ultimate loyalty was to the reader. People read her reviews to decide where to go for dinner and she would never, ever mislead them.

I remember being part of a panel discussion with her at a Chef's Conference. One of the chefs protested that reviewers did not understand the pressures they were under. 'Sometimes a chef is tired. Sometimes, at the end of the evening, he cannot give his best,' he explained. 'Oh yes,' retorted Sabina. 'And when the chef is tired, does he give the guest a discount? Or does he charge full price anyway?' Her point was valid, just as her loyalty was clear. If restaurants charge money then they must be prepared to be judged. Nevertheless, it took guts to be as blunt to an audience full of hundreds of chefs. But then, Sabina was nothing if not blunt. Her contribution to the food world cannot be underestimated. A terrific cook herself (her momos beat the hell out of any restaurant version), she was also a curious eater. Whatever money she made from her journalism (especially after her husband Shantanu started making lots of money from his websites) she spent on eating. Talk to Sabina about London restaurants and she would have eaten at all of the best ones, blowing up vast sums on large meals. Mention molecular gastronomy and she would tell you how Ferran Adria cooked for her at the Singapore Gourmet Festival. Discuss Pacific Rim cuisine and she would tell you about restaurants in Sydney and the strengths of Tetsuya's cooking. She brought that formidable knowledge and experience to bear on Delhi's restaurant scene, showing no patience with restaurateurs who were content to churn out the same old rubbish and being unfailingly encouraging of anyone who tried to do something new, different or difficult.

Of course I shall miss her as will her many, many friends. We will miss her laugh, her loyalty, her affection, her exuberance, her wit and her astonishing cooking. But the loss is not just personal. India's food scene has lost one of its pioneers, a critic who dared tell it like it was; who pulled no punches; who knew more about food than most restaurateurs and many chefs; and who showed us the way forward. The next time you go to a restaurant and have a good meal, think of Sabina. If she hadn't forced our restaurateurs to push for innovation and quality, we would all be eating very badly today.■

Anti-terrorism Squad chief Hemant Karkare was doing his job—both in Malegaon and Mumbai
Mukul Kesavan

New Delhi, November 28: THE DEATH OF Hemant Karkare, the chief of Maharashtra's Anti-terrorism Squad, in the battle against *jihadi* terrorists in Mumbai, puts the recent squabble over the term 'Hindu' terror into perspective. The alleged involvement of Sadhvi Pragya Singh Thakur, Lt Col Purohit and Swami Dayanand Pandey with the terrorist explosions in Malegaon had lazy journalists using the term as a kind of tabloid shorthand.

Spokesmen for the BJP and commentators sympathetic to the Sangh Parivar objected to the use of Hindu in this adjectival way and they were right. To assimilate a large law-abiding community to the violence of a few bigots is not just politically incorrect, it is dangerously polarising. Hindutva or Hindutva-vadi terror is more accurate and more appropriate, just as the term 'Islamist' is used to distinguish violence by *jihadi* Muslims from Islam in general or Muslims as a community. But the Sangh Parivar's objection to the term doesn't spring from such intellectual scruple. It is born of the need to deny that Hindus can be associated with terror at all. For L.K. Advani and Praveen Togadia, the offence lies in the suggestion that there can be any equivalence between violence by Muslims and violence by Hindus. The reason Hindus can't be terrorists is that in Hindutva lore, Hindus have historically been victims and victims can't be perpetrators.

This, however, was not something that could be categorically stated in a situation where Anti-terrorism Squads, hitherto notable for their pursuit of Muslim suspects, had begun to brief the press about the evidence they had accumulated against the Sadhvi, the Swami and the Colonel. Notorious as Indian police agencies are for their inability to make prosecutable cases against alleged terrorists, the chance that they did have the goods on the Malegaon suspects forced the Sangh Parivar to make its case for blanket Hindu innocence in a more roundabout way.

The opening gambit was to say that justice should take its course and the guilty ought to be punished. This was read by some to mean that the BJP and the RSS were distancing themselves from the more extreme Hindu groups like Abhinav Bharat, which have been linked by the police to the Malegaon suspects. But after a momentary hesitation when the story broke, the Sangh Parivar embraced the accused.

The BJP announced its intention to provide them with legal aid (this after becoming apoplectic when the vice chancellor of Jamia Millia Islamia extended the same facility to students arrested for an alleged involvement in terrorist incidents), it accused the ATS of torturing Pragya Singh Thakur, it criticised Karkare for doing the bidding of his Congress masters, it lobbied for the case to be removed from the jurisdiction of the ATS and called for a judicial investigation. The next rhetorical move was to argue that unlikely though it was that Hindus could be terrorists, even if it were allowed (for the sake of argument) that the suspects had been responsible for setting off the Malegaon bombs, the context of their actions absolved them morally, or, at the very least, mitigated their guilt. This context was, of course, the historically constant state of victimhood in which all Hindus lived. It followed, then, that if Hindus were guilty of terror, it was terror of a lesser order, it fell under the category of 'understandable' violence. One commentator even found a term for it: 'retributive terror'. From 'retributive terror' it is a short step to the 'cleansing violence' so beloved of ethnic hygienists.

The opportunism, the dishonesty, the moral squalor of this

position has been thrown into high relief by the deaths of policemen like Hemant Karkare, Ashok Kamte and Vijay Salaskar. These men who died fighting Islamist terror were the same people who had been investigating the possible involvement of Hindu suspects in terrorist explosions in Malegaon and elsewhere. For this they were pilloried by the BJP; now the leaders of that party are queuing up to hail them as Indian heroes, as martyrs in the war against terror. Gujarat's chief minister Narendra Modi decided to visit Karkare's family to offer his condolences and a crore of rupees. The ATS chief's widow didn't meet him and refused to take his money.

A party that condemns policemen one day for investigating terror suspects and then commends them the next day for dying while fighting the good fight against terror (because it sees Hindus as intrinsically innocent and Muslims as congenitally guilty) is unfit to rule. To defeat terrorism India needs intelligence that's gathered and acted upon by clear-eyed, even-handed policemen. The last thing we need is to have these policemen bullied by politicians who are blinkered by prejudice and made stupid by bigotry.■

The four stages of terrorism
Pramit Pal Chaudhuri

THE NATURE OF contemporary militant Islamicism keeps changing, with new tactics and new organisational structures being introduced. Such tactics are hardly exclusionary—terrorist groups will try old, new and different tactics all at the same time. They only want to know what will work. But using al-Qaeda and its affiliates as weathervanes, it is possible to make a case that *jihad* has evolved and that Mumbai may be the beginning of a new era.

1980s–1990s: Era of backyard Islamicist struggles
Ideologically focussed on overthrowing specific regimes, like the non-democratic governments of Algeria and Egypt, or fighting countries seen to be occupying Muslim lands like Israel and India.

- *Spectacular example:* Assassination of Anwar Sadat of Egypt in 1981 was probably the most famous terrorist act of this period.
- *Preferred tactics:* Mimicking the methods of secular leftwing and nationalist terrorist groups like the Palestinian Fatah or the Irish Republican Army. Hence hijacking of aircraft, assassination of political figures and kidnapping of foreigners. Few of these attacks had much of a ripple outside the region that they took place. Largely seen as a local law and order issue rather than an international menace.

1990s–2001: Rise of spectacular global *jihad*

Osama bin Laden and the Egyptian Ayman al Zawahiri argue local Islamicist struggles need to combine forces so they can replicate Soviet defeat in Afghanistan. To bind such groups together, they conclude, requires targeting the US and ensuring attacks are a quantum leap higher in terms of casualties.

- *Successful attack:* The obvious answer is 9/11, still the world's most lethal and media-friendly terrorist attack. But it was preceded by attacks on US warships and embassies in Africa and the Persian Gulf.
- *Preferred tactic:* 9/11 stamps suicide bombing as the preferred *jihadi* tactic but also raises the bar on how spectacular the attack must be. From roughly 2002 onwards there is a huge surge in suicide bombings across the world, spreading into places like Kashmir, Chechnya and so on where they had previously been rare.

2001–2007: Maturing of local guerrilla terrorism

Losing its Afghan base, al-Qaeda turns to local *jihad* affiliates to keep up the momentum of attack. Transit attacks in Madrid and London follow. But US invasion of Iraq and Afghanistan provides a new outlet for *jihadi* wrath. Abu Musab al Zardawi, head of al-Qaeda in Mesopotamia, begins to replace Bin Laden as the terrorist of the moment.

- *Successful attack:* The entire campaign against the US military in Iraq which soured the US public to the war and led to a consensus on the need for the US to withdraw from Iraq as soon as possible.
- *Preferred tactic:* In Europe, it's the bomb in the bus or terror on the train. In Iraq it is a more straightforward guerrilla style war with roadside explosive devices, suicide bombers. Zardawi introduced such niceties as the execution video à la Daniel Pearl and a strong touch of anti-Shia sentiment.

2008: Possible start of global guerrilla terrorism

Suicide bombing hurts al-Qaeda sentiment among mainstream Islam. Surveys have shown declining support for such tactics since 2005 onwards. Proves increasingly ineffective against new security methods and in terms of winning media attention. Al-Qaeda now has a base and a large pool of local *jihadi* fighters it can influence in the Pakistan–Afghan border areas.

- *Tactical experiment:* The use of small bands of suicide fighters, trained like professional soldiers, that simultaneously strike local and global targets. Mumbai is now being seen as the most intricately coordinated and most successful Islamicist terrorist attack since 9/11. This could well be the dawn of a new era of such terrorism.∎

Urban *jihad* comes to town
Daveed Gartenstein-Ross

MORE THAN 24 hours after terrorists unleashed a wave of violence across Mumbai, standoffs continued at the Oberoi hotel and a Jewish center. The loss of life was considerable—more than 150 dead, with the toll almost certain to rise. In the aftermath, there are more questions than answers, particularly questions about the future of terrorism.

The first set of questions involves the reach of American, British, and Indian intelligence. Though it isn't clear how many attackers were involved, informed observers put the number around

20. Yet none of the intelligence services expected an attack of this magnitude. Nor do these services know much about the organisation assumed to have perpetrated the attacks, the Indian Mujahideen (IM). Past IM operatives who have been captured have been low level, leaving intelligence services with scant information.

A second set of questions involves the goal of the attacks. Terrorists typically seek to strike fear, damage symbolic targets, and hurt the economy of the target country. These attacks on India's financial hub accomplished all of these goals. But they could have taken even more lives. Why, for example, did the attackers focus almost exclusively on American and British citizens, and Jews? Almost certainly, one consequence will be further damaging relations between India and Pakistan. There is already peripheral evidence of Pakistani involvement. There are reports of involvement by Lashkar-e-Tayyeba, a Pakistan-based terrorist group with a complex set of connections to the ISI (connections that have become weaker under Pervez Musharraf, and now Asif Ali Zardari). Will the ensuing tensions cause Pakistan to mobilise forces to the Indian border? If so, one likely consequence of the Mumbai assault will be Pakistan drawing its military away from Bajaur and Swat, where it has been in heated combat against Islamic militants.

A final critical question: will the world see a move toward an urban warfare model? Certainly urban warfare offers a number of advantages to attackers. A suicide bombing is over as soon as it happens, though occasionally there are follow-on attacks aimed at first responders.

The Mumbai attacks, in contrast, still were not resolved after a full day. It caused a citywide lockdown. They were coordinated among dozens of terrorists and kept secret from multiple intelligence agencies. In contrast, building a bomb—even a sophisticated one—requires only a handful of people.

The Mumbai attacks represented the evolution of a different model of terrorist attack, and by any metric they succeeded wildly. Nobody should count on this being the last time terrorists employ urban warfare.■

The future of terrorism
Pramit Pal Chaudhuri

THEY MAY CALL the next several years the 'Era of Mumbai Terror'. An increasing number of counterterrorism specialists say the nature of the attack is clearly different from the South Asian norm and possibly even by any global measure. And because it was so successful—a score of armed men holding an entire country to ransom for three days—it may become a model for the next wave of *jihadi* fighters.

Colonel Jonathan Fighel of Israel's International Institute for Counter-Terrorism is among those who has pointed out that the Mumbai attacks are 'unusual not only for India, but also on the international scale'. The subcontinental norm has been a 'series of explosions undertaken simultaneously by radical Islamic organizations aiming to kill' masses of people. This was an 'all-out offensive, with clear military hallmarks.'

The military nature of the attack is striking. Indian commandos have been interviewed as saying it was like fighting regular soldiers whose training was not unlike their own. And contrary to the common perception, the militants largely avoided the taking of hostages or using civilians as shields. The innocents were either executed or got caught in the crossfire. Lashkar-e-Tayyeba and its ilk have over the years developed a *jihadi*-making process that churns out ideologically-driven cannon fodder. This attack indicates they, probably with the assistance of al-Qaeda grey matter, have shifted to quality over quantity. US intelligence sources say they rate the Mumbai attack as being more sophisticated and logistically complex than even 9/11.

Slam-bang terrorism may make way for a special forces variety. Why would *jihadi* master-blasters feel the need to try a new tactic? The reason is that their cause is in the grip of its own global meltdown. The movement's main fighting force, al-Qaeda in Mesopotamia, is in retreat—ironically because of attacks by infuriated Arab Sunni tribal groups. The enemies that Osama bin Laden has often declared to be his number ones—the US, Israel and Britain—haven't had their hair seriously ruffled now for several years. Al-Qaeda affiliates in Saudi Arabia, Southeast Asia and the Caucasus are subprime and falling.

It's not as if militant Islamicism doesn't have its bright spots. The Afghanistan–Pakistan border and the Maghrib are still in turmoil. But this is a far cry from 9/11. The movement is struggling to find a new clarion call and, as important, offer evidence it remains a potent force against the infidel. It is clearly flailing. The latest set of videos by Ayman al Zawahiri and Bin Laden are noteworthy for their weirdness. Comparing Barack Obama to Malcolm X or offering leftwing analyses of the world financial crisis indicate the message is in trouble.

The medium of terrorism isn't faring too well either. Terrorism needs to show a steady stream of successes to win hearts and minds. Outside of the governance wilderness of Afghanistan, Islamicist terror is struggling against security and intelligence establishments that have surpassed it in thoroughness. Islamic terrorist groups haven't really gone beyond the same old hijack aircraft formula. Their long-awaited technological leap forward to liquid bombs, biological and chemical agents, dirty bombs and the like show no signs of ever materialising. When US presidential voters rate potholes on roads a greater concern than terrorism, it's time for any self-respecting mujahideen to consider joining the Boy Scouts.

Mumbai 26/11, with its mix of military force and managerial nuance, may come to be seen as a major tactical shift by terrorists. Terrorism expert Bruce Hoffman famously said a terrorist is an 'intellectual gone bad'. The new definition may be an 'MBA holder gone bad'.

India should worry. Terror attacks of such complexity are most easily detected and disrupted by a developed country which has deep pockets and efficient systems. A country like India, with a foothold in three centuries, provides both porous lines of defence and excellent, globally important targets. Rohan Gunaratne, author of *Inside Al Qaeda*, points out that 'the world's top four countries that suffer from terrorism are Afghanistan, Iraq, Pakistan and

India.' Take out the failed and rogue States and only India is left. Or, to put it another way, you won't find a Chabad-Lubavitch guesthouse in the other three. Other major cities are bombarding New Delhi with questions about the tactics, methods and whatnot that the attackers used. Mumbai's terror experience, an assault that invoked Che Guevera as much as it did Sayid Qutb, may be a dry run for it is a new template of blood.■

'We've never felt scared. This is the first time we've been made to feel like Jews.'
Naresh Fernandes

AS A CHRISTIAN, I occasionally remind my Jewish friends that I owe my faith to them. Indian tradition maintains that a few years after Christ's death, one of his apostles, Thomas ('the Doubter'), sailed to Kerala to share the Good News with his co-religionists. Jews have lived in India for thousands of years, perhaps arriving on a mission from the court of King Solomon to trade in 'elephant's tooth, peacocks and apes'. The Jews of Cochin are said to have been less than receptive to Thomas's message, though he did make many other converts.

India's ancient Jewish history, evidence of the country's tolerance for people of all faiths, has long been a source of pride for us. But an even greater cause for satisfaction has been the fact that Indian Jews have never faced persecution. Indian Jews have flourished, and nowhere is that more evident than in Mumbai. Some of the city's best-known landmarks, including Flora Fountain, have been built with donations from Jewish philanthropists who grew prosperous on trade and manufacturing. Most notable among them were the Sassoons, a family from Iraq. Their name is etched in plaques in at least four schools, a magnificent library, a dockyard and at least two of the city's nine synagogues.

A more chilling reminder of the city's role as a sanctuary for Jews is to be found on another set of marble tablets in a cemetery in Chinchpokli in Central Mumbai. One wall bears memorials to people who died in faraway concentration camps such as Auschwitz. It was donated by friends and relatives who found refuge here. Many of these exiles had arrived in India because of the intervention of Jawaharlal Nehru. 'Few people can withhold their deep sympathy from the Jews for the long centuries of most terrible oppression to which they have been subjected all over Europe,' Nehru wrote, as he lobbied the British government to allow Eastern European Jews into India. 'Fewer still can repress their indignation at the barbarities and racial suppression of Jews which the Nazis have indulged in during the last few years.' Many of the exiles soon became an important part of Mumbai society, serving as catalysts for the modern Indian art scene. Rudolf von Leyden, Walter Langhammer, and Emanuel Schlesinger had brought with them full-colour reproductions of European masters and a world of ideas and discussion. They proved vital in helping the Mumbai artists discover a new way of seeing. These ideas found expression on canvas when painters such as M.F. Husain, F.N. Souza, and K.H. Ara founded the Progressive Artists Movement in 1947, bound together by the desire to find a new way to depict the stories of their newly independent nation.

Despite the significance of the contributions of the Baghdadis or the European exiles, the Jewish community that has left the deepest impression on the city are the Bene Israelis, who believe their ancestors were shipwrecked just south of Mumbai in 175 BCE. Centuries later, many of them migrated to Mumbai, where they built a synagogue in 1796.

Perhaps the best-known member of the community was Nissim Ezekiel, one of the pioneers of Indian poetry in English. My favourite of his poems is 'Island', a tribute to my home city. The first stanza says, 'Unsuitable for song as well as sense/ the island flowers into slums/ and skyscrapers, reflecting/ precisely the growth of my mind./ I am here to find my way in it.'

Though thousands of Indian Jews have emigrated to Israel over the years, many of those who stayed behind have an ambiguous relationship with the country that offers them the Right of Return.

Among them is my friend Robin David, the author of *City of Fear*, a gem of a memoir that describes the horrors he witnessed as a reporter during the anti-Muslim pogrom in Gujarat in 2002. He also explains his frustration with Israel, a country to which he has attempted to emigrate three times, only to return. 'I realised that the Promised Land was not my country,' he writes. 'Even the strong fragrance of spices, wafting in from the Arab market through the yellowing Jerusalem sandstone, did not help. Just like Teen Darwaza [in Ahmedabad], but not quite home.' There's another aspect to the relationship that goes unnoticed by most Indians. Each year, an estimated 20,000 Israelis take their vacations in India after finishing their three-year compulsory military service stints. Their 15,000-shekel bonuses go much further in India and, as one Israeli told me recently, 'It's nice to be in a place where you don't always have to watch your back.' The beaches of Goa and the slopes of Kulu and Manali rank high on the visitors' itineraries. The massive numbers of Israelis in the subcontinent prompted the Brooklyn-based Lubavitcher sect to open its first Indian mission centre—known around the world as Chabad Houses—in Pune in 2000.

Two years ago, I travelled to Pune to interview Rabbi Betzalel Kupchick, who ran the centre. By offering his hundreds of Jewish visitors a year of free meals and the chance to chat in Hebrew, Rabbi Kupchick believed he was opening an opportunity for dialogue. 'There are many ways that God brings people to Him,' he told me patiently. 'Here, without the pressure of family and society, Israelis are more open-minded. Often, this is their first exposure to spiritual things. When they come to India, they're searching.'

Mumbai's Jewish community doesn't have much to do with the Israeli visitors. The ultra-orthodox leanings of the Lubavitchers have been regarded with some suspicion by liberal Indian Jews. That divide disappeared on Wednesday night. When I spoke to Robin David on the phone on Friday, he was still trying to make sense of it all. 'The Indian Jewish identity is the only one that hasn't been created by persecution,' he said. 'We've never felt scared. This is the first time we've been made to feel like Jews.' That, to me, has been among the most tragic casualties of this terrorist attack. In a barrage of grenades and bullets, a part of the Indian dream that's 2500 years old has now been buried in a pile of bloody concrete shards.■

Defeat or victory isn't determined by the success of the strike itself, but by the response
Amitav Ghosh

SINCE THE START of the terrorist invasion of Mumbai on November 26, the metaphor of the World Trade Center attacks has been repeatedly invoked. In India and elsewhere commentators have taken to saying, over and again, 'This is India's 9/11.' There can be no doubt that there are certain clear analogies between the two attacks. In both cases the terrorists were clearly at great pains to single out urban landmarks, especially those that serve as points of reference in this increasingly interconnected world.

There are similarities too, in the unexpectedness of the attacks, the meticulousness of their planning, their shock value and the utter unpreparedness of the security services. But this is where the similarities end. Not only were the casualties far greater on September 11, 2001, but the shock of the attack was also greatly magnified by the fact that it had no real precedent in America's historical experience.

Our experience of terror attacks, on the other hand, far predates 2001. Although this year has been one of the worst in recent history, the year 1984 was arguably worse still. That year a burgeoning insurgency in the Punjab culminated in the assassination of Prime Minister Indira Gandhi. This in turn led to riots, which took the lives of some two thousand Sikhs. I was living in Delhi then and I recall vividly the sense of besetting crisis, of extreme fragility, of being pushed to the edge of an abyss. It was the only time I can recall when the very project of the Indian republic seemed to be seriously endangered.

Yet for all its horror, the portents of 1984 were by no means obvious. In the following years, there was a slow turnaround; the Punjab insurgency gradually quietened down; and although the victims of the massacres never received justice in full measure, a process of judicial retribution was indeed initiated.

This has been another terrible year. Even before the invasion of Mumbai several hundred people had been killed and injured in terror attacks. Yet, let us recall that the attacks on Jaipur, Ahmedabad, New Delhi and Guwahati did not succeed in setting off chains of retaliatory violence of the sort that would almost certainly have resulted ten or fifteen years ago. Nor did the violence create a sense of existential crisis for the nation, as in 1984. Thus, despite all its horrors, this year could well be counted as a victory not for terrorism but for India's citizenry. The question now is: will the November invasion of Mumbai change this?

Although there is no way of knowing, this at least is certain: if the precedent of 9/11 is taken seriously the outcome will be profoundly counterproductive. As a metaphor, the words '9/11' are invested not just with the memory of what happened in Manhattan on September 11, 2001, but also with the penumbra of emotions that surround the events: the feeling that 'the world will never be the same', the notion that this was 'the day the world woke up' and so on. In this sense '9/11' refers not just to the attacks but also to its aftermath, in particular to an utterly misconceived military and judicial response, one that has had disastrous consequences around the world.

When commentators repeat the metaphor of '9/11' they are in effect pushing the Indian government to mount a comparable response. If they succeed in doing this the consequences are sure to be equally disastrous. The very power of the 9/11 metaphor blinds us to the possibility that there might be other, more productive analogies for the November invasion of Mumbai. One such is the Madrid train bombings of March 11, 2004, which led to a comparable number of casualties and created a similar sense of shock and grief. If 9/11 is a metaphor for one kind of reaction to terror, then 11-M (as it is known in Spanish) should serve as shorthand for a different kind of response: one that emphasises vigilance, patience, and careful police work in coordination with neighbouring countries.

This is exactly the kind of response that India needs now: a refusal to panic, heightened vigilance, and most particularly, judicious cooperation with those elements of the Pakistani State who have come around to a belated recognition of the dangers of terrorism.

The choice of targets in Mumbai clearly owes something to the September bombing of the Islamabad Marriott. Here already there is common ground between the two countries—for if this has been a bad year for India in regard to terrorism, then for Pakistan it has been still worse. It is clear now that Pakistan's establishment is so deeply divided that it no longer makes sense to treat it as a single entity. Sometimes a crisis is also an opportunity. This, if any, is a moment when India can forge strategic alliances with those sections of Pakistani society who also perceive themselves to be under fire.

Much will depend, in the coming days, on Mumbai's reaction to the invasion. The fact that the city was not stricken by turmoil in the immediate aftermath of the attack is undoubtedly a positive sign. The fact that the terrorists concentrated their assault on the most upscale parts of the city had the odd consequence of limiting the disruption in the everyday lives of most Mumbaikars.

Chhatrapati Shivaji station, for instance, was open within a few hours of the attack. Although there was much fear and uncertainty, the city was not panic-stricken. But with each succeeding day, tensions are rising and the natural anxieties of the inhabitants are being played upon.

But this is not a moment for precipitate action. If India can react with dispassionate but determined resolve then 2008 may yet be remembered as a moment when the tide turned in a long, long battle. For if there is any one lesson to be learnt from the wave of terror attacks that has convulsed the globe over the last decade it is this: defeat or victory is not determined by the success of the strike itself. It is determined by the response.∎

THE INVESTIGATION

DECEMBER 2008

Terror commands came from Nariman House
Abhishek Sharan

New Delhi, November 30: '*UNKE COMMANDO HAIN, maaro, maaro
&%$# (Their commandos have reached there, kill them)'
   '*Uda do (Shoot them)*'
   '*Grenade phenk, grenade phenk (Throw grenade)*'
   '*Jalaa de (Set fire)*'
These were some of the instructions being sent out by cellular
phone from one of the terrorists—killed by the National Security
Guards on Friday night at the Jewish residential complex of
Nariman House in south Mumbai—to his comrades, according to
telephone intercepts available with the Intelligence Bureau.

This man, as yet unidentified, allegedly the 'operations controller'
of the ten-man Lashkar-e-Tayyeba *fidayeen* unit that went on a
62-hour killing spree on 26/11, issued many of those instructions
after watching live television coverage of the siege at all three
locations, a senior IB officer tasked with monitoring these
conversations told *HT*, requesting anonymity as he is not authorised
to speak to the media.

'This suspect, who was killed along with another associate at the
House but not before they allegedly killed five hostages, was the
leader of the *fidayeen* team,' said the officer. 'Till he died on
Friday, for over 44 hours since his team began attacks across the
Taj Mahal, Oberoi and Trident hotels, this man was directing his
eight other associates in their tactical manoeuvres and armed
actions against the NSG, marine commandos and even the hostages,'
said the IB officer. 'He [the controller] was the man who issued
instructions on the type of offensive, defensive measures his men
needed to take against the advancing commando teams,' the officer
said.

The suspected team leader 'kept an eye on the round-the-clock coverage of the ongoing commando operations carried out by news channels', the officer said. Alarmed by his alerts, security officials requested news channels to 'not show current positions of the commandos, to use earlier footage'.■

Saved by the skin of the teeth
Sujit Mahamulkar

Mumbai, November 30: CHIEF FIRE OFFICER A.V. Sawant can never forget how he came face-to-face with a terrorist at Taj hotel on Friday. He was dangling on the aerial ladder platform, the ladder with a cage on the top, outside a window on the fifth storey during rescue operations when he saw the terrorist. Sawant was saved in the nick of time because he quickly changed position of the ladder and came down before the terrorist could blink. Sawant's story is similar to many of the 300 firemen, who were part of the rescue operation at the Taj, Trident and Nariman House along with the NSG, and police.

But Sawant got lucky twice. He was on duty at the Taj from Wednesday night to Saturday morning. On Thursday morning, he was discussing and planning further strategy with Joint Fire Officer P.D. Kargoppikar and Assistant Divisional Fire Officer P.S. Rahangdale at 7 a.m., when there was a lull in the firing.

'A terrorist threw a grenade towards us, it fell right between us and rolled under one of our vehicles. We were lucky because it was pinned properly and did not explode,' said Sawant, adding this was an incident he was unlikely to forget because it had given him a fresh lease of life.

Rahangdale recollected another chilling experience at the Trident. He and two other officers were on the ladder rescuing guests, when terrorists lobbed two grenades at them. 'They were not aimed properly and exploded away from us. We were plain lucky.' The firefighters were among the many unsung heroes of the last three nights. They had started operations by Wednesday night before the NSG commandos got on the field.

At Taj, they controlled fire at least 40–45 times, said Sawant. 'They [terrorists] wanted to set the entire hotel on fire. Our job was to control it. The jawans did me proud.' ∎

Doctor walked into danger to treat wounded at Taj
Dr Mursalin Shaikh (29), Critical care specialist
(As told to Chitrangada Choudhury)

ON WEDNESDAY NIGHT, I was sitting down for a rare dinner with my mother at my flat in Kala Ghoda, when a staff member from Taj hotel, which has a tie-up with my employer, Bombay Hospital, gave me a call. 'There seems to be some sort of fight here at the hotel, please come across,' he said. I had no inkling of the long night that lay ahead.

When I drove in to the hotel with my department head, I was surprised that there was no security at the entrance. I walked in to the lobby, and I saw some bodies, mostly foreigners, lying on the floor. I caught a fleeting glimpse of a man with a rucksack firing indiscriminately and running up the stairs. I tried to run out, but a policeman at the door told me that the roads were also not safe with grenades being lobbed all over the place.

I called my wife, also a surgeon at Bombay Hospital, and she said, 'Stay where you are. There has been a shootout at the Metro cinema. The area seems unsafe.'

We, the hotel's general manager and my department head, decided to attend to the bodies, even as the sound of firing continued incessantly from the floors above.

I remember rushing to an elderly European man who had gone blue because of bullet injuries and I began administering resuscitation. He was put in an ambulance, but I do not know where he was taken and if he survived. Grenades were being lobbed in our direction, so we moved to the old wing, but we could see a fire there.

I felt scared, especially when there were two big blasts in the hotel before the army came in. We had already spent three to four hours inside. I would call my surgeon wife every hour, and she was at Bombay Hospital treating the injured. She said, 'I am missing you, and your medical expertise while treating the injured.'

My mother phoned me. 'Are you the only doctor in the city?' she cried. 'Please come home.'

But there was no question of leaving. Those who were dead had been lost. But those who were unconscious needed to be rushed to hospitals. We moved about 20 patients into ambulances. We finally left the hotel at six in the morning. I stopped at home, and then went to the hospital. Doctors had come in through the night to help treat over 80 patients who had been brought in from various sites of attack. I am happy I could be of help to some people, and am relieved to be alive.■

From Manipur to Jaipur, this is an Indian tragedy

Team *HT* (Alka Dutt & Rakesh Verma in Patna; Ashok Das in Hyderabad; Salil Mekaad in Indore; Sobhapati Samom in Imphal; K.S. Tomar in Jaipur; Amit Roy in Chandigarh & Rajesh Kumar Singh in Lucknow)

Mumbai, November 30: THE INVITATIONS WERE out, the caterer booked, the sweets distributed, the shopping over. The wedding was next week.

That is when the phone rang late Wednesday at the Patna home of software engineer Khusboo Jha. Hundreds of kilometres to the south in Mumbai, her fiancé Malayesh Banerjee, a venture capital executive, had been killed by terrorists as he dined with friends at Mumbai's Leopold Café. Phones were ringing with news of death and injuries through the next several days in cities and towns around India. In India's cosmopolitan hub, Mumbai's terrorist attacks were India's tragedy—possibly the first time when homes across the country were together affected by terrorism at such a staggering scale.

Three days ago, Jha's doctor father and lawyer mother had completed a pre-wedding ritual sitting on a mat at their home in Patna's Srikrishnapuri neighbourhood.

A thousand kilometres to the south-west in Indore, another coffin brought in another body on Friday. Neighbours rushed to help carry it to the home of 27-year-old Gaurav Jain. Jain had finished dinner and was standing by the roadside with two friends on Wednesday night when terrorists fired from a moving police car they had seized.

He is survived by three sisters and his parents Kanta and Balchandra Jain, a retired government official. Gaurav Jain had completed his schooling from Indore before getting an MBA degree from Dubai, and working briefly in Singapore. Minutes before the bullet got him, Jain had spoken to his mother Kanta, telling her about her day and that he was having dinner with friends.

Maibam Bimolchandra, 30, had last spoken to his parents in Manipur two days before he died. 'He never wanted to work there [Mumbai] . . . he promised he would construct a new house for us. But everything is gone now,' said his father M. Nandababu, mourning at his home in the Khurai Ningthoubung Leikai village in Manipur's Imphal East district. The son worked as an assistant manager at the reception of the Oberoi hotel.

Three bullets hit Bimolchandra on Wednesday night, as he fell at the hotel lobby. Hundreds of men and women in traditional mourning attire took part in ceremonies held in Imphal and his native village before he was cremated. Bimolchandra was a national handball player and had had represented Manipur in many national championships. He was to travel to Britain on December 1 for a six-month training course before a foreign posting. 'Everything was ready for it, but all of a sudden, it was all over,' said Nandababu, who works for the state's public works department.

At another end of the country in Hyderabad, a family quietly mourned the 20-year-old woman who had just finished a day of sightseeing in Mumbai. Ameena Begum, daughter of a labourer, stood at the Chhatrapati Shivaji Terminus, waiting to board the Devagiri Express to return home to Nizamabad, 180 kilometres from Hyderabad.

She was returning after 12 days of prayer from a Sufi shrine in Bijapur town, where she prayed that her poor health—which was affecting her seven-month-old marriage—be cured. Then she went to visit a sorcerer in Mumbai. She wanted to come back soon. That was when the terrorists started firing indiscriminately and she received three bullets—one in her jaw, another in the chest and the third in the stomach. The terrorists had noticed her as she stood up to pull her niece and father to safety. Her teeth ripped out by the bullet, Ameena whispered to her mother Shanu Begum to give her some water. Within seconds, she was dead. 'What harm did Ameena do to deserve a death like this? Islam never teaches one to take another's life,' said her father Rasheed, as he wept.

Lawyer Laxmi Narayan Goel, 55, from the Andhra Pradesh capital of Hyderabad had missed his return train to Hyderabad and rang his family from CST to inform them. Seconds after he boarded a taxi to his sister's home, it became a ball of fire after grenades thrown by terrorists exploded on it. Goel is survived by his wife and four daughters. His badly mutilated body was identified from the documents on his body.

In a dusty town in eastern Uttar Pradesh, a son had not kept promise made to his father. 'I will earn enough to ensure that all my three sisters are married into well off families,' industrial worker Mohammad Umar had told his father Abdul Khaliq. 'He was the only earning member in the family as I am too old to work in the fields,' Khaliq said. Mohammed had promised to get other jobless men in his village employment in Mumbai.

Four other men from the Sant Kabir Nagar district in Uttar Pradesh were killed, three of them emerging from the Taj hotel after meeting a Bahujan Samaj Party (BSP) politician, seeking help with jobs.

If they were looking for jobs, Niti Kang was looking for peace of mind. 'Brother, please ask Panditji to prepare my horoscope, I feel very dejected these days,' Niti Kang, who died in terrorists attack in Mumbai, told her cousin Sachin Bhatnagar in Jaipur on November 22. Kang, wife of the Taj general manager Karamvir Kang, died with her two children.

'I was planning to go to Panditji to get a horoscope for her but the Almighty had a different plan,' Bhatnagar said. Kang was to move into their new home—four days after she was killed.■

26/11 could have been stopped
Vir Sanghvi

New Delhi, December 1: AS THE INVESTIGATION into the intelligence failures that preceded the Mumbai attacks proceeds, there is evidence that even quite specific information that was gathered was either not properly analysed or not acted on. The Research and Analysis Wing, India's external intelligence agency, had provided several intercepts from signals intelligence over the last three months. These suggested that a terror strike on a Mumbai hotel was imminent. But they were largely ignored.

On September 18, R&AW computers intercepted a satellite phone conversation between a known Lashkar-e-Tayyeba asset and an unknown person. The LeT asset said that an operation to target a hotel at the Gateway of India in Mumbai was being planned and that the sea route would be used.

On September 24, R&AW's computer recorded another satellite phone conversation. This time, the LeT asset identified the hotels that were being considered for the attack by name. They were the Taj, the Marriott, the Lands End and the Sea Rock. A possible attack on the Juhu airfield (used by a flying club) was also discussed. All these hotels have one thing in common: they are easily accessible from the sea.

The Taj is on the Apollo Bunder waterfront, the Marriott is on Juhu sea face and the Lands End and the Sea Rock are both on the sea-facing tip of Bandra. This should have been enough to let police know that: (a) Hotels were the target. (b) The attackers would use the sea route.

On November 19, R&AW listeners picked up another unexplained satellite phone conversation. A voice said, 'We will

93

reach Bombay between nine and eleven.' R&AW trackers identified the exact coordinates of the call and discovered that it came from the sea near Mumbai, 40 kilometres west of Jhol. This was clear evidence—at the very least—of an attempt being made to enter Mumbai illegally by people armed with advanced satellite phones. R&AW passed on the information contained in each intercept on the very day it was received to the centralised intelligence group set up by the National Security Advisor. Its officers say that R&AW's job ended there—it does not have the authority to operate on Indian soil.

Despite repeated attempts by *HT*, National Security Advisor M.K. Narayanan did not take calls.

On November 26, the day of the attack, but several hours before it had begun, R&AW trackers recorded a conversation between the LeT's Muzammil, who has been under surveillance for some time, and a Bangladesh number. Muzammil said that five SIM cards would be required for the operation.

R&AW analysts are still making sense of the conversation. Was Muzammil referring to another operation? Why would he ask somebody in Bangladesh for SIM cards to be used in Mumbai on the day of the operation? One theory is that the LeT was unwilling to phone its Mumbai assets directly for fear that they would be traced. The Bangladesh number was either a relay station from which the call was forwarded to Mumbai or perhaps the LeT communicated with its Mumbai cells through Bangladesh based cut-outs or intermediaries.

The revelations about the phone intercepts (which R&AW has documented) are certain to lead to questions about the government's inept response to the attack, especially as the intercepts make it clear that (a) Mumbai hotels were being targeted (b) that the sea route was being used and (c) that the attacks were imminent. The Mumbai Police say they had no specific inputs from intelligence agencies. But these intercepts were clear, detailed and specific. So, are the police lying? Was this information not passed on? Or was it just incorrectly processed? So far, there are no answers.■

Terrorists got caught—and got away

Stavan Desai

Mumbai, December 1: THE HIJACKED FISHING trawler that brought the ten-man squad of terrorists to Mumbai's shore on the night of November 25 was actually stopped by an unidentified Indian coastal patrol vessel—and let off because the suicide fighters flashed fake Gujarat government cards issued to fishermen, the lone terrorist now in police custody has revealed. Inquiries are now under way with the coast guard, the coastal wing of the customs and the Border Security Force (which patrols a disputed area called the Sir Creek area) to identify the vessel.

In a disclosure that indicates yet another failure in stopping the hit squad of suspected Lashkar-e-Tayyeba (Army of the Pure) terrorists, Ajmal Amir Kasab from Pakistani Punjab told his interrogators that they were aboard the *MV Kuber* 300 nautical miles (556 kilometres) from Mumbai, off the coast of Jhakhau, Gujarat, when they were stopped. They escaped by flashing Fisherman Identity Cards, issued by the Gujarat government. These cards were found on the *Kuber*, whose captain was killed after he guided the boat to Mumbai's western shore. Maharashtra too on December 1 announced it would issue smart cards to its fishermen. The Gujarat Department of Fisheries of Gujarat issues these smart cards to fishermen of the state to help them prove their identity on the high seas and to get a mandatory customs okay needed before each fishing trip into international waters. On the same day the ten terrorists sailed along the coast of Gujarat enroute to Mumbai, a police station at the port town of Mandvi registered a case against 'unidentified persons' for faking Fisherman Identity Cards. 'We have registered the offence and are investigating it,' said Police Inspector S.N. Jhala of Mandvi police station. 'Till now we do not know who has been forging signatures of the authorities to get these cards issued from the Department of Fisheries.'

Earlier, on August 27, 2005, the local crime branch of the

Kutch police arrested a man called Salim Amad Jat and found 76 fake smart cards with him. Central security agencies are now investigating how these smart cards wound up with the terrorists. Kasab, injured in a gun battle with commados, is now in the custody of the Mumbai Police and is being held in a safe-house at an undisclosed location.■

24x7 coverage undermined ops
Chitrangada Choudhury (Inputs from Rahul Singh & Vijay Dutt)

Mumbai, December 1: DID THE DETAILED, real-time coverage of the 60-hour battle between commandos and terrorists by Indian TV channels endanger the success of the operations and the safety of the hostages? Sources close to the NSG said the lack of restraint on the part of the channels seriously undermined the commando operation.

'Television channels airing live feed of commandos being air-dropped on to a building captured by terrorists not only compromised our safety but also took away the element of surprise, which is critical in operations of this nature,' they said.

Veteran print and TV journalist and now Media Studies professor at the University of Bristol, Prasun Sonwalker, felt 'the initial coverage soon collapsed into overkill of the channels' infotainment practices, where sensation is king. Journalists were clearly unable to deal with the trauma that was unfolding, and went overboard.'

Not everyone is as critical, though. 'This was a huge story, in a very competitive field,' said Somini Sengupta of the *New York Times*, who was among the journalists camping outside the Taj hotel, adding: 'At the same time, reporters must observe some basic rules—you cannot touch evidence; and you cannot walk around a scene of crime.' The criticism of the media's conduct has already resulted in introspection. The News Broadcasters Association of India, which is a little over a year old, will meet this week to evolve a code of conduct for the industry to follow in such situations.

It is long overdue, conceded Rajdeep Sardesai, President of the Editors' Guild of India and Editor-in-Chief of CNN-IBN. 'We need more restraint and higher ethical standards. And the challenge . . . will be to ensure we actually implement the code we frame.'

Dr Peter Lehr, Senior Researcher at the Centre for the Study of Terrorism & Political Violence at St. Andrews College, UK, pointed to the Defence Advisory in the UK that suggests a code of conduct for the media while reporting on security and intelligence issues. It advises the media to treat information of a sensitive nature carefully so as not to hamper any operation or give away information that helps terrorists.■

'Kasab calm, composed; shows no fear or remorse'
Kanchan Chaudhari

Mumbai, December 1: AJMAL AMIR KASAB, the lone terrorist captured alive during the 26/11 terror attacks, reportedly shows no remorse for his killing spree. Instead, the 21-year-old alleged Pakistani national has been telling Arthur Road Jail personnel '*maine jo kiya achchha kiya* (Whatever I did was good)', jail sources told *HT* on condition of anonymity.

Kasab has been shifted to the jail for the test identification parade. Several witnesses have identified him before a special judicial magistrate. A witness who participated in the parade on Sunday said, on condition of anonymity, that it was being conducted in an open hall within the jail premises where policemen connected with the investigation were not allowed.

Explaining the process, the witness said the parade was held before a magistrate and two panch witnesses. Kasab was lined up with six identically dressed people and the witness was called in to identify him. 'The magistrate told me that one of the people present is an accused who fired indiscriminately in the Chhatrapati Shivaji Terminus on November 26 and asked me whether I can identify him,' he said. 'I moved forward and touched and pointed towards him.'

But some witnesses were nervous, he said. 'Some of the witnesses were scared even to face the terrorist. Two of them, probably Kolis from Badhwar Park [where the ten terrorists landed and entered the city] were very scared,' he said. 'One of them somehow gathered courage and identified him.' Kasab was composed, he said. 'The young man clad in t-shirt and pants was dressed identically to the other people standing with him.' He was not tall but had a 'strong, well-built body', the witness said. 'Every time after the identification the magistrate would ask the terrorist his name, he would shout "Ajmal Amir Kasab".'

Kasab is being identified primarily in connection with three cases—the killings at CST, the encounter at Girgaum Chowpatty and hijacking of a Skoda owned by hotelier S.R. Arasa.■

Kasab squeals, nails Lashkar role in attack
Presley Thomas

Mumbai, December 2: AJMAL AMIR KASAB (21), the terrorist arrested by the Mumbai Police, has started singing. He has told investigators that dreaded Lashkar-e-Tayyeba commander Mohammed Muzzamil, who is known by aliases such as Yusuf and Abu Gurera, controlled the entire operation, codenamed 'Operation VTS', to attack Mumbai.

Kasab, who was made to listen to intercepted telephone conversations, has identified the voice of Muzzamil. Police sources said the terrorists, who had entered the city with five prepaid SIM cards, were in constant touch with Muzzamil, who kept barking out orders through the operation. Two of the five SIM cards have been traced to Delhi, while the remaining three were brought from Kolkata. 'They were procured on the basis of bogus documents and were smuggled to Pakistan,' said an investigator.

According to police sources, Muzzamil had called the terrorists holed up at the Taj Mahal Palace & Tower, Oberoi Trident and

Nariman House using a Voice Over Internet Protocol (VOIP) telephone. The US Federal Bureau of Investigation (FBI) has helped investigators track the VOIP telephone to a computer in Lahore.

Kasab has told interrogators about the various Lashkar camps that he has attended since 2007. He has also told investigators about Lashkar's base camp where Jamaat-ud-Dawa chief Hafiz Mohammad Sayeed and others deliver fiery speeches to motivate the cadre. Ajmal also disclosed to investigators the inflammatory films that were shown to brainwash Lashkar recruits.

According to police sources, Kasab revealed that LeT conducts regular training camps at Danna, Abdul-bin-Masud, Mangla Dam and Um-al-Qura camps in Muzaffarabad and Badli in Kotli. He has also disclosed that LeT has opened two new camps for handpicked cadre to train for suicide missions at Akas in Muzaffarabad and another camp in an area known as 'Point'. He also told investigators that LeT commander Zaki-ur-Rehman Lakhvi had promised his poor family in Faridkot a large sum of money in return for his participation in the attack on Mumbai.

Based on Kasab's revelations, the Crime Branch of the Mumbai Police is preparing a dossier on the banned terror outfit, which will be handed over to the Ministry of Home Affairs, the National Security Advisor and the FBI.

The dossier will also be handed over to the Pakistan government, which has been seeking evidence against LeT from the Indian government. Deven Bharti, Additional Commissioner of Police (Crime), confirmed that a dossier on the entire operation was being prepared. Meanwhile, investigators are examining the Garmin GPS and walkie-talkie set used by the terrorists to track the exact route the terrorists took to enter Mumbai from Karachi.

FBI grills Kasab

For the first time, India has granted permission to a foreign agency to question a terror accused arrested on its soil. The FBI, the federal criminal investigative body of the US Department of Justice, was allowed a brief interaction with Ajmal Amir Kasab, the terrorist arrested by the authorities, after the US offered help to fight the ongoing war against terrorism, said police sources.

The FBI, which undertook a guided tour of the Taj and Oberoi hotels, Nariman House and Leopold Café, and met senior police officers and officials from central intelligence agencies, has also offered technical expertise to assist the probe, added sources.■

Terrorists conducted several dry runs along sea route
Haidar Naqvi

Kanpur, December 2: THE SEA ROUTE taken by the terrorists who attacked Mumbai last week—that took India's security agencies by surprise—has seen some pretty heavy traffic in recent times.

According to the Jammu & Kashmir Police, it arrested two Lashkar-e-Tayyeba militants who entered India via this route on March 11, 2007. Abdul Majid of Nawabshah in Sindh and Mohammad Jamil of Manshera were part of an eight-member group that was launched from Karachi by their commander, Cheema, in a fishing trawler. The group, after entering Indian waters, moved to another boat waiting for them and reached Mumbai on March 5, 2007, where they divided into four groups of two militants each.

A senior J&K police officer said his department had informed both the coast guard and the Mumbai Police about this new infiltration route following their arrest. Another report was sent detailing the plans and descriptions of the remaining six who are still at large.

The sea route was in the spotlight once again when the police in Kutch arrested two LeT operatives, Abdul Khaliq Tayyab and Abdul Gafoor Qasim Chaba—both Pakistani nationals—on July 13 last year with Rs 24 lakh in fake Indian currency and a GPS device. A case was registered against them at the Dayapar police station in Kutch. These two told their interrogators their trip was part of a series of dry runs on the Karachi–Mandvi and Karachi–Jhakhau sea routes being conducted by their handlers. They said their handlers had built a network of local fishermen who were paid Rs 5 lakh each time they landed a consignment on Indian shores. 'Tayyab and Gafoor carried a GPS they used to navigate and reached Dayapar in Lakhapat area of Kutch. They were instructed by Amanullah Khan Parocha, a key LeT operative, to undertake sea journey and meet certain other operatives,' the FIR lodged at the Dayapar police station says. Then, in April, the Hyderabad Police arrested a UAE national, Alkaz Khamis Obaid Kamal, who confessed to having shipped Rs 1.72 crore using the sea route.■

Gafoor makes it official: Only ten terrorists
HT Correspondent

Mumbai, December 2: POLICE COMMISSIONER HASAN Gafoor said on Tuesday that there was no proof of 'immediate local support' for the November 26 terrorist attacks. He was, however, quick to add: 'We are interrogating many suspects, but none of them have been detained.'

Discounting reports that the terrorists had knowledge of the Taj's layout, he said: 'It does not seem that they knew about the hotel from before. They were just running from one place to the other.' Gafoor said the police had not received any 'specific intelligence' of the attack, though scrambled intelligence in the form of an alert to beef up security at hotels, including the Taj, had been sounded soon after the Marriot blasts in Pakistan in September.

Almost a year ago, the police had received intelligence about a possible attack from the sea in Gujarat and some South Indian states, but not Mumbai, Gafoor said. He also dismissed reports that the terrorists had an escape plan, adding: 'It appears to be a suicide attack.' He also sought to quash rumours that five terrorists were at large, saying there had been ten, of whom nine were killed and one was captured. There was no woman in the group, as reported in a section of the media, he asserted. He said the terrorists had reached the coast in rubber boats and split into five groups of two each. They had assault rifles, pistols, grenades, ammunition and a time bomb for every group. Of the five bombs, they planted one each below the front seats of the two taxis that blew up in Mazgaon and Vile Parle respectively. The rest were planted in a passageway between Leopold Café and the Taj, at a turning near the Taj and one inside the Oberoi hotel. Luckily, none of these went off.

The terrorists, said Gafoor, could not do more damage at Chhatrapati Shivaji Terminus because of wrong information supplied by their bosses. They had been asked to climb to the first floor of the station and fire from vantage points. However, there is no first floor, which confused them. When asked what proof the police had of Pakistani involvement, Gafoor pointed out that the ship under investigation, *Al Hussaini*, was boarded by the terrorists at Karachi. He also referred to the arrested Pakistani terrorist Ajmal Amir Kasab.■

Black Cats could have cut terror short
Rahul Singh

New Delhi, December 2: THE COMMANDOS OF the National Security Guards could have launched operations in Mumbai at least three hours earlier had they been alerted on time, given a special aircraft immediately and provided clear roads for their movement.

Top NSG sources told *HT* that these factors handicapped rapid response that could have saved many more lives. The terrorists had more time to hole themselves up in defensive positions. The Black Cats stationed in Manesar, near Gurgaon, were alerted at midnight on Wednesday, two and a half hours after the terrorists struck. They had to drive to the Palam airport in trucks because air force helicopters did not have night flying capabilities. After loading equipment, ammunition and stores in trucks, the commandos took an hour to reach the airport. The police had made no arrangements to facilitate swift movement as laid down in the rulebook.

An NSG commando, who took part in the Trident-Oberoi operations, said: 'We can launch operations 30 minutes after being alerted. The commandos were ready for combat at 12.30 a.m. [Thursday]. We could have reached the hostage sites at least three hours earlier.' A military transport (IL-76) was provided by the Aviation Research Centre, which is a part of the Research and Analysis Wing, to fly the Black Cats to Mumbai. Its crew had to be woken up and the plane refuelled. The NSG does not have its own fixed wing aircraft. The home ministry has not responded to its demand for an aircraft.

The NSG can charter a plane but that takes time. K. Subramanyam, a member of the Kargil Committee Report, told *HT*, 'The NSG should have been based closer to an airfield. It must have its own aircraft that are operationally ready at all times.' Operations at Trident-Oberoi began only at 10.30 a.m., 13 hours after the terrorists had taken control. NSG sources said, 'The outcome of the operations could have been different had we been given early warning and briefed in advance.' ■

Low IQ: Why India fails
Varghese K. George

New Delhi, December 2: AN ADVANCE TEAM of security personnel securing the Oberoi in Mumbai for Prime Minister Manmohan Singh's visit at a function on November 29 had no idea of persistent terror alerts for several sea-facing hotels in that city.

These alerts had been sounded by the country's external intelligence agency, Research and Analysis Wing not once but four times, as reported exclusively by *Hindustan Times* on Tuesday. *HT* has learnt that a team of the Special Protection Group (SPG), the outfit that protects past and present PMs and their families, left the Oberoi barely minutes before terrorists struck on November 26. This paper reported on Tuesday that R&AW had four intercepts starting September 18 about an operation being planned and launched by the terrorist outfit Lashkar-e-Tayyeba against Mumbai hotels using the sea route. Though the Oberoi was not among those named in the intercepts—the alerts were against sea-facing hotels. Those named were the Taj Mahal, the Marriott, the Taj Lands End and the Sea Rock. The Oberoi also faces the sea. But the SPG had no clue to these alerts.

Every public place that is to host the prime minister for any length of time is checked and sanitised by the SPG one or two days in advance. And every threat perception is considered before the visit is allowed. Each of these alerts was sent to a centralised intelligence group set up by the National Security Advisor M.K. Narayanan. Sources in the intelligence agency told *HT* they don't know what happened to these alerts. They didn't at least go to the SPG as it was not aware of these alerts. Officials in the group refused to discuss this issue when contacted for comments. Hotel sources said that the SPG team was asked to stay for dinner. But they declined, and left the hotel minutes before it was stormed by the terrorists.■

Lashkar chief is key motivator: Kasab
Presley Thomas

Mumbai, December 3: HAFIZ MOHAMMAD SAYEED, the *amir* (chief) of Jamaat-ud-Dawa, is the key motivator of Lashkar-e-Tayyeba recruits, captured terrorist Mohammed Ajmal Amir Kasab has told investigators.

Lashkar is the militant wing of the Jamaat-ud-Dawa. Kasab, the 21-year-old Rawalpindi thief-turned-terrorist, the only survivor of the terror squads that attacked Mumbai, has cast new light on Lashkar's methods.

Sayeed, who has denied links with Lashkar, visited its training camps in Rawalpindi, Muzaffarabad and Kotli regularly and gave inflammatory speeches, he told investigators. Kasab, who along with Mohammed Ismail Khan attacked Chhatrapati Shivaji Terminus, said it was a Sayeed speech at Rawalpindi and a meeting with Lashkar co-founder Abu Waleed Zaki-ur-Rehman Lakhvi that drew him to the terror outfit. Sayeed is among the 20 men whom India has sought from Pakistan. Once at a Jamaat-ud-Dawa camp, Sayeed convinced Kasab that Lashkar and its suicide missions were for the glory of the religion. He told investigators Lakhvi kept referring to Sayeed. Police sources said the Lakhvi–Sayeed link dates back to 1990 when they formed the Markaz al-Dawa wal Irshad with the help of al-Qaeda operative Sheikh Abu Abdel Aziz. Lakhvi, a trained Afghan–Arab terrorist, then scouted for cadres in and around Pakistan. But Lashkar got a boost only after Pakistani dictator Zia-ul-Haq gave Sayeed 200 acres of land near Muridke. Kasab said Lakhvi was the key plotter. Kasab, who finished his training last year, trusted the Jamaat-ud-Dawa after his family was pulled out of abject poverty. Lakhvi also promised to give his family Rs 1.5 lakh if he agreed to go on the operation.

Kasab said he was given weapons training for six months, while training for tactics and explosives lasted four weeks at two different camps in Rawalpindi and Kotli. Later, handpicked cadres were taken to Mangla Dam in Muzaffarabad for eight weeks of marine and commando training.∎

LeT chief denies role in attack
Abhishek Sharan

New Delhi, December 3: IN A DEPARTURE from the past, 'Professor' Hafiz Mohammad Sayeed, Ameer, Jamaat-ud-Dawa Pakistan and the alleged chief of the dreaded Lashkar-e-Tayyeba, has sought to distance himself from the group which carried out the deadly terror attacks in Mumbai last week.

'We would like to clarify once again that Jamaat-ud-Dawa and Lashkar-e-Tayyeba are two entirely different organisations, and to name Professor Hafiz Mohammad Sayeed as being the head of Lashkar-e-Tayyeba is completely incorrect and untruthful, and a deliberate attempt to mislead people,' Sayeed's spokesperson, Abdullah Muntazir was quoted as saying on the terror group's (unofficial) website, www.jamatdawah.org. Sayeed's name figures in the list of fugitives India handed over to Pakistan on Monday night.■

Pak says 'no'
V. Krishna & Amit Baruah

Washington/New Delhi, December 3: PUNCTURING HOPES OF cooperation between New Delhi and Islamabad, Pakistani President Asif Ali Zardari has ruled out handing over wanted fugitives to India and questioned the Pakistani nationality of the Lashkar-e-Tayyeba terrorist captured during the Mumbai 26/11 attacks.

'At the moment these are just names of individuals. No proof, no investigation, nothing has been brought forward,' Zardari told CNN in an interview when asked if Pakistan would hand over to India fugitives such as gangster Dawood Ibrahim and terror chiefs Masood Azhar and Hafiz Sayeed. If there was proof, he said, they would be tried in Pakistani courts. Zardari did not stop at India's old list.

'We have not been given any tangible proof to say that he is definitely a Pakistani. I very much doubt . . . that he's a Pakistani,' Zardari said on Tuesday about Ajmal Amir Kasab, the LeT terrorist arrested by the Mumbai Police. With Zardari rebuffing India's demands for the handover of the 20-odd fugitives, the stage is set for a further escalation in the ongoing row between the two countries.

Responding to Zardari's comments, external affairs minister Pranab Mukherjee said on Wednesday that India was still awaiting a response from Pakistan on its démarche, or diplomatic protest, lodged with Islamabad, demanding that the wanted fugitives be handed over. Mukherjee made it clear that India's future course of action would depend on the response New Delhi got from the Pakistani side.

'The gunmen, plus the planners, whoever they are, they are Stateless actors who are holding hostage the whole world … the State of Pakistan is no way responsible,' Zardari said as Lashkar boss Hafiz Sayeed gave an interview to a Pakistani television channel. Sayeed feared an attack by Indian forces on his Muridke headquarters, considered to be the base of the LeT front, the Jamaat-ud-Dawa. India, Sayeed said, should focus on investigations into the Mumbai attacks.

Zardari said he would not know if the LeT was involved in the 26/11 Mumbai carnage. Like al-Qaeda, it operated outside the system, he said. 'I'm a victim. The State of Pakistan is a victim. We are the victims of this war, and I am sorry for the Indians,' said Zardari, widower of former prime minister Benazir Bhutto. 'I've seen this pain. I feel this pain every time I see my children.' Zardari downplayed the potential for another war with India, saying 'democracies don't go to war.' Pakistan, he reiterated, would never be the first to use a nuclear weapon.

He was asked about US President-elect Barack Obama's statement during the campaign that if Islamabad did not act after receiving specific intelligence, the US had the right to attack terrorist targets in Pakistan. 'That would never arise,' said Zardari. 'The minute we get any actionable intelligence, we shall act ourselves.' When his attention was drawn to a report that Pakistan could be an unwitting source of a terrorist attack on the US, possibly with weapons of mass destruction, Zardari said, 'Ever the more reason that Pakistan needs more help … It's part of the war in Afghanistan.' On the Pakistani intelligence agencies' record of supporting militant movements, Zardari admitted, 'In the past, lots of mistakes have been made.'■

Terrorists' bodies: Not in a Muslim graveyard
Tasneem Nashrulla

Mumbai, December 3: IN A STRONG gesture of rejection, the Muslim Council of India issued letters to the Jama Masjid Trust and the Mumbai Police demanding that the nine bodies of the terrorists should not be buried in the Bada Kabrastan at Marine Lines.

Sarfaraz Arzoo, general secretary of the Council, said: 'The terrorists' acts are un-Islamic. In name they are Muslims, but not in their actions. Thus, we do not want them to be buried in a Muslim burial ground.' He added that the police have assured the Council that their demand will be considered. The Council's view is supported by South Asia's holiest Muslim shrine, Ajmer Sharif. Said Syed Salman Chishty, a *khadim* (hereditary custodian) at the shrine: 'The terrorists are like the *munafiqin* (hypocrites) described in the Holy Quran, who pretended to be Muslim only to accomplish their own agenda. Let the Mumbai Police send these bodies to Pakistan if they wish. They should not lie in a Muslim burial ground.'

However, Hanif Nalkhande, a trustee of the Jama Masjid Trust that manages the 7.5-acre Mumbai graveyard, the only one in the city for unclaimed bodies, said: 'The government [has] stated that the bodies will be buried in an undisclosed location outside Mumbai.' To this, Arzoo responded, 'It is the police's prerogative where to bury the bodies as long as it's not in the Muslim burial grounds under our jurisdiction. Let them keep the location a secret.'

A policeman from the JJ Marg station, whose officers are on security duty at the JJ Morgue where the bodies are presently kept, said that they have not received orders yet to bury the terrorists.■

How heroes were born at CST
Rajendra Aklekar

Mumbai, December 3: WHEN AN UNSPEAKABLE horror descended on Chhatrapati Shivaji Terminus on Wednesday night, the actions and reactions of security personnel and Railways employees would play a crucial role in saving innocent lives. Senior Police Inspector Sandeep Khiratkar, Police Inspector Kiran Bhosale and Constable Jhullu Yadav were among the dozens of Railway Protection Force personnel who fought the AK-56-wielding terrorists.

Fifty-one-year-old Yadav, in an exceptional display of bravery, took a rifle from a colleague, ran towards the terrorists and fired at them. 'He was the bravest among all, and that too at his age,' Khiratkar said. 'This was the first time I had a gunfight with terrorists after years of training,' Yadav said. 'I wanted to kill them.' Khiratkar chased the two terrorists till the rear end on the station. Bhosale, who was posted in the main-line concourse, joined him. 'It was a fight to save passengers and the station,' the 29-year-old Bhosale said.

Mohammed Sheikh, known as Chhotu around the station, serves tea at the booking ticket counter and is quite familiar with the station. He helped many commuters find a safe exit. 'Chhotu entered the booking office and locked the door behind him, shouting at us to lie low,' said Ajay Bhatia, a booking supervisor. Brushing aside his role, Sheikh said, 'Whenever I remember what happened, I just break down.'

Senior ticket checking officer R.H. Dubey, who was posted on the Harbour line section, shielded passengers from the bullets, even helping an old woman carry her luggage, while a fierce gun battle raged. 'I could not think,' Dubey said. 'I only knew I had to help the passengers to safety.'

Outstation terminus manager A.K. Tiwari and his team took charge after the carnage was over. 'We had to restore normalcy as early as possible,' Tiwari said. 'Cleaning out blood and bodies and restoring trains was the priority.' The first train left CST at 2.34 a.m. on Thursday, just hours after the bloodbath. 'There were so many bodies; we had to pick them up, put them in parcel handcarts and take them to St. George Hospital,' said parcel agent R. Selvan. 'It is a sight I will never forget.' At least 57 people died at the station and 87 were injured. For their bravery, a Rs 10 lakh award was announced for Yadav and Rs 5 lakh each for Khiratkar and Bhosale. Railways announcer Vishnu Dattaram Zhende, who kept a cool head and directed people to safety, was awarded Rs 10 lakh.■

With you, for you, always: A tribute to the unknown policemen who died on 26/11

Lina Choudhury-Mahajan, Soubhik Mitra, Joydeepa Sarma, Hussain Khanbhai, Riddhi Shah, Mauli Buch & Mini Pant Zachariah

Prakash More, Police Sub-Inspector

It's not hard to find out where Police Sub-Inspector Prakash More used to live. A giant hoarding with a condolence message has been erected just outside Deen Dayal Nagar, a tribute to a man who served the force for 28 years and lost his life to eight bullets fired by terrorists on November 26.

His widow Madhvi, like most policemen's wives, is unhappy with what More had to go through in the force. He was harassed and pressurised, she said, adding: 'He never got a holiday or leave. We never had a proper family life.' The last holiday the family took was in May, to her village in Mahad. But More could be with them for just a few hours as he had to attend a training session in Nashik.

Madhvi is adamant on not allowing her son or daughter to join the force. 'I will never support such a decision,' she said. She lamented that her husband, like the entire force, was ill-equipped to deal with terror attacks. 'All he had was a small handgun. How could he fight those terrorists? He didn't even have a bulletproof jacket.'

Arun Chitte, Vijay Salaskar's driver

Few know encounter specialist Vijay Salaskar didn't die alone when he took on the terrorists. Salaskar's driver Arun Chitte (37) was with him, refusing to abandon his boss of many years. A bullet in the chest snatched away the patriarch of the family—that included his wife Manisha (28), and three daughters, Komal (10), Snehal (9) and Khushi (4)—that resides at the Dharavi police quarters. The family has gone to their native village, Veergaon, for the funeral rituals. 'We miss Chitte's quiet presence. As he was away the entire day on work, we met him only at night,' said Raju

Ghadi, another neighbour. 'He was a family man. On Sundays, he would love to spend time with his daughters.'

Over the phone, Chitte's elder brother Pandari Nath explained how he went to collect the body and brought back the family to their village. 'He was cremated with a gun salute and the Mumbai and Nashik police were present,' he said with a hint of pride in his quivering voice. Baburao Mane, chairman of Chhatrapati Shivaji Vidyalaya, where Chitte's daughters study, has said he will take care of the girls' education. 'I have decided to waive the fees for his daughters. The family need not worry about that.'

M.C. Chaudhary, RPF Inspector

One bullet was all it took to shatter a humble dream. Six years away from retirement, Railway Protection Force Inspector M.C. Chaudhary was content with the marathon struggle of bringing up his family comprising parents, seven brothers and three sisters. The bullet, amongst the several rounds fired indiscriminately on November 26 hit his left arm, pierced his chest and ended the journey before he could see his children settle down.

The 55-year-old, who died in the firing at Chhatrapati Shivaji Terminus, has a daughter of marriageable age and a school-going son. 'His entire life was spent nurturing the family. Now his brothers have grown up, but he is not alive to reap the fruits of his hard work,' said Snehalata, his wife.

Born in a lower-middle-class household in Khandesh near Bhusalwal, the eldest son had little freedom to chase his own dreams. 'For the 26 years we were married, his daily schedule comprised 10 to 12 hours of work and three hours of commuting between Ambernath and CST,' said Snehalata in their single-room flat—her only possession.

Vijay Khandekar, Police Constable

Constable Vijay Khandekar is survived by wife Shraddha (32), daughter Samrudhi (4) and mother Nirmala—all too stunned to speak. 'We didn't know how serious the situation was. We didn't think that anyone would harm policemen,' said brother

Ashok (41). The family was informed of Khandekar's death the morning after the attack. In a trance, Ashok went to GT Hospital to claim the body and sent his wife Akshata to his brother's home to break the news. The family knew what had happened when it saw Akshata in tears.

Khandekar was very close to his mother and dedicated to his family. 'He would ask Nirmala for advice on everything—even on shoes. He had no vices and his record was flawless,' said Ashok. Khandekar was on leave when he got news of the attacks. He rushed to Cama Hospital and is believed to be the only constable from the Azad Maidan police station actively involved in the incident.

Shashank Shinde, Senior Inspector, RPF

Shashank Shinde (46) was one of the first officers to be shot at by the terrorists at CST. He rushed out of his office as soon as he heard the first shots. He returned fire, but his service revolver was no match for the terrorists' assault rifles.

'Shinde's [action made an impact]. The terrorists were forced to flee CST. But before that, they attacked him from behind. He was hit by four bullets, died within minutes,' said Uttam, his brother. Shinde is survived by his wife Manasi and two daughters aged 18 and 14. 'My brother always gave his duty top priority. He would hardly meet us on days when he was on duty, but he was always there at family gatherings,' said Smita Bhonsale, Shinde's elder sister.

Baburao Dhurgude, Police Sub-Inspector

We just thought there was some rioting. Nothing more,' said Dhurgude's 18-year-old son Vishal. Dhurgude had been watching the match with his son when his cellphone rang and he left in a hurry. 'There's no cable at home, so we had no access to the news. Our father had it removed so we could concentrate on our studies,' said 21-year-old Poonam. It was only when the newspapers arrived the next morning that the Dhurgude family realised the magnitude of what had been happening.

'My mother told me to call my father to make sure he was okay. I couldn't get through, so I called his friend. We thought he was just injured. But when I got to the hospital, I was asked to identify his body,' said Vishal. Working with the Anti-terrorism Squad, Dhurgude's job was fraught with danger, but he never took his work home. 'He never talked about work. He was simple— enjoyed cricket and old movies,' said Neelam, a second-year student.

Ambadas Pawar, Constable
Ambadas Pawar (29) would have been home in Kawte village in Satara by December 1 for his brother Sunil's wedding. Instead, two bullets from terrorists ended his life. Shivam Salukhe, his room-mate and friend, was the first to learn of his death when he called Pawar on his mobile phone. Someone at St. George Hospital answered to tell him about the fatal shootout. 'It took us two hours to find Pawar amid the mounting bodies,' recalled Salukhe. In the one-room dwelling Pawar shared with three friends, a bundle of blue polythene lies in a corner. 'These are the saris Pawar had bought to take home for the wedding,' said Rahul Dewde, another room-mate.■

Sole terrorist survivor reveals he was being trained in Pak
Tushar Srivastava

New Delhi, December 4: THE MUMBAI TERROR attacks have been in the works for at least a year. The interrogation report on Ajmal alias Abu Mujahid, who the media have been referring to as Ajmal Amir Kasab, reveals that he underwent 21 days of physical training and *Darsh-e-Quran* (Quran recital) at a Lashkar-e-Tayyeba camp at Muridke in Punjab in Pakistan last year. This training programme was called *Daura-e-Shufa* (Era of Simplicity). 'He does not remember the date, but recalls that he was in training, along with 24 others, when Benazir Bhutto was assassinated,' the interrogation report states. Bhutto was assassinated on December 27, 2007.

This timeline is corroborated by the confessions of Fahim Ahmed Ansari, who was arrested, along with four others, by the UP Special Task Force in February this year. Following this, after a gap of one or two days, Ajmal, the only terrorist captured alive by the police, was sent to Manzera in Pakistan-occupied Kashmir (PoK) for another 21-day training programme called Markaz-e-Tayyeba (Centre of the Pure). He was taught how to use automatic rifles, including AK-47s and M-16s, and pistols. On completing his arms training, he had to undergo two months of *khidmat* (service) training—as a cook in the camp kitchen.

The courses were very intensive and gruelling and not all recruits made the cut. Ajmal did, and was then sent to another LeT camp in the Cherapadi Pahadi region of Muzaffarabad in PoK in June-July this year. For the next two-and-a-half months, he received advanced training from *ustads* (teachers) in firing AK-47s, rocket launchers and mortars and was also taught how to use GPS systems and marine compasses. The camp commander was a terrorist called Saif-ur-Rahman, alias Chachu (who his fellow terrorist Ismail was trying to call when they were cornered in Mumbai). Ajmal was also trained by terrorists who had returned from Jammu & Kashmir. This bunch of battle-hardened desperados were highly respected by members of the camp and called 'Gazi'.

Apart from arms training, Ajmal and the other 'students' were also taught how to withstand intensive interrogation and mislead interrogators. The methods were primitive and brutal—they were thrashed for several days during training to prepare them for 'hostile interrogations'. Having 'qualified', Ajmal and his cohorts were taught to operate maritime vessels. His handlers now considered him a finished product. He proceeded to Azizabad in Karachi where he and nine others were briefed about their deadly mission.

The group of ten started in a medium-sized boat from an isolated creek in Azizabad on November 23. Three or four nautical miles into the sea, they boarded *Al Hussaini*, a larger, sea-faring vessel. They were given a bag each, which contained eight grenades, one TT pistol with one or two magazines, an AK-47 with three double magazines, a gas lighter, a dry fruit packet weighing 500 gm, loose ammunition, one mobile phone with an Indian SIM card and a walkie-talkie. Each of them was also given fake ID cards. By 12.30–1.00 p.m., they were within reach of Mumbai, but the instructions were to launch the operations only after nightfall. So, they slowed down and waited for the sun to set. At 6.30 p.m., the group of ten boarded a rubber speedboat, fitted with a new Yamaha engine and came ashore in India's financial capital at 8.30 p.m.■

'I've never been convicted on any charge': Hafiz Mohammad Sayeed
Nagendar Sharma

New Delhi, December 4: THE FOUNDER OF terrorist outfit Lashkar-e-Tayyeba, Hafiz Mohammad Sayeed, a fugitive wanted by India for his involvement in many terror attacks, says he cannot be extradited since he has never been convicted either in India or Pakistan.

Sayeed, whose name figures in the list of 20 fugitives wanted by India from Pakistan after the Mumbai attacks, has called the demand for his handover a 'crude attempt' to divert people's attention from the failures of India's intelligence and security agencies.

In an interview to *Outlook* magazine (the issue will hit the stands on Saturday), Sayeed said, 'I have never been convicted either in India or in Pakistan on any charge. On the other hand, a criminal case is still pending against BJP leader L.K. Advani for masterminding Mohammad Ali Jinnah's murder.' He said Pakistan never demanded 'Advani's extradition despite this pending case'. On the other hand, the Indian leadership was using Pakistan as a punching bag to cover its failures at home, Sayeed said. He said the LeT would fight alongside Pakistani forces in case India

115

launched an attack. 'Like any other patriotic Pakistani, we will stand with the army if there is any aggression,' he said.

About India's accusation that the Mumbai attacks were masterminded in Pakistan, Sayeed said it was not the first time India was making the charge, and it would again be proven wrong. 'The Indian leadership was quick to blame Pakistan for masterminding the blasts in Samjhauta Express and Malegaon,' he said. 'Yet their own security and intelligence agencies have finally arrested an Indian army officer as the actual mastermind.' About the arrested Mumbai attacker's admission that he was a Lashkar militant from Pakistan, Sayeed said it was a 'cooked-up confessional statement'.

Completely denying any LeT involvement in the Mumbai attacks, he said, 'Lashkar does not believe in killing civilians.' Sayeed said India was not interested in properly investigating the Mumbai attacks. 'They are only interested in blaming Pakistan, evident from the fact that they started naming Pakistan even while the operation was still under way,' he said. Former Pakistani president Pervez Musharraf had banned the LeT after the 9/11 attacks. Since then, it has been operating under the name of Jamaat-ud-Dawa as a religious organisation in Pakistan.■

26/11 planning started a year ago, and we had the evidence
Manish Pachouly, Presley Thomas & Haider Naqvi

Mumbai/Kanpur, December 4: THE PLANNING FOR the November 26 terror attack started a year ago, and security agencies had evidence of it—nine maps plotting the attack sites recovered from a Lashkar-e-Tayyeba terrorist arrested in Uttar Pradesh on February 10. But the evidence was buried in a bulky chargesheet.

The story began in 2003 in Dubai, where Fahim Ansari, originally a resident of Goregaon (West), was looking for a job. Fahim, already an activist of the banned Students' Islamic Movement of India, was spotted by a Lashkar recruiter. Police sources said Fahim was indoctrinated and sent to Pakistan by sea.

He was trained in Muzaffarabad, Pakistan-occupied Kashmir, in handling computers and arms. Last year, he was sent to Mumbai with orders to scout various locations, most of which were attacked on November 26 by the ten men who came to the city by boat, said police sources. The chargesheet against him said that in Mumbai, Fahim called himself Shahil Paskar and stayed at Sunlight Guest house near Grant Road from November 28 to December 10, 2007. He surveyed spots in south Mumbai and drew out maps by hand. The maps—part of the UP police chargesheet and copies of which are with *HT*—gave directions from Cuffe Parade and Backbay Reclamation to Gateway of India, Lions Gate (the naval dockyard), the state police headquarters, Chhatrapati Shivaji Terminus, Mantralaya, Vidhan Bhavan, Churchgate and the police commissioner's office, among other places. Some maps even gave the time it would take to commute between locations.

On November 26, the ten terrorists landed in a rubber dinghy near Cuffe Parade and Backbay. They then split up into different teams, attacking Taj hotel at the Gateway, CST, the Oberoi and Nariman House in Colaba. Fahim—who was arrested for the December 31, 2007, attack on a Central Reserve Police Force camp in Rampur, UP—confessed to surveying the sites and preparing the maps. A separate first information report filed on February 10 by the Civil Lines police station in Rampur, after Fahim's arrest, mentioned this. The FIR also mentioned the seizure of the maps.

The UP police also seized Fahim's Pakistani passport (BM6809341), which gave his name as Hassan Hammad, a false identity. It was issued on November 1, 2007, and was valid till October 30, 2012. The STF then flew Fahim to Mumbai, where he was kept for three days. During this time, he showed the Mumbai Police all the sites that were eventually attacked on November 26, said STF sources. 'Our officers took Fahim to Mumbai,' confirmed A.K. Jain, Inspector General of Police, UP ATS. 'He told the Mumbai Police everything he told us.' Added Amitabh Yash, then Senior Superintendent of Police, STF:

'Later, the Mumbai Police got a court remand allowing them to take custody of Fahim as well.'

'Fahim guided the ATS to all the attack sites, particularly the Taj and CST, which he'd surveyed. He had sent the information by email to somebody in Pakistan,' said a senior STF officer in Lucknow. Fahim also told the STF that he was asked to arrange for safe-houses as close to the sea as possible and for Maharashtra-registered vehicles, said an STF officer.

But, K.P. Raghuvanshi, currently in charge of the ATS, told *HT*: 'At present, we are not following the Fahim angle.' Investigations showed that Fahim was managed by Muzammil, a Pakistan-based Lashkar commander who was later found to have also 'handled' the ten terrorists who attacked Mumbai.

'Fahim used more than 16 email accounts to communicate with his handlers. He sent them nine scanned copies of handmade maps. His disclosures were later cross-checked with another Pakistani militant Sabauddin, who was arrested for the Rampur attack,' said an STF officer. Fahim was arrested with two others at the Rampur bus stand with grenades and a pistol. Another team nabbed Sabauddin, Imran Shehzaad and Mohd Farooq Bhatti while waiting for Fahim in Lucknow. From them, the STF seized three AK assault rifles, a 9-mm pistol and eight grenades. All of them were to catch the Pushpak Express for Mumbai, where Fahim had established a safe-house for the Rampur attackers. STF sources said he also provided them logistical support.■

Mosques send out anti-terror messages
Team *HT* (Inputs from Tasneem Nashrulla, Mumbai; Tariq Khan, Lucknow; Ashok Das, Hyderabad; Arun Kumar, Patna; Anirban Choudhury, Kolkata & Hyder Naqvi, Kanpur)

New Delhi, December 5: MUSLIM CLERICS ALL over the country on Friday came out strongly against the November 26 terror attack in

Mumbai, showing solidarity with the victims and the government in their after-prayer sermons. They said the community would support every step to curb terrorism, 'even if it means attacking militant hideouts in Pakistan'. But at the same time, the clerics made it clear the government should relentlessly chase those responsible for the Malegaon and Samjhauta Express blasts and no innocent Muslim should be harassed in the name of investigation. Noorur Rehman Barkati, Shahi Imam of Tipu Sultan Mosque in Kolkata, said the government must ensure terrorist activities by Hindu outfits in Malegaon and Hyderabad are strongly dealt with. 'They are evil and must be destroyed,' he said. Meanwhile, imams in Mumbai, Delhi, Kolkata, Hyderabad, Jaipur and Patna were unanimous in urging people to observe the Babri Masjid demolition anniversary on Saturday peacefully. In Mumbai, clerics urged Muslims to stand up and be counted as Indians. At the Dharavi mosque, the imam declared, 'Humanity is the biggest religion,' while at the Jama-e-Hidayaa in Bandra, the imam said, 'They [the terrorists] went against the basic tenets of Islam.'

In Lucknow, Maulana Khalid Rashid Firangi Mahali said, 'We are Indians. We are with the government in whatever action it takes. The government must not think Muslims will oppose action against Pakistan.' Mahali and All India Muslim Personal Law Board vice-president Maulana Kalbe Sadiq said it was high time Muslims joined the fight against terror. In Hyderabad, attendance at mosques was thin though the police had made elaborate security arrangements. Clerics and religious leaders held a street meeting in Kolkata under the banner of the All India Majlis-e-Shoora just after Friday prayers. Shia leader Maulana Athar Abbas Rizvi, however, sounded discordant at the meeting: 'Hemant Karkare [Maharashtra ATS chief] was the *massiha* of Muslims. He was killed to stop the Malegaon investigations.' In Patna, Imarat-e-Shariat secretary Anissur Rehman went a step farther, saying terrorists' 'limbs need to be amputated so that others could also get a lesson'.■

The mourning in Malegaon
Chitrangada Choudhury

RESIDENTS OF THIS bereaved town, 285 kilometres north-east of Mumbai, are now pushing for the 500-metre stretch to be named.

It was a bomb planted in a motorcycle outside Abdul Ansari's shop on September 29 that has now morphed into one of India's most divisive religious and political debates. Textile transporter Ansari (75) has been here in Malegaon's 200-year-old eastern quarter since 1962. Outside his spartan office is a half-kilometre street of shops selling cosmetics, *hijabs* and glasses of steaming tea. This is the street Malegaon wants named 'Shaheed Hemant Karkare Road', in memory of senior police investigator Hemant Karkare. He was among the 183 people killed in Mumbai's November terror strikes.

As chief of Maharashtra's Anti-terrorism Squad, Karkare was probing the 2008 blast where a bomb planted in an anonymous motorcycle left outside Ansari's office went off on a September night, killing six. In Ansari's office, the pockmarked walls and a frozen clock mark the bombing and its time: 9.38 p.m.

'Karkareji ko maara gaya hai kyonki sab khulaasa kar rahe the, aur kya? Ek umeed ki kiran thi hum logon ke liye, who bhi chali gayi. (Karkare has been killed because he was exposing the real forces behind the Malegaon blasts. We had one ray of hope, he too is gone),' said Ansari. It's an unwavering conclusion—Karkare's killing was a targetted assassination meant to stifle the uncomfortable revelations of the blast probe—that echoes across a cross-section of the over four lakh Muslims who make up 70 per cent of the residents of Maharashtra's poorest town.

Two blasts, a funeral
The probe under Hemant Karkare led to the arrest of nine Hindus—including former and serving soldiers and a *sadhvi*—and sparked a divisive national debate.

In weary Malegaon, however, Karkare's findings were greeted with a collective sigh of relief because they suggested to the rest of India what its residents had been pleading for long—that terror is not synonymous with Muslims alone. 'When the news first broke, I could not believe what I was reading. I kept going back to the newspaper through the day,' said Dr Sajid Sidiqi, who also runs a foundation that propagates inter-faith dialogue. 'My wife and I asked each other if India's police could really charge people other than Muslims?' Scarred by periodic communal riots and police action, Malegaon's Muslims have a history of deep mistrust of law-enforcement agencies. This lack of faith peaked two years ago with the ATS investigation into serial blasts in the city in September 2006, which killed 32 people. Today, nine Muslims from the city in their 20s and 30s are in jails across Maharashtra awaiting trial. The Central Bureau of Investigation took over the case in 2007. The town is convinced that policemen fabricated evidence, a view backed even by the city's Shiv Sena MLA Dagadu Bhuse. Once a government engineer, Bhuse said: 'Malegaon's *awaam* (people) does not believe these arrests are correct. I also wrote to the police asking them to reinvestigate the matter.'

Chemist Shafiq Khan, who lost his teenaged son and nephew in the blasts, said: 'My heart refuses to believe that Muslims could have carried out the blasts in a Muslim-dominated area.' Garage manager Nooruddin Shamsoda (22), whose brother Noorulhuda (25) has spent the past two years in jail, charged with carrying out the blasts, said: 'Present proof. Hang the guilty. None of us will tolerate breaking of the law. But this investigation is completely fabricated.' Shamsoda likened Karkare's death to 'losing a family member. He would have reinvestigated the 2006 case for links with the 2008 blast. Our hopes have died again.'

Why Malegaon?
Malegaon is neatly divided into Hindu and Muslim ghettos, a ramshackle city. None of its major roads have sewers or storm-water drains. It is a city of looms, built through waves of migration of weavers and workers from across northern India.

On the banks of the putrid Mausam river, which cleaves Malegaon into two, stands a fort that marks the head of the Muslim quarter. Here, English troops battled Arab fighters in 1740. The river's west bank houses the Hindu community. The houses are larger and set in neat gardens. There are banks, ATMs, even a shopping mall. There is no ATM in the Muslim quarter, where 62,000 people are packed into every square kilometre, among India's most-crowded areas.

'Any Muslim who suffers after riots in India finds refuge, and work, in Malegaon,' said Sudhir Raut, who heads the town's municipal body, founded in 1893. 'Their condition is no better than bonded labourers though.' The poverty is a direct outcome of crippling power cuts, which ensure that the British-era power looms, purchased as scrap from India's defunct textile mills, today stand silent for 10-12 hours each day. The municipal corporation runs on a deficit of Rs 35 crore to Rs 40 crore, a third of its budget. That means it is bankrupt, surviving on largesse from Mumbai.

The most damaging impact is on Malegaon's 116 civic schools, where children regularly drop out to join looms, and teachers haven't been paid in months. In June, then Chief Minister Vilasrao Deshmukh announced a Rs 9 crore special grant so they could be paid: It's still tangled in redtape in distant Mumbai.

This administrative callousness is common to towns across India, but Malegaon's Muslims view it through the prism of discrimination. The common refrain: 'We could have been as good or better than Nashik [the town next door], but see where we are.' It is this alienation that fuels the suspicion around the death of Karkare, the officer who had come to be viewed as Malegaon's messiah.

In the office of the Malegaon chapter of the Jamiat-Ulama-i-Hind, a 1919 national socio-religious body built by figures like Maulana Abul Kalam Azad, lawyer S. Sheikh is putting final touches to a petition to move the Supreme Court. It will ask that the 2006 blasts be reinvestigated in the light of Karkare's findings around the town's second blast. The silver-haired, urbane lawyer said: 'Why was Malegaon bombed in 2006 and 2008? Who directly benefits from Karkare's killing? We need credible answers to these questions.'■

Life finds a way

'November 26 is a day I will never forget'
Rajendra Aklekar

BACK ON HIS job of checking passenger tickets at Mumbai's Chhatrapati Shivaji Terminus, senior ticket checker R.H. Dubey is relaxed until he hears any mention of the horrific terror attacks at CST on November 26. Memories come flooding back—of shrieking passengers, bodies lying in a pool of blood and the deafening sound of gunshots that reverberated in the stately building.

'It feels good that things are back to normal. But November 26 is a day I will never forget. My thoughts had just numbed. I knew I had to help the passengers before the situation went out of control,' Dubey recalls.

A resident of Kurla, Dubey was at the ticket checking office on Platform 1 on the Harbour Line section of CST when the terrorists opened fire. The CCTV footage shows how Dubey helped commuters move out of the station even as RPF Head Constable Jullu Yadav engaged terrorists in a gun fire battle on Platform 3.

In the footage, Dubey is seen helping an old woman pick up her luggage, and escorting her to safety. 'My duty was to end in two hours time when I heard loud bursts and cries from the adjacent outstation train terminus. I knew something was wrong. There was very little time and I had to move fast,' he says. Dubey had his back towards the terrorists even as he was helping passengers get out of the station.

'Dubey actually stood between the terrorists and the passengers as a shield without caring for his life,' a senior official who has witnessed the footage, points out.

'I could not think. I only knew I had to help the passengers to safety. It was all by instinct,' Dubey recalls. His instinct saved many lives that fateful night. 'As the terrorists ran towards the subway entrance, some commuters felt it would be safer to hide inside the train. But I asked them to move out of the station and escorted them through the rear exit,' says Dubey.

A father of three daughters, Dubey has been in the Indian Railways service for a decade. Central Railways General Manager V.K. Manglik gave an 'On-the-Spot' cash award of Rs 5,000 to Dubey for his exemplary courage.■

'I regret I could not kill the terrorists'
Rajendra Aklekar

HEAD CONSTABLE JULLU Yadav is back at the Chhatrapati Shivaji Terminus doing what he is trained to do—protect the commuters that pass through the heritage precinct every day. Posted at the entrance of the Central Railways general manager's office, his eyes dart from one area of the station to another as he instructs a constable. Many pairs of eyes are focused on him as he goes about his business. Yadav is a hero for his colleagues, the city and for the nation but he cannot fathom what the fuss is all about.

'I only did my job. Please spare me all this media attention,' says the 51-year-old head constable of the Railway Protection Force, who returned fire at the terrorists at CST on November 26.

Had it not been for Yadav engaging the terrorists in a daring gun battle, the official toll of 56 dead and 95 injured at CST would undoubtedly have been much higher. The CCTV footage on the night of terror attack at CST shows Yadav running across a passage in full view of the terrorists, grabbing a rifle from a colleague too stunned by the attack to react, and opening fire at the terrorists. Yadav was the only security personnel who stood his ground when all others panicked and fled. The moment Yadav sensed tension at the premises, he rushed to the main entrance of the building to lock the huge iron gates. After shutting the gates, an unarmed Yadav ran towards the terrorists, who were firing indiscriminately at hapless passengers. He flung a chair at them to distract them before grabbing a rifle from one of his armed colleagues to return fire.

'I opened fire at them, but they jumped between the train and

124

the platform to take cover and opened fire,' Yadav recalls. After a long night of blood and gore, Yadav returned home to his wife and three sons in the northern suburb of Dombivli. 'It feels good to be back on the job,' says Yadav, thankful that the city is slowly regaining its rhythm.

Central Railways General Manager V.K. Manglik gave an 'On-the-Spot' award of Rs 5000 and a commendation certificate while Railways Minister Lalu Prasad Yadav has announced a reward of Rs 10 lakh for Yadav's bravery. 'I do not think I have done anything great. We are trained to protect people,' says the self-effacing Yadav.

Was he scared to face the terrorists? '*Darr to laga tha. Par hamne toh training li hai* (I was afraid but I have been trained to meet such situations),' says Yadav who last fired a rifle in January during his annual training at the Thane-Pokhran range. 'This was the first time I had an actual gun fight with terrorists since my last training session. My regret is that I could not kill those terrorists. They had sophisticated weapons,' Yadav says.

What Yadav lacked by way of equipment he compensated with his presence of mind and grit. As his boss and senior RPF inspector Sandeep Khiratkar says, 'Yadav is as small as an AK-47 gun, but he was the bravest among everyone his age.'■

Dal, rice and a new beginning
Neha Bhayana

IT WAS A simple fare of *dal,* rice, *chappatis* and *bhaji* served in a steel *thali*. But Anamika Gupta (26) was thrilled when a nurse laid it down in front of her on Thursday afternoon. Gupta, a beautician, had been shot thrice in the stomach in the firing at Leopold Café on November 26. The bullets were surgically removed at St. George Hospital just hours after the incident. She was moved to JJ Hospital the next morning and was kept on a dose of glucose-water.

A complete chatterbox, Gupta was quiet for once as she relished her first meal since the fateful day when the urge for Chinese food had landed her in the line of fire. Gupta had moved to Colaba just a month ago to start her own parlour. She and her friends Rashika Sawant and Sarika Upadhyay had been shopping for Gupta's brother's wedding on December 12. They were exhausted and famished so they decided to go to Leopold, their favourite hang-out. 'We had ordered fried rice, vegetable manchurian and noodles but the food had not arrived so we were busy checking out boys,' says Gupta. Of all the boys in the café, two sitting at the table next to theirs caught Gupta's attention. 'They were so good-looking. Both were wearing cargo pants and had sports bags slung across their shoulders. One of them had a beige shirt on,' she says.

Little did Gupta know that the two 'mysterious men' she was ogling at were terrorists. Moments after her eyes first fell on them, one stood up and threw something, possibly a hand grenade, at the manager's desk and the lights went off. Gupta and her friends thought it was a short circuit but then they heard firing. Gupta's friends ran out of the café but she froze. 'I couldn't take my eyes off them. I wanted to reach them somehow. I felt like kicking them, making them stop but I couldn't move,' she adds. The next thing Gupta remembers is a doctor saying: 'You are a lucky girl, Anamika. You are the first one we operated on.' Gupta knows a social worker called Francis had brought her to the hospital. Ten days after the attack, Gupta is the most cheerful patient in JJ's ward 11.

But behind Gupta's smile lies the trauma of one who was seen the face of death. 'Every time I close my eyes to sleep, I can see their faces. I can hear the sound of gunshots and the screams. I prefer staying awake,' she says. Gupta plans to go straight to her rented flat in Colaba when she is discharged. 'I am dying to play with my cats—Jimmy and Maria. They must be missing me,' she says.■

'We must overpower terrorism, not terrorists'
Soumitra Ghosh

AS ERIC ANTHONY, the 33-year-old manager of Leopold Café pushed past a crowd to walk back into his workplace of ten years on December 1, he felt an acute sense of violation.

'Just days before, the terrorists came to our café, ate at our tables and then opened fire at our guests. I wanted to scream and protest loudly but after a moment, as we resumed our services, I felt like we just need to pick up the pieces and move on,' said Anthony, who escaped a bullet on November 26.

'Since the attacks, I've had the same dream thrice—that Leopold is safe, and no terror attack took place. But every morning, I wake up to the reality—two of my boys, Peeru and Kazi, dead along with five of our customers. I remember showing the table to the foreigners who were shot dead along with three Indian customers,' recalled Anthony, who lives in a room in Colaba.

The day after Leopold opened to much media attention, a couple, both foreign nationals, walked in. 'It reopened my wounds. I couldn't help but recall the horror of that evening. I couldn't speak and managed to only signal them to a table,' said a visibly shaken Anthony, recounting the deaths of his peers. 'I ran outside the café with a slight bruise as a bullet whizzed past me, and Peeru tried to follow me but was hit and fell to the ground bleeding profusely. Kazi came rushing to help me pick up Peeru but he felt giddy at seeing all the blood. So he went across the street to call for help but got shot.'

But he is already seeing signs of normalcy: Customers walking in without fear, prayers being said, staff filling in for the deceased, Peeru and Kazi. 'We'll recruit new staff members soon and replace our broken cutlery. Customers are showing their support by visiting our café, but I don't know if that's called getting back to a normal life. I'm waiting for the day I can go back to my room, put on my sound system and sleep.'

Anthony's colleague, 25-year-old Thomson Fernandez, captain of Leopold, was manning the cash counter on November 26 when the terrorists opened fire and a grenade went off under the table in front of him. 'Before Leopold reopened, I felt immense hatred towards the two terrorists. I had a lump in my throat as I entered the café the day it reopened. The horrific events of the night of the 26th flashed before my eyes: the terrorists with guns, the firing, the bodies we put in the ambulance, the mayhem. I couldn't look away from the spots where Peeru and Kazi collapsed, where the bullets were sprayed. But as we reopened, with support from guests and peers, I felt a transformation taking root within me. It's time we overpower terrorism rather than just those two terrorists.' Fernandez, who has worked at Leopold for three years, believes the day of the reopening was not just a symbolic victory but also the most meaningful day of his life.

'The whole atmosphere was electrifying—the tables, chairs, counters, cutlery . . . everything seemed to have a new life. It's as if the objects, along with the people, were saying, "Look, we are back." I silently thanked Jesus and made a silent resolve: For the last three years, I only did my job but now on, as long as I work here, I will help represent the victory of life over terrorism,' he declared. ∎

How a plot was lost
Prem Shankar Jha

THE FRANTIC SCRAMBLE within the intelligence agencies to find out what went wrong, and their willingness to enlist the media in proving that they were not to blame, has unleashed a flood of information. This deluge shows that the government not only knew that an attack was being planned, but had a pretty accurate idea of when it would take place and how and where it would be launched. And yet the Indian State was able to do nothing to stop it.

The Intelligence Bureau first got wind that the Lashkar-e-Tayyeba was developing a sea route to India via Mumbai as far back as March 2007 when a coast guard ship to intercept a trawler carrying eight *fidayeen*s let them go after accepting a bribe. But the authorities managed to plant a bug in their belongings and traced them all the way through India, before arresting them in Jammu. The movements of this group did not specifically suggest that Mumbai could be their target. That came to light in February

2008, when the Uttar Pradesh Police arrested an LeT operative, the UP-born Fahim Ahmed Ansari, along with seven others. He and two others had been infiltrated into India from Pakistan specifically to travel to Mumbai and blow up the stock exchange building. The UP case files against him include maps he had drawn of the fort area of Mumbai, with specific references to Oberoi hotel and the Chhatrapati Shivaji Terminus. The LeT may have decided upon the sea route only after this group was arrested. Confirmation that the Taj was also likely to be a target came on September 18 when the Research and Analysis Wing picked up a satellite phone conversation between a known LeT operative and some other person in which the former said that 'the target' was a hotel near the Gateway of India. Another intercept, six days later on September 24, revealed that four luxury hotels, all of them at the edge of the sea, were being considered as possible targets.

By the end of September, therefore, all that the agencies had not put together, between them, was the timing of the attack. But they did this too within the next six weeks. On November 19, the R&AW received an 'intelligence input' (possibly from the Americans), based upon the interception of another satellite phone call that originated at a point due south of Karachi and four days sailing away from Mumbai, that the 'cargo' was on its way to Mumbai.

All that the government had to do was to put the navy on high alert, move in the National Security Guards and commandos quietly, identify the most likely drop off points and be waiting for the terrorists when they arrived.

But this required five things:

- A sharing of the information between the agencies
- Discerning the pattern that was emerging
- Informing the prime minister and all the concerned executive agencies
- Issuing an alert to the state governments and the targeted hotels and buildings that was sufficiently precise to mak them sit up and take notice

- Moving the NSG and naval commandos into key locations without allowing our media to get wind of it and blow the gaffe.

Not a single one of these things was done. Someone has got to pay.

But so far, all that the Manmohan Singh government has done is to decide upon whom to make its scapegoats. The real culprits are going scot-free. Shivraj Patil, Vilasrao Deshmukh, and R.R. Patil may have been indifferent ministers who needed to be replaced anyway. They may have lacked the minimum understanding or experience needed to deal with issues of security, but none of this is relevant, for they could have done nothing even if they had had it. For none of them, not even the Home Minister, was given either the information they needed or the wherewithal with which to prevent the attack. That information lay buried in the police and intelligence agencies of the country—i.e., in its vast and sprawling bureaucracy. If it did not reach the executive branches of government in a usable manner, the fault lies in the chain of command that stretches from those whose business it is to collect the intelligence to those whose business it is to collate and analyse it, and recommend the appropriate course of action. That entire function, and the Secretariat that performs it, is located in the Prime Minister's Office, and is presided over by the National Security Advisor (NSA).

The Tower of Babel
India has no fewer than 16 intelligence agencies dealing with security and another three that deal with economic intelligence. The task of collating all the information they collect is performed the Joint Intelligence Committee (JIC).

JIC is the third tier of the National Security Council the second being the National Security Advisory Board. consists of representatives of the army, navy and air ctorates of intelligence, the IB, the R&AW, the Border rce (BSF), the Centre Bureau of Intelligence (CBI), the

National Terrestrial Remote Sensing Organisation, the Signals Intelligence Directorate. It meets every Thursday. The meeting is currently chaired by the head of the National Security Council Staff (NSCS), and a weekly intelligence report to the government is submitted.

The NSCS consists of a number of analysts. They should be doing the job of collating the information provided by the agencies and armed forces over a period of time to identify connections, discern patterns and thereby anticipate threats. But in fact they write long papers that no one reads.

The NSC was a brainchild of former prime minister V.P. Singh, but was actually set up in November 1998 to become the central focus of all strategic planning for the government. Security was only the fourth of its four areas of concern, coming well below 'political' and 'economic' and even energy.

The need for a central coordinating focus for intelligence had been pointed out by the Subramaniam Committee in 1998, when it said that the agencies passed on less than 25 per cent of the information they received. So complete has been the failure of the system that today, according to insiders in the security establishment, they do not pass on even a tenth. The agencies send junior officers to the JIC's weekly meetings, and the brief with which they come is not to impart information but 'to find out what the others know'. The agencies also depute officers to the NSCS, but they have made it a dustbin for unwanted officers.

The way to give the NSC countervailing power is to bring it directly under a heavyweight cabinet minister. The head of the NSC is the prime minister. But since the PM plays no more part in its day-to-day work than he does in the Planning Commission, its real head is the NSA.

In its first year or two, the JIC used to be chaired by the NSA (then Brajesh Mishra). But during the UPA government, it has been chaired by the head of the NSCS. This job was held by Satish Chandra, a former civil servant for the first four years and then by R.D. Pradhan till September 2007. Neither had the clout to make the agencies more forthcoming. Things took another turn for the worse when, two years ago, M.K. Narayanan, who had taken over external, in addition to internal, security after the death of J.N. Dixit, appointed three deputy NSAs. The distance between him, and therefore the PM, and the JIC, therefore increased, and the status of the latter in relation to the intelligence agencies sank even further. According to insiders, two small nails completed the sealing of the coffin. Satish Chandra converted the NSCS into an NSC Secretariat by requiring the staff members to not only present their assessments to him, but also to rewrite their papers after incorporating his comments on the subject. This eliminated the scope for independent thinking within the NSCS and the little possibility that had remained for the airing of diverse opinions. And the creation of three deputy NSAs has divided not the work, but the staff itself. In an expansive moment, one of them claimed that he was the 'single point military advisor to the prime minister'. The armed forces brass' reaction was: 'We shall see.'

When the terrorists struck, the country had an NSA who was wholly preoccupied with making domestic and foreign policy on behalf of the PM; deputy NSAs of whom only one, Lila Ponappa, enjoyed any repect in the armed forces; a demoralised NSCS staff split between Ponappa and Shekhar Dutt, the PM's military advisor, and a joint intelligence council that received next to no intelligence from the agencies and the armed forces.

Add to that the fact that the UP government probably did not forward Fahim Ahmed Ansari's hand drawn maps to the central government, and we begin to get our first inkling of why 200 people had to die last week in Mumbai.■

Live from India-Pakistan
Mohammed Hanif

LAST WEEK, AS the television news channels on both sides of the border turned the Bombay tragedy first into 'patriot games' and then into 'ratings wars', I ended up contributing to the hysteria in two TV studios. One in Delhi, and one here in Karachi.

I am one of those sad journalists who has managed to survive in the profession without succumbing to the charms of television news. Some of us still hang on to that outdated notion that a notebook and a ballpen are all the gadgets that a journalist needs to get to the heart of a story. Whenever I have to face a TV camera, I squirm and mumble and promise myself never to do it again. Then why did I do it twice in two days? It must have been a seasonal bout of vanity, because I actually hoped that I might have something to add to the debate. Because what I was watching on the TV screens had a macabre disconnect with what the anchorpersons were saying.

On the one hand, horrifying pictures of people caught in a prolonged certain-death situation, and on the other, shrill voices demanding more and immediate violence, and their Pakistani counterparts responding with the chorus of 'They did it to themselves.' I kept asking myself: why aren't these people sad? Why aren't they mourning? So I was quite nervous as I was whisked off to a TV station in Noida. I was told in vague terms that I'll be talking about the current situation between India and Pakistan. The producer who received me at the station told me the topic: Should India attack targets in Pakistan? I asked if I could go out for a smoke. I was hoping to do a runner but then realised I'll never find my way out of Noida and will probably get arrested for having a Punjabi accent. An SMS poll was already underway when the programme started and 90 per cent respondents wanted India to go ahead with these strikes. By the time the programme ended 91 per cent wanted these attacks. I have no idea how I might have contributed to this rousing demand for a televised war because I only mumbled some basic facts: yes, there are lawless areas in Pakistan but these areas were not Muzaffarabad or Muridke as the presenter seemed to suggest. At one point, frustrated at my failure to stop the war rhetoric, I said that people of Pakistan have gotten over their 'India obsession' but India hasn't. That again is a fact I know first hand. In my own village in central Punjab, which was the centre of Indiabashing till a decade ago, nobody talks about India as Enemy No. 1. In fact nobody talks about India.

It's not that we have converted to some form of Gandhi-ism; it's just that we are faced with far bigger problems ranging from local Taliban to 12-hour power cuts. Who has the time? But there is something about television formats that by the time you get to mention your village, the anchorperson has moved on to that retired general who always wants to give you four strategic options.

On my way back from the TV station, I did what all old-school travelling reporters do. I asked the cab driver if India should attack Pakistan. He seemed startled by my rude suggestion. 'But we don't even know yet who has done it.' It seemed driving all those journalists to the TV station he had picked up some basic journalistic training. And then with a healthy cynicism, probably mixed with an urge to please a guest, he said: 'Maybe your people have done it, maybe our people have done it, who knows?'

When I got back to Karachi the next day, I was asked for a repeat performance—on a very popular prime-time show on a very popular channel. Still reeling from the previous night's experience, I asked a friend what I should say. He told me to say the same things I said in India the night before. I was surprised at my own response: 'I said those things because I was in India.'

The Pakistani presenter asked me what it was like being in India. I said inane things about how normal it seemed, how there were traffic jams. There was no hostility. None at all. I tried to make a word-play on an Urdu expression—a favourite with our presenters—*ghum-o-ghussa* (sadness and anger). I said people were sad and the media were angry, very angry. I pointed out that the Pakistan media were also very angry. This, of course, I was told, was a reaction to the Indian media's anger. I managed to slip in that while the governments seemed quite cautious with their words, TV presenters were gagging for war. All this while a ticker was running on the monitor: 'Pakistan army's high command meets to deliberate India's *junooni* behaviour.' I wondered if somebody had actually seen the meeting's agenda and whether it says: 'How to tackle India's *junoon*'.

There was a question about whether India is increasingly looking for military solutions. I rolled out an emphatic and wishful 'No!'

134

on behalf of the Indian people conveniently ignoring the SMS poll. I said that there is an emerging middle class in India that wants new accessories like pilotless drones. This pleased the presenter. To dilute the effect I rolled out a cliché about five year olds begging on the streets of Karachi as well as Delhi. My time was up.

I think the problem with TV is that it doesn't allow for mourning unless it's of the variety observed by photogenic people with candles and Facebook accounts. With pen and paper, or even with a laptop, between typing one sentence and struggling to write another, you can let out a sigh of desperation and admit to yourself that you don't know what the hell is going on. You have no idea if there will be a solution in your lifetime.

Try saying that to an anchorperson.■

Intelligence agencies identify ISI handler
Abhishek Sharan

Mumbai, December 7: THERE ARE STRONG indications that Pakistan's Inter-Services Intelligence's colonel Mehmud Hasan had allegedly played a role in assisting the Lashkar-e-Tayyeba plot the Mumbai attacks, according to a senior Intelligence Bureau officer who is monitoring the probe.

Hasan, the officer told *HT*, allegedly 'played a role in rustling up logistics required for the Mumbai attack perpetrated by the LeT. Among the things he arranged were retired armed forces and ISI personnel, who trained the Lashkar's suicide attackers. Hasan, a serving officer, works with an ISI division named Joint Intelligence (Miscellaneous). Hasan, the officer said, has been tasked to interface with '*jihadi tanzeems* (*jihadi* outfits) like the Lashkar that operate in India to aid and guide their operations.' Hasan's jurisdiction, added the officer, 'is the rest of India, barring Kashmir that is looked after by another specialised division.

'The LeT would not have dared to orchestrate its Mumbai attacks without the approval of their mentors in the ISI. They knew the ramifications would be great,' he said. Intelligence sources revealed that another ISI division named 'X' had allegedly 'played a role in fine-tuning the attack plans'. Indian enforcement and intelligence have come across the names of a few other ISI officers who allegedly aided the LeT in carrying out the audacious, clinical attacks having the 'precision of a commando operation'.

According to revelations made by Mohammed Ajmal Amir Kasab, the arrested alleged Pakistani Lashkar attacker, he and nine other associates involved in the attacks had undergone a year-long training, divided into specific modules of between six to 12 weeks-long, in Muzaffarabad, Manshehra and Karachi. The training, apart from tutoring in Islam and *jihad*, focussed on imparting skills—in handling arms, explosives, navigating the sea with instruments like the GPS, among others—required by conventional commandos in land/sea operations.

When *HT* asked Mumbai Crime Branch's Additional Commissioner of Police Deven Bharti about the alleged role of Hasan, he said: 'We are interrogating Ajmal Amir but he is only a Lashkar foot soldier who would not know such details. But he has said that retired personnel from the ISI and the Pakistani armed forces would attend the training camps and especially hold *taqreer*s (discussions) on how to handle tactical situations in such a terror attack.'■

The facts of life
Ajit Doval

WHATEVER OUR INFIRMITIES, we can ill-afford to demoralise the team which has to fight the battle. Even if with a heavy heart, every Indian should stand by the government and help it do whatever it can to reclaim the nation's lost honour. This is not the best time to ask for heads; it will only cheer our enemies. Media has a crucial role to play in not sapping the will of the nation. Let us first win the battle; accountability can follow. Let us prove our enemies wrong in estimating India's tolerance as infinite just because a few people do not measure up to the responsibilities destiny thrust on them. India's intrinsic power is far beyond the weaknesses of the few and given the support, it can even make its C-team win. Depending on the US or any other country without our taking the lead role will not prove productive. No one is going to subordinate his interests for our sake. But if we rise to the occasion with speed and determination, many will support us. Let the opposition parties, media, intellectuals and public lend full support to the government and not force it to do things against its better judgement. Just as it was regrettable that hysterical public opinion and a TRP sensitive media forced the government to release terrorists in the Kandahar hijack against its wishes, the nation may regret some day that it forced the government to do things in the aftermath of Mumbai which were not in India's best interests. This may be a chance to improve things both within and without. Let it not be one more missed opportunity. A national response in a democracy cannot be without the support of the main opposition. Such initiatives are not for scoring political points but historic watersheds to convert a government's response into a nation's response. People's anger and anguish against their political parties and leaders can drive change but their cynicism against the system can be fatal.■

Pakistan arrests 26/11 plotter Lakhvi in PoK
HT Correspondent

Islamabad, December 8: ELEVEN DAYS AFTER the 26/11 Mumbai terrorist strikes, Pakistani authorities reportedly arrested Zaki-ur-Rehman Lakhvi, a top Lashkar-e-Tayyeba operative, following a raid on a Lashkar front organisation outside Muzaffarabad in PoK on Sunday. Indian investigators have directly implicated Lakhvi as one of the plotters of 26/11. Nineteen other Lashkar men were caught in the raid, which the *Dawn* newspaper described as a 'quiet crackdown' on the group, banned by Pakistan in 2002, but which has maintained a solid presence in the country.

'I saw an army helicopter hovering over the area and around 5 p.m. I heard two or three loud explosions,' a woman who lives in the area told the newspaper. Another person said, 'The helicopter ... may have airlifted people detained or injured during the operation.' There were unconfirmed reports of an exchange of fire. Pakistan said it would investigate. There was no official statement from Islamabad on the 'arrest'. Hafiz Sayeed, chief of the Jamaat-ud-Dawa, the Lashkar front, condemned the attack on his group, which has been held responsible for the Mumbai terror attack.■

Orphaned by 26/11, Afroz wants to move on
Prasad Nichenametla

Mumbai, December 8: '*JOH SOCHTE HEIN wahi hota hai kya ... (isiliye) sochne se kuchh nahi hota,*' said Afroz Ansari when asked what he would like to become when he grows up.

Afroz (the police say he is 13 but he insists he is 12) has a reason to pursue this philosophy. He lost his parents, along with four other relatives, on 26/11—a day which Mumbai and the nation will never forget. Afroz, who would have been celebrating Bakr Eid in his hometown of Mananpur in Nawada district of Bihar, is now lying in ward 19 of JJ Hospital, recovering from a bullet injury in his back. Afroz's father, Abbas Ansari, was working as a taxi driver, while his mother was a homemaker.

While Abbas's first two sons are in *zari* work, the third is studying; the youngest one, after Afroz, remains at home. Afroz said he missed his village. The family residing in Mumbra was on the way to their hometown in Bihar for Bakr Eid when the tragedy struck at CST.

'*Amma aur abba ko to goli lag gayi thi, aur mujhe bachaate huye Iliyaz mamu maare gaye,*' Afroz said, while trying to preoccupy himself with a video game gifted by one of the visitors. Doctors at the hospital said though he was recovering he needed more medical attention. 'We would also provide him psychological care for some more time,' Dr V.S. Jaiswal, CMO on duty, said.

Meanwhile, help is pouring in from all sides with people even from the US offering to take care of Afroz. And this seems to be giving him confidence. He said he knew there were people outside his family who were willing to take care of him. Afroz wants to continue his studies wherever he is.

But Afroz's brother, Shagir Ansari, said they were awaiting the compensation announced by the government for the kin of the dead. Afroz, who had lost the sight in his left eye while playing cricket, said English was his favourite subject, followed by Urdu. He was in class V in his village and was attending private tuition in Mumbai. Afroz, who wants go and stay with his married sister in Nawada, said: 'There is no pain now. I don't know when I will be discharged. Doctors are saying I will be discharged in two three days from last two three days.' But will he comeback to the city, which took away almost everything from him? 'I like being with my sister but my brothers are here. *Abhi tho utna socha nahi . . . baad mein dekhenge* (I haven't thought about it. Let's see later.).'■

View from Pakistan: It is an eyewash
Irfan Husain

IN THE WAKE of 9/11, many moderate Pakistanis had hoped that in the process of ridding Afghanistan of the Taliban, the Americans would also help Pakistan roll back the forces of extremism that were threatening to tear the country apart. Over seven years later, the Taliban are resurgent, and their Pakistani clones have tightened their grip on the country's jugular. So what went wrong? First, Iraq diverted the West's military might and focus. And in Pakistan, Pervez Musharraf's need for support from Islamic groups gave extremists political space as well as protection. Since the rigged elections of 2002 until recently, mutations of the Wahabi/Salafi Islamic militias have become stronger and better organised in the tribal areas.

Financed largely by Pakistani and Gulf businessmen, these groups trained their volunteers—largely drawn from Pakistan's mushrooming madrasas—in bomb-making, as well as other ways of creating mayhem. A number of hard line Islamists drawn from the ranks of retired army and intelligence agency officers served as trainers, and the graduates of this Terror Academy became increasingly active in the region. But Pakistan was the biggest victim of this campaign, with over 50 suicide attacks claiming nearly a thousand lives (including that of Benazir Bhutto) last year alone. This, then, was the situation Asif Zardari inherited when he was elected President. Always suspect in the eyes of the army for being a Sindhi, as well as a member of the PPP who was married to a Bhutto, his grip on power is tenuous at best. The reality of the power equation in Pakistan is that the army is the most organised and powerful party around. And although the present military leadership would prefer to stay out of the limelight after nine years of Musharraf's high profile rule, it still calls the shots where Pakistan's regional policy is concerned.

In at least two recent episodes, the generals have shown the political leadership exactly where power resides. When the government announced a couple of months ago that the ISI would henceforth report to the Interior Ministry, it took barely six hours for this notification to be withdrawn.

More recently, when Prime Minister Yousaf Raza Gilani announced that General Ahmed Shuja Pasha, the director general of the ISI, would go to India to help in the investigations of the November 26 Mumbai attacks, he was forced to retract his offer within hours.

Given this reality, it is difficult to see how terrorist groups like the Lashkar-e-Tayyeba and the Jaish-e-Mohammed can be reined in. Both have received official blessings and support in the past. Even if formal links with the ISI have been severed, training camps are difficult to shut down permanently, given the sympathy these groups enjoy in sections of the military, the police and the judiciary.

Since Zia's poisonous rule in the 1980s, extremism has seeped into every level of the bureaucracy. Many Pakistanis are in denial about the extent to which their country has been infected by this plague. Under these circumstances, the arrest of an individual like Zaki-ur-Rehman Lakhvi, a commander in the LeT, is meaningless. In the past, too, top terror suspects like Masood Azhar of the Jaish-e-Mohammed and Hafiz Sayeed of the Lashkar-e-Tayyeba have been scooped up in the wake of terrorist outrages, only to be released a few weeks later.

One major reason the army is unwilling to completely sever its links with extremists is that it fears an alliance between India and Afghanistan that would see Pakistan encircled. Having an army of proxy warriors is an insurance policy military planners are reluctant to surrender. Years ago, a general said to a colleague: 'By supporting the mujahideen in Kashmir, we have tied down at least four Indian divisions there. What could be a more cost effective strategy?' Now, this same strategy has come to haunt Pakistan and the region.■

Lashkar's local support group still a mystery
Abhishek Sharan

Mumbai, December 9: ABOUT 20 MONTHS after an eight-member team of suicide attackers allegedly belonging to the Lashkar-e-Tayyeba infiltrated into Mumbai via sea using a fishing trawler in March 2007, the Maharashtra police and central security agencies are yet to identify the dozen-odd local Lashkar operatives who provided them logistics back-up, a senior Intelligence Bureau officer told *Hindustan Times.*

Even as these key local operatives are yet to even be identified, the Kolkata Police last week arrested J&K police constable Mukhtar Sheikh who had been cultivated to launch a covert operation

141

within Lashkar-e-Tayyeba cadres by sourcing 23 SIM cards. As reported by *HT* on Tuesday, details of all 23 SIM cards were relayed to the Intelligence Bureau and were under surveillance. One of these cards was found on the terrorists involved in the November 26 attack and in a desperate move, Sheikh was arrested, compromising his counter-terrorism operation and his contacts.

An IB officer, requesting anonymity since he is not authorised to talk to media, added: 'A team of around a dozen local Lashkar logistics handlers in Maharashtra helped the eight-member Lashkar team from the moment they landed at a place in and about the coast near Palghar. Around two days later, they had taken the Punjab Mail to reach New Delhi on their way to Kashmir.' He added: 'It is very disturbing that till now, these local aides, who we now suspect of having provided similar logistical support to the ten-member Lashkar team that executed the attacks in Mumbai on November 26, have remained faceless and untracked.'

Of the eight Pakistani nationals, two—Mohammed Jameel and Abdul Majeed—were arrested along with Mohammed Zuber, a local aide, last March in a joint operation by the Rajouri and Poonch police in Kashmir. While Jameel was from Mansehra, Majeed belonged to Nawabshah town; the local aide, Zuber retired as a Lance Naik attached with the Jammu & Kashmir Rifles. Admitted a senior officer of the Maharashtra Anti-terrorism Squad, who had supervised the months-long futile search for the 12-odd local Lashkar logistics handlers: 'We had sent a team to Kashmir to interrogate the two arrested Pakistani Lashkar operatives and later scoured the coastal areas in and around Mumbai to nab the local Lashkar aides but the efforts proved futile.' 'The two Lashkar *fidayeen* [Mohammed Jameel and Abdul Majeed] had revealed that their Lashkar handlers, Muzammil alias Yusuf and Qafa Ali, had instructed them not to exchange a word with local operatives, who they'd described as guides,' the IB officer told *HT*.

'The Lashkar team and local logistics team had taken care not to use mobile or landline phones, which had made the task of picking their trail difficult,' said the officer. 'It was only in the later stages of the journey, when they reached Chandigarh from Delhi enroute to Kashmir, that a source alerted us,' he added. After landing near Panvel, the eight-member Lashkar team (six are still 'missing') had stayed in a one-room safe-house near Titwala. The local aides had booked reserved tickets for them through *tatkal* facility to reach Delhi from Kalyan via the Punjab Mail train and got them photographed in a photo studio for the purpose of making identity cards, according to the interrogation report of Majeed and Jameel accessed by *HT*.■

Pak rules out access to Lakhvi

New Delhi, December 9: PAKISTAN RULED OUT giving India access to Lashkar-e-Tayyeba commander Zaki-ur-Rehman Lakhvi, alleged to be behind the Mumbai terror strikes, saying questioning could be done only by Pakistani authorities to ascertain whether he had any link to the attacks. Defence Minister Chaudhary Ahmed Mukhtar said India's 'concerns' can be discussed through a joint investigation mechanism that Islamabad has proposed to be set up to probe the Mumbai attacks. 'We do not have to rush into things. We have to move slowly to get hold of the right kind of people who could be involved or are alleged to be involved [in the Mumbai strikes].'■

On the trail of Masood Azhar
Neelesh Misra

YOU COULD SAY the father and brother of one of India's most wanted men were my phone friends. It was February 2000 and I was working on my first book, *173 Hours in Captivity: The Hijacking of IC-814.* I was trying to get all the information I could on Masood Azhar, the militant leader freed in Kandahar in exchange for the passengers of the seized flight. And who better to tell me about him than his own father, former school teacher Allah Baksh Sabir? Friends in the Indian security establishment had given me Azhar's interrogation report, and friends in Pakistan had given me his landline telephone number at their poultry farm-cum-home in Pakistan's Bahawalpur town.

I decided not to call from home; my phone records could land me in jail if someone decided to call me a terror conspirator. So I'd walk to a PCO in Noida every second day and talk with the soft-spoken Sabir in hushed tones from a cubicle. He referred to his son as 'Maulana Saab'. Azhar is part of big family—he has five brothers and six sisters. Four of Sabir's sons had been away for a long time. Azhar was in a Jammu prison, Abdul Rauf Asghar in Karachi, Jehangir Akbar at a madrasa near Bahawalpur. Ibrahim Athar—the main hijacker—was planning his mission, though the father told everyone he was on a pilgrimage. It is unclear if Sabir knew the truth. That left another brother, Mohammed Tahir Anwar, in charge of the farm, and Class 9 student Mohiuddin Alamgir to help out at home.

The long ring would often go unanswered at first, and I'd wonder: Was it the old-style phone with a dial? Was it in a big house guarded by armed men? Would the maulana himself pick up the phone one day; would I encounter the voice of the obese, stern-eyed man we had been watching on TV for weeks? I kept my name vague and did not reveal I was calling from India. Azhar was never home. He was busy—he had just formed the militant group Jaish-e-Mohammed. Over the next few days, Sabir and I began making small talk. 'You know, Maulana Saab just got married, a day after Eid . . . the child teaches in a religious school here.' 'Maulana Saab has just bought a house in Karachi.' 'He has a mobile phone, but I don't have the number.' One day I asked: 'Are you ok? You don't sound so good.' He said: 'No, just a slight cold.' One day he didn't pick up; it was a boyish voice instead. I realized it could be the youngest son mentioned in the interrogation report. '*Beta*, is that Alamgir?' '*Ji!*' said the boy. We soon became friends. Alamgir gave me Azhar's mobile number, but muddled up one area code and I could never speak to him.

The book was published, and weeks later, I read a newspaper report about a man who featured in it, who'd bought a copy at the Mr Books store in Islamabad: the London School of Economics-educated Ahmed Omar Saeed Sheikh, one of the other two top militants released with Azhar.■

15 days on: Life goes on, but the pain remains

After the grief, waiter's family struggles with bills
Prasad Nichenametla

Mumbai, December 10: '*KEEDE PADKE MARENGE* (They will rot to death),' said Munira Sheikh about the terrorists who gunned down her father Peerpasha Mehboob Sheikh, a waiter at Leopold Café, on the night of November 26.

The eldest of Sheikh's five children, Munira—a Class 9 student—said: '*Hum Hindu ke saath rehte hein. Quran mein yeh kahi nahi likha hein ki Islam ke naam pe kisiko bhi maardo ya auron ke mazhab ko mitaado* (We live with Hindus. It's not written anywhere in the Quran that in the name of Islam you can kill anyone; neither can you erase someone's religion.).' Munira and her sister and brothers haven't gone to school since their father died, though they plan to do so soon. Their father used to spend whatever he earned on their education. 'He used to feed us himself. We fall ill frequently and he used to rush us to the doctor every time. Now who will do that,' she asked, crying. The 15-year-old tried to put up a brave face. 'If you cry, we will also cry. *Abba* won't like this,' she said to a relative who broke down.

Though the Maharashtra government has given them Rs 5 lakh in compensation, the family is clueless about the future as Sheikh was the only earning member. 'What can we think as of now? The one who should be taking care is gone,' said Husseinbi, Sheikh's widow. Sheikh, who originally hails from a village in Karnataka's Gulbarga district, had moved to Mumbai around 30 years ago. He did odd jobs before joining the famous cafe in Colaba.

The family lives in a tiny room down one of the narrow alleys of Janata Sevak Society in Mahim. Residents of the locality—most of them Muslims—say no politician has visited the family since the tragedy. 'All these attacks are to provoke the public. But the government and the police seem to be weak, that's why these kinds of attacks are happening,' said a resident, refusing to give his name.■

Wasabi worker's family proud of their hero
Prasad Nichenametla

Mumbai, December 10: 'HIS DEATH IS a great loss for me but I am happy he died a hero, saving the lives of others,' said Sunu Varghese, wife of Varghese Thomas who fell to terrorists' bullets while rescuing guests at the Taj hotel. Thomas, a senior captain at Wasabi restaurant, served the hotel for 30 years.

Thomas, who spoke to Sunu at 1.30 a.m. on the night of 26/11, collapsed within a couple of hours. 'Don't worry, I will be there with you tomorrow,' were his last words to his wife. He is survived by his two sons, Wesley (20) and Rynell (14). The family, for whom Thomas was a good husband and a caring father, said that only after the incident did they realise how great a human being he was. 'We never had to ask for anything. He was not like others. But through his act of courage he has made us proud. He has given us such sweet memories that we can live with them now,' Sunu said. 'I realised how great my son was after he laid down his life carrying on his duty,' his mother Gracy Thomas said.

Residents of the Dharavi Cooperative Housing Society, where the Syrian Christian family has lived for years, are extending their support. While Prakash Shinde, a Shiv Sainik and friend of Thomas, is helping with the formalities, their Muslim neighbours were seen bringing food to the family on Eid.

A man of deeds instead of words, Thomas encouraged his elder son to take up nursing as a profession. Younger son Rynell said he wanted to get into hotel management like his father. Thomas was also a favourite among celebrities at the Wasabi and a fun-loving, devotional worker whom his colleagues held in high regard.

The family said it was touched by the warmth of their neighbours and by Ratan Tata's assurance of help, apart from the compensation provided by the government. Sunu even said she had no hatred for the terrorists who killed her husband. 'I cannot even blame them. They are trained like that. Let God decide [what should be done with them]. I only wish no one else faces such tragedy.'■

'Welcome to the headquarters of the Lashkar-e-Tayyeba. You think a terrorist organisation will be based a few metres from the Grand Trunk Road?'
Harinder Baweja

'YOU ARE IN an educational complex, but you are from India, so it will take you time to change your mind.'

That's what my guide and spokesperson Abdullah Muntazir told me within minutes of reaching Muridke, commonly believed to be the headquarters of the Lashkar-e-Tayyeba in Pakistan's Punjab.

It was the first time that permission had been granted to any Indian journalist to visit the sprawling campus 40 kilometres out of Lahore. The barricade that leads to the complex is heavily guarded. No one can enter without prior consent. The guided tour took me through a neatly laid out 60-bed hospital, schools for boys and girls, a madrasa, a mosque, an extravagant swimming pool and a guest house.

Nestled between trees and a wire-mesh boundary, the 75-acre complex has manicured lawns, turnip farms and a fish-breeding centre. The students who enroll in the school pay a fee; those who study in the madrasa don't. Everyone learns English, Arabic and computers. Students peer into microscopes and work on electrical circuits. Muntazir's sarcasm continued. 'Welcome to the headquarters of the Lashkar-e-Tayyeba. You think a terrorist organisation will be based just a few metres away from the main Grand Trunk Road?'

Trimmed lawns, conversations of *jihad*

The administrators of the complex, drawn from the LeT's political wing, Jamaat-ud-Dawa, try hard to disassociate themselves from the Lashkar.

Of course there are no firing ranges, and though the gates have been opened—after clearance from Pakistan's security agencies (read ISI)—to dispel the impression of Muridke being a terror-training camp that 'India has made it out to be', the conversation is not about the school syllabus. It's about the enemy: India

I met a family whose sister-in-law lives next to the complex. 'But of course it's a training ground,' they said. 'You hear slogans for *jihad* from loudspeakers at full volume, and you sometimes hear gunfire.' During the two hours that I spent within the complex, there were enough conversation about *jihad,* even if there were no signs of a Lashkar sanctuary and a hideout for al-Qaeda men, including one of the conspirators of the 1993 World Trade Centre bombing. ∎

Here is the evidence, direct from Pakistan

By special arrangement with *Dawn*

Karachi, December 12: 'I WAS IN denial for the first couple of days, saying to myself it could not have been my son,' Amir Kasab, father of Ajmal Kasab, one of the ten terrorists who attacked Mumbai on 26/11, has told *Dawn*. 'Now I have accepted it,' he said in the courtyard of his house in Faridkot, a village of about 2,500 people just a few kilometres from Deepalpur on the way to Kasur. 'This is the truth. I have seen the picture in the newspaper. This is my son Ajmal.' After his brush with crime and criminals in Lahore, Ajmal is said to have run into and joined a religious group during a visit to Rawalpindi.

Along with the others, claimed the Indian media, he was trained in fighting. Amir, a father of three sons and two daughters, said Ajmal disappeared from home four years ago. 'He had asked me for new clothes on Eid that I couldn't provide him. He got angry and left.'

While Amir was talking, Ajmal's two 'sisters and a younger brother' were lurking about. To Amir's right, on a nearby charpoy, sat their mother, wrapped in a *chador* and in a world of her own. Her trance was broken as the small picture of Ajmal lying in a Mumbai hospital was shown around. They appeared to have identified their son. The mother shrunk back in her *chador* but the father said he had no problem in talking about the subject.

Amir Kasab said he had settled in Faridkot after arriving from the nearby Haveli Lakha many years ago. He owned the house and made his earnings by selling pakoras in the streets of the village. He modestly pointed to a hand-cart in one corner of the courtyard. 'This is all I have. I shifted back to the village after doing the same job in Lahore. My eldest son, Afzal, is also back after a stint in Lahore. He is out working in the fields.' Faridkot is far from the urbanites' idea of a remote village. It is located right off a busy road and bears all the characteristics of a lower-middle-class locality in a big city. It has two middle-level schools, one for girls and the other for boys, which Ajmal attended as a young boy.

The approach to Faridkot also points to at least some opportunities for those looking for a job. There are some factories in the surroundings, rice mills et al, interspersed with fertile land. But for the gravity of the situation, with its mellowed and welcoming ambience, the picture could be serene.

It is not. Amir Kasab described the people who snatched Ajmal from him as enemies, but had no clue who these enemies are. Asked why he didn't look for his son all this while, he countered: 'What could I do with the few resources that I had?' Otherwise quite forthcoming in his answers, Amir Kasab, a mild-mannered soul, is a bit agitated at the mention of the link between his son's actions and money. Indian media has claimed that Ajmal's handlers had promised him that his family will be compensated with Rs 150,000 (one and a half lakh) after the completion of the Mumbai mission. 'I don't sell my sons,' he retorted.

Journalists visiting Faridkot since *Dawn* reporters were at the village say the family has moved from their home and some relatives now live in the house. Perhaps fearing a media invasion, nobody is willing to say where the family has gone.■

Lashkar money trail led to Dawood
Presley Thomas

Mumbai, December 12: MAHMOUD MOHAMMAD AHMED Bahaziq, the 65-year-old Saudi Arabia-based chief financier of the Lashkar-e-Tayyeba, was in touch with underworld gangster and designated global terrorist Dawood Ibrahim.

Bahaziq, also known as Abu Abd al-Aziz, approached Dawood in the late 1990s to fund the LeT. Sources in the Intelligence Bureau said Dawood acceded to Bahaziq's demands and also promised him foot soldiers for the LeT in India.

The Indian-born Saudi national has been key to the LeT's establishment and activities, and was a popular visitor to the Jamaat-ud-Dawa's—the parent body of the LeT—centre in Muridke in Pakistan. In certain cases, Bahaziq used video-conferencing to stay in touch with Dawood and top Saudi-based businessmen to raise funds for the LeT. Sources added that Bahaziq created fictitious charitable trusts after the US listed the Al Rasheed Trust as a terror front aiding the al-Qaeda. Aid Organisation of the Ulema, Pakistan, Al Amin Welfare Trust Al-Madina Trust are among the few front organisations Bahaziq created. Though there is no birth certificate available, police sources said, Bahaziq was born in Hyderabad and later went on to procure Saudi nationality. How he got Saudi nationality is still a mystery to police officials, who are trying to ascertain the person who stood by Bahaziq.

A key functionary for the LeT since the 1980s, Bahaziq's name first surfaced when police officials launched a hunt for Mohammed Azam Ghauri—the LeT's India operations commander, who was gunned down in April 2000 in Andhra Pradesh—and his partner Abdul Karim Tunda. Sources said Bahaziq had visited India in 1999 as a Saudi national and stayed at a plush hotel in south Mumbai. This is where Bahaziq met Ghauri and later helped him get to a safe haven in Saudi Arabia, said police sources.

Bahaziq, police sources said, is believed to have met members of the proscribed Students' Islamic Movement of India (SIMI) and Tanzim Islahul Muslimeen (TIM). He also met Mohammed Ishtiaq alias Saleem Junaid—a Pakistani LeT operative who was later arrested in Hyderabad—in Mumbai and helped him with finances.■

'Without doubt, India is the enemy'
Harinder Baweja

MOHAMMED AJMAL AMIR Kasab, the lone terrorist who was captured alive in Mumbai, is supposed to have studied here in the Jamaat-ud-Dawa camp in Muridke, Punjab, according to his interrogators, and it was time to ask my minder, Abdullah Muntazir, some straight questions.

So did Kasab study here, in Muridke?

'Even if he did, we are not responsible for what any one of our students do after passing out.'

Do you support the Lashkar-e-Tayyeba?

'We used to.'

You used to?

'Yes, we were like-minded but the group was banned after Indian propaganda following the attack on its Parliament, which was done by the Jaish-e-Mohammed and not LeT. We used to provide logistical help to the Lashkar, collect funds for them and look after their publicity.'

Did you provide them with arms?

'They must have bought weapons with the money we gave them. They were obviously not using the money to buy flowers for the Indian army.'

The Lashkar has claimed responsibility for the attack on the Red Fort in Delhi and the airport in Srinagar.

'We do not consider Kashmir a part of India. It is a part of Pakistan. Those who attack the security forces are not terrorists, they are freedom fighters.'

President Musharraf moved away from the position that Kashmir either secede or be given independence. He proposed joint control.

'Musharraf did not have any legitimacy. He had no business making such proposals.'

Do you consider India an enemy?

'Without doubt. India is responsible for the attack on Islamabad's Marriot hotel, for the bomb blasts in Peshawar. Sarabjit Singh has been convicted for being a R&AW agent.'

Your *amir*, Hafiz Sayeed, has given calls for *jihad*.

'He supports the freedom movement in Kashmir. We think it is right. It is ridiculous to call him a terrorist. Even when India is pricked by a thorn, the whole world stands up. Why did Condoleezza Rice not put pressure on India for handing over Narendra Modi after the Gujarat carnage?'

Kashmir is no longer entirely indigenous. Foreign fighters, like Maulana Masood Azhar, were arrested in Anantnag.

'He was a journalist and still is an inspirational writer. Anyone from here can go to Kashmir. We don't see it as part of India.'

Did you sanitise this place before bringing me in?

'This is an educational complex and the Jamaat-ud-Dawa is a charitable organisation. There are very few people here because of the Eid break.'

Does the Inter-Services Intelligence support you?

He just laughed.

A Pakistani Hamas

The Jamaat-ud-Dawa, banned by the US in 2005 for being a Lashkar alias, draws patronage from the ISI and though proscribed abroad, has a free run in Pakistan. It has branches all across the country and is as famous for its social work as for its terror activities. It sees itself as a movement and not an organisation and has appealed to many in rural and urban areas.

When a correspondent from London's *The Observer* newspaper went to Kasab's village in Faridkot, close to the border with India, to establish if he indeed was a Pakistani, he was told 'religious clerics were brainwashing youth in the area and that LeT's founder

Hafiz Sayeed had visited nearby Deepalpur. There was an LeT office in Deepalpur but that had hurriedly been closed down in the past few days. The LeT paper is distributed in Deepalpur and Faridkot'.

The Jamaat-ud-Dawa has a wide base and operates 140 schools and 29 seminaries in different towns and cities of Pakistan. According to the Jamaat's website: 'Islam does not mean following a few rituals like performing prayers, keeping fasts, performing the pilgrimage to the Ka'ba (Haj), giving alms (*zakat*), or donating to charitable works, but in fact, it is a complete "Code of Life".'

That is why Jamaat-ud-Dawa's struggle is not limited to any particular aspect of life only; rather, it addresses each and every field of life according to the teachings of Islam. The Jamaat-ud-Dawa is a movement that aims to spread the true teachings of Islam, and to establish a pure and peaceful society by building the character of individuals according to those teachings.'

Its appeal extends to urban professionals like doctors who were out in large numbers in Muzaffarabad (the capital of Azad Kashmir or PoK, depending on which side of the Line of Control you are on) in 2005, after a devastating earthquake. Unlike the Taliban, the Jamaat is modelled after Hamas and is not merely an army with gun-toting members but a complex and intricate organization with a social and political agenda. It has a huge following and reports have often indicated that in its annual congregations, where Hafiz Sayeed gives a call for *jihad*, as many as 100,000 people are present in the sprawling Muridke compound.

It is groups like the Jamaat and Jaish—started by Maulana Masood Azhar, soon after he was set free in Kandahar—that both India and Pakistan are up against.

Not the time to pick a fight
The complete U-turn, post 9/11, when Musharraf lent complete support to George Bush, saw Pakistan take a slow but sure journey that has today placed it in a dangerous cross hairs. While Musharraf joined the war against terror—forced to by Bush, who had infamously said you are either with us or against us—he also got

isolated from his own people. They took to the streets, openly protesting his support of America that was bombing and strafing civilians, first in Afghanistan and then in Iraq.

The last straw came when his own army stormed the Lal Masjid in Islamabad in mid-2007. Reports of machine guns being used against innocents trapped in the *masjid* converted many within the army and the ISI and those who had retired from these outfits. It was the tipping point, said former ISI chief Lieutenant General Assad Durrani. 'It was the most blatant homage paid to the Americans. The mosque is located under the nose of the ISI headquarters, and you can't first allow it to become a fortress and then fire on people who were willing to surrender.'

The storming of the Lal Masjid was a tipping point in more ways than one. If the release of Masood Azhar and the subsequent formation of the Jaish saw the advent of *fidayeen* attacks in Kashmir, the Lal Masjid operation led equally to the birth of intense attacks by suicide bombers.

The suicide attacks were not just targeting civilians, they were seeking men in uniform and the figures, in fact, tell the story. The first half of 2007 saw 12 such attacks all over Pakistan between January and July, and an estimated 75 people were killed.

But after the Lal Masjid operation, which reduced large parts of it to rubble, 44 suicide attacks took place between July and December, killing 567 people, mostly members of the military and paramilitary forces, ISI and the police.

December also saw the assassination of Benazir Bhutto, a grim reminder of the fact that the militants had declared war against their ex-masters. The attack on Islamabad's Marriot hotel—the city's most high-profile landmark—only confirmed the fact that terror can strike at will, any time and any where.

It confirmed also that terror was not restricted to Pakistan's tribal belt alone. Musharraf himself had, in fact, also survived three assassination attempts and now lives under extremely tight security.

The terror threat in Pakistan can, in fact, be gauged from the fact that both President Asif Zardari and Prime Minister Yousaf

Raza Gilani, in a complete first, offered Eid prayers at their respective residences on December 9.

The wave of suicide attacks in Pakistan and neighbouring Afghanistan does not just testify to the revival of the al-Qaeda and the Taliban networks but as Ahmed Rashid, strategic writer and author of several books on the *jihadi* networks, said: 'The army is embroiled in fighting these forces in the Frontier and one third of the country is not even in the State's control. This is hardly the time to pick a fight with India.'

'More Lashkar than Lashkar'

The ratcheting up of tension and animosity between India and Pakistan after the Mumbai terror attacks on 26/11, points to another dangerous faultline—while the Pakistani army joined the global war against terror, it never completely gave up its support to the *jihadi* network that is active on its border with India.

Even after the Lashkar and Jaish were banned, neither were their bank accounts frozen, nor was there any attempt at forcing them to shut shop. The army and ISI continued to support fronts like the Jamaat-ud-Dawa, which does more than just equip men with arms. It motivates and indoctrinates minds and, as Rashid pointed out, 'Musharraf used to place Hafiz Sayeed and Masood Azhar under house arrest for Western consumption. He may have stopped infiltrating them into Kashmir too under international pressure but there was no attempt to stop their activities in Pakistan after they were banned. They were just allowed to hang loose.' Former interior secretary Tasneem Noorani said: 'There was no effort to mainstream the radicals.'

Kasab's journey from a remote village in Faridkot to Mumbai is a testimony to this. So is his revelation to his interrogators that he was trained by a 'Major'.

Zardari may have been right when he attributed the Mumbai attack to 'non-State actors' because the Major does not necessarily have to be a serving officer employed with the ISI. 'Retired ISI officers are helping the Pakistani Taliban and they have become more Lashkar than the Lashkar,' said Rashid. Any number of strategic and security analysts will testify to this dangerous trend—to how ex-ISI officers are still in business because they have now attached themselves as advisors to militant organizations like the Lashkar and the Jaish.

'You don't need large training camps,' admitted one such analyst who prefers not to be named. 'Ex-servicemen are imparting arms training within the compounds of their homes. Different officials are attached with different groups.'

The switch from one alias to another—Lashkar-e-Tayyeba, Markaz-e-Tayyeba, Markaz-e-Dawa-Irshad, Jamaat-ud-Dawa—speaks of the Establishment's (the army and ISI combine is referred to as the Establishment in Pakistan) more than subtle support of groups that are used against India. The long-standing relationship between the Establishment and the India-bound militants is now under pressure. The overriding message from America after the Mumbai attacks is for these groups to be reigned in and this is testing not just the army's carefully crafted support for the militants but has also focused attention on yet another faultline—the equation between the Establishment and the civilian government.

The effect of Indian television

Committed to better relations with India, Pakistan's top-most civilian representatives responded instinctively to the horror in Mumbai, in keeping with what Zardari had told the *Hindustan Times* Leadership Summit, held a few days before the gun and grenade battle at Nariman House and the Taj and Oberoi hotels.

In what took the Indian government by surprise, Zardari committed Pakistan to a no-first-use of nuclear weapons. It was the first major security-related statement to come from Pakistan's government after the February 18 election, and more than just surprise the Indian government it caused unrest amongst its own Establishment. The next statement, made by Prime Minister Gilani—and confirmed through a press release issued by his office—pertained to the civilian government agreeing to sending its topmost ISI officer, Lieutenant General Ahmed Shuja Pasha, to India on Prime Minister Manmohan Singh's request.

The sequence of events following Gilani's offer and Zardari's quick retraction, saying they had agreed to send a director and not director Lieutenant General Pasha, in fact speaks of the internal battle of supremacy between the Establishment and the civilian authorities, especially on the crucial issue of national security which the army believes to be its exclusive domain. As Imtiaz Alam, a peacenick and head of the South Asian Free Media Association, who had dinner with Zardari a day after the Mumbai attacks, explained: 'Zardari is very firm on terrorism. He thinks democracy is a better weapon but the terrorists have succeeded in creating a psychological gulf between India and Pakistan. Instead of Pakistan fighting the *jihadi*s, it has become a fight between India and Pakistan.'

Senior journalists in Pakistan admitted that briefings from the ISI changed the post-Mumbai discourse. Reacting perhaps to the loud, jingoistic demands on Indian television channels, for action against Pakistan, the ISI told a select group of journalists that India had in fact 'summoned' their chief. Jamaat-ud-Dawa *amir* Hafiz Sayeed—with a clear nod from his handlers—appeared on one news channel after another, making the same points: that India's list of 20 most wanted, which also includes him, was old hat; that India was playing the blame game without evidence; that India had its own band of 'Hindu terrorists'; and that India should give freedom to Kashmir and end the matter once and for all. The leak, soon after, of the hoax call, purportedly made by External Affairs Minister Pranab Mukherjee to President Zardari, sealed the debate—India bashing was back in business. The jingoism overtook the more important debate of the threat Pakistan itself faced from terror networks flourishing on its soil.

Who's in charge? Not Zardari

Pakistan's news channels went on overdrive and as some even blared war songs, the question that gained importance through all the din was: Who really runs Pakistan? Who is in control?

The answers to the questions are both easy and complex. Mushahid Hussain, chairman, Foreign Affairs Committee in the Senate, was clear about the answer: 'War on terror, national security and relations with India, Afghanistan and China are the domain of the army. Thanks to India, the army has been rehabilitated and the war bugles are all over. No one person, no one institution is running Pakistan. Musharraf ran a one-window operation and the army and the ISI used to report to him, but now decision-making is murky and that is causing confusion. The hoax call and the ISI DG controversy are symptomatic of that.'

There are other examples. Only a few months ago, Zardari quickly retracted his effort to bring the ISI under the control of the Interior Ministry. And even as the Pakistan government's response to Indian pressure to rein in the terror networks plays itself out on a day-to-day basis, it is evident that the civilian authorities have had to embrace the Establishment's point of view vis-a-vis India. Therefore, the talk that India should provide concrete evidence. Therefore, Zardari's statement that the guilty—if found guilty—will be tried on Pakistani soil. That the 20 most wanted will not be handed over. Even on sourced reports, put out in the local media, that Masood Azhar had been put under house arrest, Prime Minister Gilani went on record to say that no such report had come to him yet.

If India believes that Pakistan's response has been poor—two Lashkar men, Zaki-ur-Rehman Lakhvi and Zarrar Shah, have been arrested in Muzaffarabad—it is because the government here is tied down by the Establishment and pressure from its own people. It cannot be seen to be buckling under pressure either from India or America.

Some moves seem to be on the cards, including the banning of the Jamaat-ud-Dawa. But the Lashkar was banned in the past, as was the Jaish. Prime Minister Gilani has committed to not allowing Pakistani soil to be used for terror attacks, but then Musharraf had made the same exact promise on January 12, 2002, soon after the Parliament was attacked in Delhi.

Former prime minister Nawaz Sharif has gone as far as to say that 'Pakistan needs to set its own house in order' but he is in the Opposition and he can afford to make such statements. If Pakistan has begun to resemble a house of terror, it is because the army and the ISI are yet to change their stance, not just vis-a-vis India but vis-a-vis the terrorists it creates and supports. Until then, the sprawling compound in Muridke will continue to remain in business. If the Jamaat-ud-Dawa does get banned, all it will need is another alias.■

With you, for you, but . . .
Neha Bhayana

Mumbai, December 14: CONSTABLE VINAY DANDGAWAL (40) looked calm and focussed as he and others from Azad Maidan police's detection staff tried to solve a theft at Pydhonie on Saturday evening. But his mind was far from peaceful. A terrorist bullet had grazed Dandgawal's back at CST on November 26. Blood was spurting out of the cut but he valiantly continued his duty till the next afternoon when the pain became unbearable. His family was hysterical because they were watching the television news at their home in Ambarnath and couldn't reach his cell phone. 'I am mentally disturbed since the attack. I was lucky but my friend constable Rajiv Khanderkar was killed at Cama Hospital,' he said. 'My wife is insisting that I transfer to Nashik but that's not what I want.'

Dandgawal is not the only policeman who is feeling traumatised since the terrorist attack that shook Mumbai. Jaslok Hospital's Trauma Counselling Cell and a special helpline set up by two private companies on December 2 have been flooded with calls from police personnel, especially constables. 'Over 80 constables have called us over the last week,' said Jane Henry, psychiatric social worker with PPC Worldwide, an international employee assistance programme provider that worked with British army soldiers in the Iraq war. PPC Worldwide has tied up with Healthcare Solution Service to provide the helpline service as part of their Corporate Social Responsibility. The companies also held a group counselling session for the Mumbai Police—over 200 police personnel attended it—on December 5 and 6. The reasons for the calls to helplines have been varied. While some police personnel were frustrated at not being well armed, some were hurt that the public was blaming them and others were reeling under family pressure to quit the police force. Henry recounted the call from an angry, young constable who had gone to practice at the Mumbai Police firing range. 'He was so annoyed that nothing had changed at the range after the terror attack. They were given single barrel guns which have to be reloaded after every shot,' said Henry.

Counsellors said many officials were also dealing with marital discord post 26/11. 'I have got a few calls from constables who were having fights with their wives because they wanted them to quit the force,' said Henry. Dr Maya Kirpalani, who heads the trauma cell at Jaslok, counselled the wife of a police official, who is posted at a suburban station but was deployed to south Mumbai during the terror attack. 'The policeman brought his wife to the hospital because she was constantly fretting that he would be killed,' she said, adding that she had asked the lady to distract herself by chatting with neighbours or cooking when she felt anxious.■

On 26/11, his lie saved 25 lives
Kanchan Chaudhari

Mumbai, December 14: CHANDRAKANT TIKHE IS an unlikely hero. This pot-bellied man in his fifties works at Cama and Albless Hospital—as a generator operator. But at least 25 people are alive today because he showed commendable presence of mind on the night of November 26. Tikhe was standing in front of the six-storeyed hospital building with some other staff members and relatives of patients when they heard gunfire. Though they did not know it then, that was the sound of Mohammed Ajmal Amir Kasab, who was later arrested, and Ismail Khan, who was shot dead at Girgaon Chowpatty later that night, opening up with their AK-47s at Chhatrapati Shivaji Terminus. As the noise grew closer, Tikhe and the others rushed into the hospital building. Once inside, the staff on duty got into their respective wards and locked the doors and gates from within. More than a score of others who were stranded on the staircase rushed towards the terrace for cover as gunshots were heard within the hospital compound. Tikhe followed them. But as he reached the terrace, he found himself face-to-face with Kasab and Khan. The duo, after leaving CST, had rushed up another flight of stairs to the hospital's terrace.

With their guns trained on Tikhe, the terrorists asked him who he was and what he was doing there. 'I told them I am a hospital staffer on night shift and that it was my duty to ensure that all doors were locked,' Tikhe said. He managed to convince the two that there was no one else on the terrace and that he was about to close the doors. This drew the terrorists' attention away from the terrace where at least 25 people, including doctors, crouched in the dark. Kasab and Khan then wanted to know whether Tikhe was a Hindu or a Muslim.

'I replied: "*Saab, mein Hindu hoon*" [Sir, I am a Hindu],' said Tikhe. The terrorists then ordered him to lead them out of the building.

Tikhe led the way downstairs while the two followed, keeping well back. And this is probably what saved him.

For halfway down the stairs, Tikhe ran into a posse of policemen—led by Sadanand Date—who had reached the hospital and were on their way up in search of the terrorists.

Afraid that he would be mistaken for a terrorist, Tikhe shouted out to the cops not to shoot, saying he was a hospital staffer. He also held up two fingers, gesturing to the police that there were two terrorists behind him.

The policemen told him to get out of the way and moved in on

Kasab and Khan. In the crossfire, Tikhe was injured by an exploding grenade. He was released from KEM Hospital after treatment for wounds on his neck and the right side of his upper body.

The terrorists escaped from the hospital and fled towards Girgaum Chowpatty, where Khan was killed in an encounter with the police and Kasab was captured.■

Investigation agency will deal with all terror crimes
Nagendar Sharma

New Delhi, December 16: THE GOVERNMENT ON Tuesday set in motion the process to seek Parliament's nod on its war against terror with the introduction of a Bill to create a National Investigation Agency (NIA).

Union Home Minister P. Chidambaram introduced the Bill in the Lok Sabha for the creation of a new agency to exclusively deal with terror attacks. 'India has been the victim of large-scale terrorism sponsored from across the borders. After due consideration and examination, it has been proposed to set-up this agency,' Chidambaram said introducing the Bill.

The National Investigating Agency Bill, 2008, when passed, would for the first time in the country allow officers of the agency to freely crack terror cases and bring culprits to book. The Bill provides for overriding powers to NIA officers 'of or above the rank of sub-inspector' throughout India—powers equivalent to the officer-incharge of a police station in the area the officer might be at the time of investigation.

The NIA would be empowered to take over investigation of eight specifically mentioned terror-related crimes including hijacking, any terror attack, any violation of the Atomic Energy Act and anything against the law on weapons of mass destruction. The Bill empowers the Centre to hand over the investigation of a terror attack on its own. In addition, if states want to get any offence investigated by the NIA they would be able to do so.

In case of a terror attack or a related offence, the officer-incharge of the concerned police station would be required to immediately inform the state government, which in turn shall forward the report to the Centre as soon as possible, the Bill says.

The Centre would have to decide within 15 days whether the offence committed is fit to be handed over to the agency. Those accused of terror would be tried in special courts on a day-to-day basis, with the agency having its own prosecutors to elaborate the charges. In case the special court wants it, the trial would be held in-camera—meaning it would not be open to public. Any appeal against the decision of such a court would lie with a division bench of the high court.

How the agency will work

- It would be headed by a director general, to be appointed by the Centre.
- The cadre details are being worked out by the Home Ministry.
- The Centre may directly ask the NIA to investigate a case of terror attack in case it does not receive a request from a state to do so.
- NIA officers of and above the rank of sub-inspector will enjoy the powers of the SHO in the affected area.
- Trials of the terror accused would be conducted on a day-to-day basis in special courts and the NIA would have special prosecutors.
- The Appeal against the decision of a special court would lie only with a division bench of the high court, which would have to decide the appeal within three months.■

'Taj and Oberoi were warned'
Shailesh Gaikwad

Nagpur, December 17: MAHARASHTRA HOME MINISTER Jayant Patil
on Wednesday said the Mumbai Police had alerted the management
of Taj and Oberoi hotels that both the premises were under threat
of a terror attack.

On September 26, Deputy Police Commissioner Vishwas
Nangare Patil had a three-hour-long meeting with Taj officials to
brief them about security measures. He said the police had then
suggested that the Taj should keep only the main entrance open
and close the other doors.

Patil had also suggested that the height of the north court gate
be raised, that closed-circuit television monitors be monitored
every 24 hours and that all visitors be checked thoroughly, Patil
said, quoting what Nangare Patil had said in the meeting.

The terrorists had allegedly jumped over the north court gate
and entered the Taj Hotel premises on the day of the terror attack.
Patil said the hotel management had not been keen to implement
the measures, saying they were a commercial organisation and
hence did not want to trouble customers. In the case of Oberoi-
Trident, the police had given a 12-point security agenda for
enhancing security, he added.

The state government had received intelligence advisory about
threats to hotels after the attack on the Mariott hotel in Islamabad,
Patil said.■

House secures country, passes anti-terror Bills
HT Correspondent

New Delhi, December 17: THE LOK SABHA on Wednesday night
unanimously passed two Bills—introduced by the UPA government
in the wake of the Mumbai terror attacks—for setting up the
National Investigation Agency (NIA) and amending of the Unlawful
Activities Prevention Act (UAPA). But not before a heated debate

that saw politics come into full play and after an assurance by Home Minister P. Chidambaram that the government had not 'copied' the infamous POTA or used it as a bench mark.■

45,846 men to guard 13,319 VIPs; if India cuts back on these numbers we could create four new National Security Guards; double Delhi or Mumbai police forces
Aloke Tikku

New Delhi, December 17: AS THE POST-26/11 debate on whether politicians need more security than the public rages on, facts hidden in government figures show how India can be safer if only our VIPs do not turn security into a status symbol. More than 45,000 policemen protect the pool of VIPs in India that grew at 20 per cent—12 times faster than the annual population growth rate—between 2004 and 2005. This means more security personnel guard 13,319 VIPs than the number of policemen in any Indian city—Delhi and Mumbai included. This is more than the police strength of all states bar the nine largest. An estimated Rs 825 crore of taxpayers' money is spent annually on the salary of the security staff alone, assuming—conservatively—that all on duty are constables earning Rs 15,000 each. The Bureau of Police Research and Development (BPR&D) headquartered in Delhi had compiled the figures more than a year ago.

Police officers, who did not want to be named, said the actual number of policemen protecting VIPs—ministers, members of Parliament, state legislators, judges and bureaucrats among others—would be at least twice this figure. In Delhi, more than 14,000 personnel are on VIP duties. The report, 'Data on Police Organisations in India', only counted about 4,900 security personnel deployed for more than six months as on January 1, 2006. 'A total of 11,012 VIPs were provided police protection for more than six months during the year 2004 . . . It shows an increase of 20.9 per cent over the previous year,' the report said. 'The increase in the VIP protection deployment has strained the limited manpower resources of state police,' it said, suggesting grounds for providing security were skewed.

On paper, threat assessments dictate security cover and the extent of protection. Politics often replaces threat assessments in practice. Samajwadi Party general secretary Amar Singh is the latest example. His threat perception suddenly increased this year to the highest level, Z-Plus, around the same time that the UPA government's life was hanging in balance after the Left pullout. Uttar Pradesh Chief Minister Mayawati too had got herself Home Ministry clearance for her car to drive up to the aircraft at the Delhi airport after she extended support to the government more than a year ago. She withdrew support this year, but the privileges continue. BPR&D said the deployment of police for VIP protection should be rationalised by reviewing it against need-based assessment. According to figures in its report, West Bengal has the most number of VIPs—1999. Assam comes next with 1610 and Uttar Pradesh a close third at 1506. Maharashtra, on the other hand, had reported about 122 VIPs. Terror-torn Jammu & Kashmir, however, has only 170 VIPs.∎

Terror finds her a family
Naziya Alvi

Mumbai, December 17: BETTY ALPHONSO (45)—who grew up in an orphanage and lived at Chhatrapati Shivaji Terminus after being abandoned by her drug-addict husband—was admitted to JJ Hospital with a bullet wound in her leg suffered during the terror attack on November 26.

But when she is discharged from hospital next week, she will have a new home and family waiting. Alphonso shared her hospital ward with two other victims of 26/11—Sabira Khan (40), a Muslim, and Anamika Gupta (26), a Hindu—and found a home with them both. 'Lucky me, I have two homes now,' said Alphonso. She will live with Khan's family till Khan is fit enough to return home. 'I'll take care of her children, who must be missing her,' Alphonso said. Later, she will move to Gupta's home.

'We have developed such a close bond that we want to help each other even after we leave hospital,' said Gupta, a resident of Colaba, who received four bullet wounds while at Leopold Café. Alphonso used to work as a guide for foreigners. Her job earned her enough to afford food, but she could never save enough for a home. 'Only once in my entire life have I had a home and someone to go back to. But it lasted only a couple of months as the man I married turned out to be a drug addict and abandoned me,' said Alphonso.■

Channels lay out conduct code
HT Political Bureau

New Delhi, December 18: THE NEWS BROADCASTERS Association (NBA) on Thursday prohibited TV channels from providing information on security operations during coverage of incidents like the Mumbai terror attack, hijack or hostage situation.

In a new self-regulatory guideline for emergency situations, the NBA said no live coverage should be provided which gives publicity to the terrorists or hampers security operations in any way. India TV had a live conversation with a person claiming responsibility for the Mumbai attacks resulting in a show-cause notice from the I&B Ministry. Other news channels also received flak from the government and people for showing NSG commandos landing on Nariman House where terrorists were holding hostages. The ministry had issued two advisories during the attack asking channels to maintain restrain.

The guidelines prepared by former Chief Justice of India J.S. Verma also advised against live contact with victims and security personnel during a hostage situation. 'News related to armed conflicts and communal violence should be shown with public interest in mind,' Verma said. He added that self-regulation was far more effective than anything else.

The rules

- All telecast of news relating to armed conflict, internal disturbance, communal violence, public disorder, crime and other similar situations should be tested on the touchstone of 'public interest'.
- No live reporting should be made that facilitates publicity of any terrorist or militant outfit or its ideology or tends to evoke sympathy for the perpetrators or glamorises them or their cause or advances the illegal agenda or objectives of the perpetrators.
- In live reporting of hostage situations or rescue operations, no details of identity, number and status of hostages should be telecast or information given of pending rescue operations or regarding the number of security personnel involved or the methods employed by them.
- Media should avoid live contact with victims or security personnel involved or the perpetrators during the course of the incident and unnecessary repeated or continuous broadcast of archival footage that may tend to reagitate the viewers. Archival footage, if shown, should clearly indicate 'file'.
- The dead should be treated with dignity and their visuals should not be shown. Special care should be taken in the broadcast of any distressing visuals and graphics showing grief and emotional scenes of victims and relatives, which could cause distress to children and families.■

Zardari refuses to speak the truth

November 29
Said he would act swiftly if given any evidence of involvement by Pakistani groups or individuals in the 26/11 attacks.

December 3
Said: 'We have not been given any tangible proof to say that he is definitely a Pakistani. I very much doubt that he [Kasab] is a Pakistani.'

December 17
Said there was still no firm proof that the gunmen who attacked Mumbai came from Pakistan.

Media found the truth

December 7
British daily *The Observer* reported that it had established that Kasab came from Faridkot village in Pakistan.

December 12
Pakistan's *Dawn* newspaper traced Kasab's father in Faridkot.∎

This Pakistani nailed Pak govt's lie on Kasab
Renuka Narayanan

New Delhi, December 21: THE PAKISTANI WHO had a court case filed against his TV news channel on December 19 for publicly establishing Ajmal Amir Kasab's Pakistani origin says he is optimistic about a solution to terror simply because he is still alive.

Hamid Mir, Islamabad-based editor of Geo Channel, who telecast Kasab's father from Faridkot village in Okara district of Pakistan identifying his son as the captured terrorist of 26/11, told *Hindustan Times*: 'The mood of the Pakistani people is overall pessimistic. But I am optimistic that there will be a positive outcome because I am still alive. I am being observed with great attention and no one has killed me yet.'

Mir was invited to address journalism students at Panjab University, Lahore, on Saturday. 'The students asked me to explain the difference between "patriotic journalism" and "real journalism",' he said. 'I said whoever is killing innocent people, whether in India or in Pakistan, has to be exposed. That is real journalism.'

Mir squarely blames several Indian TV channels for whipping up public hysteria on both sides of the border. 'Between November 27 and December 4, every bad word said against Pakistan on these channels was taped by Pakistani news channels and then shown to the public here,' he said. 'There was general disbelief about the allegation that the Pakistani navy transported the terrorists to Indian waters, because even the common man here knows that the navy are gentlemen and apolitical, they are not like our army. Also there was some fictional Pakistani character called "Rehman Chacha" shown on an Indian channel as the trainer of terrorists. I showed such clips to an Indian journalist here. She said if Indian media was behaving irresponsibly, then we should behave responsibly,' Mir added.

Mir then hosted a discussion on his show *Capital Talk* on December 4 between Pervez Hoodbhoy, professor of nuclear physics, Qaid-e-Azam University, Islamabad, and Lt Gen. (retired) Hamid Nawaz, former federal minister for interior, who said that the Mumbai massacre was the work of Hindu extremists to discredit Pakistan.

But when Professor Hoodbhoy challenged that theory, supported by Mir, 'There was an outcry next day in sections of Pakistan's Urdu press that two Indian agents were sitting on Geo TV,' said Mir. So why did he air the findings on Kasab's Pakistani identity, knowing what the fallout would be? 'I am not doing this for India. I am doing it for Pakistan,' said Mir. 'I have been telling people here that both India and Pakistan have extreme elements. Maulana Masood Azhar's counterparts are Praveen Togadia and Babu Bajrangi. We have to tell the truth about these people or we are just benefiting those who want Pakistani civil society, media and justice to be suppressed.'■

Taj, Trident return to life
Purva Mehra

Mumbai, December 21: ON SUNDAY MORNING, the breakfast tab at the Trident was a pink rose, a prayer and a 'Thank you for your support' card.

The first patron at the five-star, Madhusudan Kshirsagar, strolled into the Trident lobby for a masala chai and cheese toast at 8.15 a.m., but left with much more than that. 'I often visit the coffee shop with friends for the masala chai. This time I was alone . . . A staffer came up to me and said he wished he had a camera to take a picture of me as I was the first patron,' said Kshirsagar, who runs a shipping company. 'I didn't realise I was the first one there . . . when I asked for the bill, I got a thank you card instead.'

Draped in crisp suits and creaseless saris, the staff welcomed every person who entered the premises—after three levels of security checks—with big smiles, folded hands and profuse thank yous. 'They have all been so fantastic,' remarked Jeff Defracitas, the first guest who checked in, at 8 a.m. 'We were told at the desk that we were the first guests to check in,' said Defracitas, who will stay here for two nights with his wife Zoe.∎

26/11 terrorist Kasab wants to meet Pakistani officials; India hands over his letter to Pak high commissioner
Amit Baruah

New Delhi, December 22: NEARLY A MONTH after 26/11, New Delhi has handed over to Islamabad a letter written by Mohammed Ajmal Amir Kasab, the Pakistani terrorist nabbed by the Mumbai Police, seeking a meeting with officials in the Pakistani High Commission.

Pakistan's Acting High Commissioner Afrasiab, who uses one

171

name, was called to South Block on Monday and the letter written by Kasab was handed over to him.

'In his letter addressed to the Pakistan High Commission, Kasab has stated that he and the other terrorists killed in the attack were from Pakistan and has sought a meeting with the Pakistan High Commission,' a brief official statement said. It is the first real piece of evidence that India has handed over to Pakistan after the Mumbai attacks. The one-page letter, reportedly written in Urdu, is dated December 19.

Afrasiab confirmed to *Hindustan Times* that he had received the letter from MEA Joint Secretary T.C.A. Raghavan. 'We have already conveyed the contents of the letter to Pakistan,' Afrasiab stated. 'Action is being taken,' he added, without providing details. With this, India has taken the first step of trying to get Pakistan to confirm Kasab's nationality. Now, if Pakistan so chooses, it will be able to meet Kasab, verify his personal details, crosscheck with Islamabad and convey to India whether he is a Pakistani or not.

The Indian action comes days after Pakistani President Asif Ali Zardari expressed doubts whether Kasab was from Pakistan while former PM Nawaz Sharif said he had no such doubts about Kasab's nationality. Already, the respected Pakistani daily, *Dawn*, has traced Kasab's father to Faridkot village in Okara district and verified that he's very much a Pakistani.

Earlier this month, Joint Commissioner of Mumbai Police Rakesh Maria had been quoted as saying that Kasab had written a letter to the Pakistan High Commission. 'Kasab's letter, which also seeks legal aid from the consulate (read high commission), has been dispatched to the Ministry of External Affairs and Ministry of Home Affairs to be forwarded appropriately,' Maria reportedly said. It is now up to Pakistan to decide what it chooses to do with the letter.

Under normal circumstances, it should seek consular access to Kasab, verify his nationality and then help with his defence. But given Islamabad's continuing denials, Pakistan could well do nothing about the letter or say that it wanted more evidence from India before responding to the letter.■

'LeT is a monster created by ISI'

Vijay Dutt

London, December 22: THE INTER-SERVICES INTELLIGENCE has definite links with the Lashkar-e-Tayyeba and other militant groups involved in terror attacks on India, *The Times* reported. 'ISI created Lashkar-e-Tayyeba which is no more under its control,' claims a senior ISI official. 'These *jihadi*s were there in Jammu & Kashmir and we supported them. I think any intelligence agency worth its name would have done the same,' a senior ISI officer said.

Commenting on ISI's links with Lashkar, the official said: 'It's a monster we created and now we can't get it back in the bottle.'

The ISI had forged ties with *jihadi* groups throughout the 1980s when the CIA used it to support the mujahideen against the Soviet army in Afghanistan and it saw an opportunity in 1989 to weaken India by creating trouble in Jammu & Kashmir, the newspaper reported.

General Asad Durrani, ISI chief from 1990–92, denied supporting LeT during his tenure, but admitted that Pakistan had an interest in supporting such groups. 'Given Kashmir's history, we can't be expected to remain uninterested,' he added. The ISI officially severed links with the LeT in 2002 after the group attacked India's Parliament, but Indian and US intelligence believe that it maintained covert support, probably through ex-ISI officers.

The Times report complied after a visit to the 75-acre complex in Muridke said that although the administrator Mohammed Abbas denied any connection with the ISI, but it was here (in Muridke), in April 2001, 'that Hafiz Mohammad Sayeed, LeT's leader at the time, called a meeting of his supporters in the 75-acre complex of red brick buildings and neat lawns. Most of the visitors wore the obligatory long beards, but among them was an elderly man with no beard, only a thin, military style moustache. He was Hamid Gul, the former head of Pakistan's Inter-Services Intelligence agency.'

Generals Hamid Gul, Durrani and the serving officer all admitted that some retired ISI agents may have shared the ideology of the militants. 'Yes, I visited there. Retired army officers used to go, too. They used to hold annual fixtures to raise funds and motivate people,' General Gul said. He also said, 'Cleansing the ISI is America's dream, but this is Pakistan's first line of defence. It keeps the country united.' All three said that it would be impossible to channel serious support to militants from inside or outside the ISI without the knowledge of the agency's leadership, *The Times* reported.

As for the Mumbai attacks, they said that it was not in the ISI's interests to antagonise Washington and provoke another conflict with India during an economic crisis.

Many Indian and Western analysts agree, saying that the ISI probably trained LeT militants but was not directly involved in Mumbai. 'There almost certainly are still ISI links to LeT, but the question is how much operational control does the ISI have?' Lisa Curtis, a former CIA analyst and South Asia expert at the Heritage Foundation, said. She and other experts have urged President Asif Zardari to appoint a civilian head of the ISI and dismantle all the militant groups it has supported.

The ISI is unlikely to accept either solution until the international community also addresses Pakistan's concerns in Kashmir and Afghanistan.■

Now, Pak army man in terror plot
Tarun Upadhyay

Jammu, December 23: PAKISTANI INVOLVEMENT IN terrorism in India resurfaced on Tuesday with the police announcing the arrest of three alleged terrorists, including a sepoy in the Pakistani army, in Jammu on December 21. All three were trained at a Jaish-e-Mohammed (Army of Mohammed) camp run by Mufti Abdul Rauf, the brother of Maulana Masood Azhar, the terror group's founder.

Azhar had been held in a Jammu jail for five years before he was let off in December 1999 in exchange for hostages on an Indian Airlines flight hijacked to Kandahar. Azhar is one of India's most wanted men; his custody has been demanded from Pakistan after the 26/11 attacks on Mumbai. Director General of Police Kuldeep Khoda said the three captured men planned to set off a massive explosion in India on the lines of the truck bomb that destroyed the Marriott Hotel in Islamabad on September 20.

With the three men confessing that they were trained at a camp near Rawalpindi in Pakistani Punjab, the arrests, police said, had provided 'clinching evidence' that terror training camps still operate in Pakistan.

'After their training, the terrorists went to Dhaka from Karachi, finally crossing over into West Bengal,' said Khoda. 'They took a train from Kolkata to Jammu.'

Gulam Fareed, from Ruperi village in Pakistan-occupied Kashmir's (PoK's) Bhimber district, was identified as the Pakistani soldier (Belt No. 4319184, 10 Azad Kashmir Regiment). Before joining the army in 2001, he was a member of the Harkat-ul-Jihad Islami, another terror outfit, moving to the Jaish in 2007. Khoda said the other two terrorists were identified as Mohammad Abdullah, from Serian village in North West Frontier Province's Haripur district, and Mohammad Imran, of Dera Nawab in Pakistani Punjab's Bahawalpur district. Imran, said Khoda, joined the Jaish in 2005, followed by Abdullah a year later. 'One of them was trained to carry out a suicide attack by ramming an explosives-laden vehicle into a target.' Khoda said the trio was ordered in August to report to the Jaish's Karachi office, located next to the Muleer army cantonment. They were provided air tickets and visas for Bangladesh by Pakistan's Inter-Services Intelligence operatives identified as Hamzala and Osama.

'They arrived in Bangladesh on September 15 and were received by another ISI operative identified as Nadeem,' said Khoda. He said the trio stayed in Khulna for about three months. 'On December 15, the terrorists began their journey to India. They crossed over into India on December 18 and boarded the Jammu Tawi Express from Malda,' said Khoda. On reaching Jammu on December 20, they initially stayed in a hotel near the station but later shifted to one near the bus stand. Fareed got himself registered as Gulshan Kumar, Abdullah as Akhilesh Parsad and Imran as Inder Kumar. All three gave Delhi addresses.

The police had been receiving inputs about a possible attack and on December 21 teams of the Special Operations Group and a Central Reserve Police Force nabbed the trio from their hotel room. Khoda said they were supposed to get a consignment of arms and the location of their target from a local guide. The guide was to have been in Jammu too but was delayed because the national highway was blocked. Khoda said the police were still trying to find out whether the trio had met Azhar, but did manage to confirm that a vast terror network is operating in Bangladesh and PoK under the guidance of Pakistan.■

26/11 was to take place earlier
Abhishek Sharan

Mumbai, December 23: THE TERROR ATTACKS on Mumbai may have taken place earlier, if four operatives of Lashkar-e-Tayyeba, the terror outfit believed to be behind the attack, had not got arrested in February, say the police.

The arrest of Fahim Ansari, Sabahuddin Ahmed and their two Pakistani associates by the Uttar Pradesh police seems to have delayed the plan as they were originally meant to execute the attack.

'We interrogated Fahim, Sabahuddin and two Pakistanis—Mohammed Farooq and Imran Shehzada. Based on their revelations, it seems their aborted attack, in terms of its planning and modus operandi, unfolded as the 26/11 attack,' a senior UP police officer, who works with the Anti-terrorism Squad, told *Hindustan Times*, requesting anonymity as he is not authorised to talk to the media.

The delay also seems to have broadened the scale of the attack.

'. . . there was of course an upgradation in the scale and the sea route was the mode of infiltration,' the officer added.

Interrogation reports of Ansari and Ahmed, of which *HT* has a copy, reveal that the duo's Mumbai attack plan was being coordinated and directed by top Lashkar leaders in Pakistan— Muzammil alias Abu Yusuf, Kafa and Zaqir ur Rehman alias Chacha.

Muzammil, as per the interrogation report, had given instructions that the weapons used in the Lashkar attack on a CRPF camp in Rampur as well as the two suicide attackers sent to execute the Rampur attack were to be deployed for the Mumbai attack.

Ansari had inspected dozen-odd target spots in Mumbai, including Chhatrapati Shivaji Terminus and the Taj Mahal hotel, for this attack. Before his arrest, in January, Ansari handed over video footage, hand-drawn maps and photographs of the target locations to Ahmed, who passed it on to their mentors.

The Mumbai Crime Branch is now ascertaining if the information Ansari collected was used by the ten-man team that attacked the city on November 26. The four arrested men—Sabahuddin, Ansari, Farooq and Shehzad—have told the UP police that they used Thuraya satellite phones to escape detection and communicate with Muzammil, like the 26/11 attackers.■

Kasab says plan was to take hostages, seek release of IM men

Debasish Panigrahi

Mumbai, December 24: THE OBJECTIVE OF the ten-member Lashkar-e-Tayyeba *fidayeen* (suicide) squad, which carried out the 26/11 attacks, was not just to kill innocent people but also seek release of terror operatives, including 20 members of the Indian Mujahideen.

This has been revealed by the lone arrested terrorist, Mohammed Ajmal Amir Kasab, during his month-long interrogation, crime branch officials told *HT*. The squad were to obtain the operatives' release by creating multiple hostage situations and seek the terrorists' release in return for the hostages. However, the plan could not materialise because of prompt police retaliation, technical problems faced by the mobile phones they were carrying and the death of the group's leader Ismail Khan early in the attack.

Sources, quoting from Kasab's interrogation details, revealed LeT's operations in India had suffered a severe setback following arrest of their cadres by security forces in different parts of the country with the last major round of arrests being that of IM operatives by Mumbai Police's crime branch. 'They were told that most of the arrested cadre were lodged at the Arthur Road prison,' said an officer. 'Telephone numbers of leading Indian TV news channels had been fed on the mobile phones given to them for making their demands during the hostage crisis.'

But the group faced its first crisis when Kasab and Ismail failed to locate the 'first floor' shelter at CST where they were supposed to take hostages. Topping it, Railway Police retaliated quickly by firing at them. Even when the duo ran out of CST, Ismail desperately tried to contact other members of the group and his handlers—Rehman Chacha and one Kazi. However, his SIM card did not work. This is when Kasab and Ismail thought of creating a hostage situation in any building they came across and Cama Hospital became the next target. But here too they were challenged by the police, forcing them to abandon the idea and run for cover. Sources also said that the group had been asked to eliminate all the hostages as soon as their demands were meet and later kill themselves too.■

Season of flip-flop across borders
Amit Baruah

New Delhi, December 24: IT'S THE TIME of year when fog settles over the cities of Delhi and Lahore. Visibility is usually low; clarity elusive. This year, the fog looks to have enveloped the entire India–Pakistan relationship.

We will cooperate fully, said Pakistan post-26/11. After deciding to send the ISI chief to India to help in the Mumbai probe, Pakistan's civilian leadership back-tracked following a rap from the military establishment. Now, there is one line from the military and civilian leadership.

On Wednesday, Prime Minister Yousaf Raza Gilani said India was trying to make a 'scapegoat' out of Pakistan. Indian ministers, too, have blown hot and cold. War is not an option, said one. All options are on the table, said another. Finally, Prime Minister Manmohan Singh stepped in to say on Tuesday, 'No one wants a war.' Even opposition politicians like former Pakistani PM Nawaz Sharif are not averse to playing to the gallery. After declaring that Mohammed Ajmal Amir Kasab was a Pakistani, Sharif said on Monday that if India didn't have any evidence on Mumbai, it should avoid making false allegations that create tension. 'The media is trying to dictate the relationship. TRPs (television rating points) dominate the show between us,' said Aziz Khan, Pakistan's former high commissioner to India, from Islamabad on Wednesday.

But, what about the Pakistani planes apparently buzzing over Lahore and Islamabad? '*Aap kehte hain ki hamare jahaz ur rahein hain, ham kehte hain ki aapke jahaz ur rahein hain* (You say it is our aircraft, we say it is your aircraft),' added Khan. 'Our TV channels are going berserk. They're trying to set the tone for the relationship,' a former Indian ambassador, who chose to remain anonymous, felt. 'The crux of the matter is terrorism. We should not say or do anything that adds to the war scare that Pakistan is trying to create,' T.C.A. Rangachari, who has worked as India's deputy high commissioner to Pakistan, told *HT*.

But, already, the US seems to be concentrating on reducing tensions, not on getting Islamabad to deliver on winding up terrorist groups. 'The nations [Pakistan, India and Afghanistan] must improve relations . . . so attacks like the one in Mumbai don't escalate closer to conflict,' Admiral Mike Mullen, America's top military official, said on Tuesday.■

Will we never learn?
Shahkar Abidi

AFTER THE SERIAL blasts of 1993 devastated Mumbai, then police commissioner A.S. Samra said the coast needed better policing. The explosives used had been brought in by sea. Fifteen years later terrorists again came in from the sea and laid siege to the city.

In 2005, the central government had come up with a plan to strengthen coastal policing in nine states and four union territories. Twelve of the 73 police stations planned across the country were to come up in Maharashtra. Mumbai was to have one police station and six chowkies—each with a watchtower. Three years later, there isn't even a separate commissionerate for the coastal police. So the officials assigned to coastal policing don't have a clue about their jurisdiction. And finding equipment is a constant struggle. 'We use rented boats, which cannot move faster than 8–10 kilometres per hour,' says Senior Police Inspector Anant Rane, who is attached to the coastal police department. Rane operates out of a temporary office on the premises of the Yellow Gate police station.

The coastal police station was proposed at one of three places— Santacruz Koliwada, Mahim Reti Bunder or Madh jetty. The chowkies already functioning are at Sewri, Sasson, Cuffe Parade and Girgaum Chowpatty. What about the coastal police stations in the districts adjoining Mumbai? Well, in Navi Mumbai, the N.R.I. coastal police station in the Nerul area has no boats. 'We are not able to operate due to lack of infrastructure,' says Rafique Bagwan, senior inspector. In Thane district, land has been allotted at Dahanu, but no coastal police station has come up.

The worst part is that morale is dipping. Most of the personnel had volunteered to serve in the coastal police when the expansion plans were announced in 2005. 'The higher authorities are doing nothing. I want to get shifted to some other branch,' said one officer. So what do the police brass have to say? The Inspector General of Police (Konkan Range) K.K. Pathak told *HT*: 'We are alert and have intensified the patrolling at points.' ∎

26/11: LIFE AFTER

I. Out of the shadows

'We forgive them all'
Shashi Baliga

SANTANU SAIKIA SPEAKS calmly and precisely, in even tones. But an undercurrent of urgency betrays the enormity of both his loss and the task confronting him.

For three days beginning November 26, Saikia and his children had kept a long, tense vigil. Finally, he was told his wife Sabina had breathed her last in a suite on the embattled sixth floor of the Taj Mahal hotel.

For those of us who knew Sabina, her most striking quality was the full-throated, upfront manner in which she dealt with all that life handed her—the joys, the pleasures, the kindnesses and the conflicts. It is now left to her family to grapple with her loss in the same manner. 'When one is dealing with a terminal illness, you have time to grieve, to adjust to the natural process of life and death,' says Saikia. 'But this was a violent, mindless event. I'm 50 years old, I'm an old horse, I'm coping as best as I can.'

But his children are another matter. 'It has been particularly hard on my 11-year-old son, Anirudhha, who was very attached to his mother,' he says. 'He hasn't shed a tear since the incident; he doesn't want to even talk about it. I've tried bringing up the subject many times, but drawn a blank. All he says is that, one day, he wants to visit the room in which she stayed. Perhaps it will be a catharsis for him.'

His daughter Arundhati, thirteen-and-a-half years old, has reacted in her own manner. 'On the day her mother died, in this seemingly inexplicable event, she became a woman. Her teenage years were telescoped into adulthood in an instant,' he remarks. A pause. Then: 'This is the tragedy of my life.' Don't search for self-pity. 'The point is,' says Saikia, 'how does one tackle this tragedy with a positive attitude, if one could use the term?' This is how

Saikia has decided they will: 'We want to face this with fortitude, with quiet dignity and take it philosophically.'

One of the results of their loss, he believes, will be that his children 'will gain in character and strength and come out of this as better human beings.' But they are young; and he does worry: 'We want to side-step this tragedy and try to lead a normal life. But three months down the line, when they realise life is normal for everyone else but not for them, it will hit them.'

As the nation goes into a paroxysm of anger against the perpetrators of the attack and the politicians who have, perhaps, led us to this pass, Saikia's emotions are at another pitch. 'When I grieve, I have no anger,' he says. 'When Sabina herself is gone, why hang on to such negative feelings surrounding this event? Terror has no religion and there is a lot of misdirected anger. I've told my children, "They did what they thought they had to do." Our sorrow overwhelms all other emotions. We have no anger, no malice, no rancour or bitterness. We forgive them all.' ∎

'The compensation won't last forever'
Neha Bhayana

SHE WAKES UP early to dress her siblings for school. Then, she cleans the house, cooks lunch and coaxes her mother to eat. In the evening, she helps her two brothers and little sister with their homework and ensures they eat the dinner she has cooked. Only then does she sit down with her own books.

At 16, Neelam Gupta has taken charge of rebuilding her family's life.

Her father Shivshankar, who used to sell bhelpuri at CST, was one of the first to fall to terrorist bullets. The 37-year-old was packing his basket to leave when the firing started. He fled through a nearby gate but was hit by two bullets outside Cama Hospital at 10.10 p.m. When his body was brought to their one-room shanty in Mankhurd's Annabhau Sathaye Nagar the next afternoon, Gupta's mother Rajkumari (33) crumbled. And Neelam grew up. The young girl comforted her siblings—Deepak (14),

Sandeep (12) and Sheetal (9)—and attended to all the condolence calls and media questions. Neelam tries to maintain a brave front for her family's sake. But sometimes she can't help herself. 'I miss my father, too,' she says, her eyes welling up.

A consistent topper who never bunked school, Neelam has not attended classes since her father's death. 'I'll go back soon and try to fulfil Papa's wish. He wanted me to study computer engineering,' she says. Rajkumari is striving to move on, too. She knows her family needs her. 'The compensation won't last forever. I have to work,' she says. I approached the Railways for a job but since my husband was shot outside Cama Hospital and not at the station, they told me I was not eligible.'

The family used to manage on the Rs 100 to Rs 150 a day Shivshankar brought home. 'When he had to close down his stall at Zunka Bhakar three years ago, I went without food for days. But I always felt secure because I knew he would take care of us,' she says. 'Now, it is my responsibility.'∎

'God has been fair'
Kinjal Dagli

A LIFE-SIZE PICTURE of Pankaj Shah beckons at the entrance of the family's fourth-floor, sea-facing flat at Worli. The smiling visage of the real estate developer, captured on camera just three months ago, tells its own story. The story of a man who lost his father at 20, took on the family business and built an empire with it, married the woman he fell in love with, had two children with her, set up the famed Tao Art Gallery with her, and at an untimely 60, fell prey to terrorists on an unscheduled visit to the Oberoi's Kandahar restaurant on November 26. But the finer hues of the grand tale, I find out, are precious memories, undocumented, but etched in the minds of the family Shah left behind—51-year-old Kalpana, his wife, and his teenage children Sarjan, 19, and Sanjana, 13.

'We have been married 28 years. He was an out-and-out romantic. A few days before his death, he called me from his car just to make me listen to one of his favourite songs: *Abhi naa jao chod kar, ki dil abhi bhara nahi*,' recalls Kalpana, her eyes moistening at the irony.

Daughter Sanjana, a student of Cathedral & John Connon School, talks to the photograph at the entrance. 'I want to fulfill two of my father's wishes. He was very particular about my hair, almost like a mother would be; he wanted me to take good care of it and keep it long and beautiful. He also monitored my height closely; I'm 5' 2" but he wanted me to grow three inches taller, and I hope I get there,' she says, with a grin. Her innocence is as endearing as her rationalisation when she says, 'I believe God has been fair. This year, I got to spend an unusual amount of time with my father. We went to Turkey, London and Germany in summer and to Dubai during Diwali. Got a chance to share all the important stuff with him before he was taken away.'

Nineteen-year-old Sarjan now has to, just as his father did, shoulder responsibility for the business and family before he gets a chance to mature into adulthood. 'I hadn't decided whether to join my dad's business or to go my own way. But now the choice has been made for me,' he says. Far from bemoaning the hand Fate has dealt the family, Sarjan believes in looking forward. 'I've been thrown into the deep end, but I'm learning to swim,' he says.

The teenager is studying at the London School of Economics, and has two more years to get his degree. He plans to manage the business from afar, with trips to Mumbai at three-week intervals. Every project must be completed according to Dad's commitment, he declares. He, too, thinks he was given an intimation of tragedy last summer, when he opted to spend a month and a half working with his father instead of taking up an eight-week internship with Credit Suisse. 'I only did two weeks of the internship, and whatever little experience I gained with my father is what's helping me now,' he says. 'I guess there was some cosmic force preparing us.' ■

'Am I responsible?'

Shashi Baliga

EVERY EVENING, TAROT reader and arts consultant Roopa Patel drops in to have dinner with her 84-year-old mother Jyotsna*ben* at her home in Shreyas, an apartment block opposite the Air India building on Marine Drive.

Around 10.20 p.m. on November 26, Roopa and her son Anirudh had finished their dinner at Shreyas. As Anirudh was staying back with his grandmother, Roopa left for their apartment on Marine Drive's A Road, where she lives with Anirudh and her husband Anup Kumar Bhardwaj. She was at the corner of the Air India building when she heard the first blast. A fire cracker, she thought. But an eerie silence followed by a frantic commotion made her rush back to her mother. There, from the balcony of the fifth-floor apartment, they could not only hear the firing and the blasts but see into the rooms on the far side of the Trident. At one window, Anirudh glimpsed a man clad in black, opening the curtains with his gun: Was he a terrorist? The face of evil? They will never know. Roopa saw 'the bodies, the blasts, the pain of the relatives, the shock and the night-long burning.' And most horrifying of all, 'We could see people at their windows, waving desperately, trying to get people's attention, asking for help,' she recalls. 'And we could do nothing for them. Did they die or were they saved—the question still haunts me.'

There was no respite from the horror—inside, the three of them sat transfixed by the images unfolding on TV. 'It was unreal, like watching two different movies of the same event,' she remembers. And painful too—'The Oberoi was like our backyard. I have all my meetings there, I go shopping there, we used to take Anirudh there to see the Christmas tree. That night saw the destruction of so many memories.'

Why did this happen, she asked herself. Then, 'Another question came unbidden . . . was I in any way responsible for any of this? I pushed the thought away but it came again and again. And I asked myself: Have I done all that I can to make this city safe? Have I done my bit?'

The answer was no, she admits. 'Was I not responsible for the government that was responsible for this? We have a say, but we don't exercise it because we are too genteel to dirty our hands with politics. Have we not sat quiet when a politician mouthed inane platitudes because it is so easy to shut our ears? Have we not looked the other way when someone spat on our roads or threw garbage on them? We set aside time for our families, relatives, friends, colleagues, even distant acquaintances. But how much time do we give our beloved city?' she argues. 'Something died in me that night,' she says. 'But a new responsibility has been born.' ■

'We can't help missing him'
Mauli Buch

SIXTY-FIVE-YEAR-OLD LAKSHMI SHINDE proudly lights a lamp in front of her son's photo every day. Lakshmi derives some satisfaction amidst her grief in the knowledge that her 46-year-old son, Shashank, a senior inspector with the Railway Police at Chhatrapati Shivaji Terminus, did his duty bravely when he was thrust into the nightmare that marks one of Mumbai's darkest episodes.

Uttam, his younger brother, says Shashank came out of the police station near the station's waiting hall as soon as he heard the first sound of firing at CST. He was armed with just a service revolver, which was simply no match for the AK-47s brandished by the terrorists. But he worked quickly to evacuate people from the hall. Home Guard Mukesh Jadhav was also working alongside.

Says Uttam, 'Shashank surely saved some lives. And while he was trying to do so, the terrorists shot him in his back. He took four bullets. He died within minutes. Shashank was one of the first officers to fall to the terrorists.' Manasi, Shashank's 43-year-old wife, has gathered the courage to face the world alone. And get on with life.

'I resumed work from Monday, December 22. I have to move on for my daughters and everyone in the family,' explains Manasi in subdued tones. She is an assistant administration officer with the Life Insurance Corporation.

Shashank's aged parents endorse her decision, as do other family members. 'It is better that she goes back to work instead of being home with her sad thoughts,' says Chandrasen (76), Shashank's father. Says Chandrasen, 'Shashank carried on my legacy—I have myself been in police service all my life and retired as a *jamadar* from the Byculla police station in 1999.'

Shashank's daughters, Aditi and Nivedita, have resumed their studies too. But are still beset by memories. Says Aditi, 'Our father is a martyr and we are very proud of him. But we can't help missing him.'■

'I wish they'd stop'
Mauli Buch

IT IS A sequence of events that has been scrutinised and analysed endlessly by the media. And become the centre of controversy too, thanks to Minority Affairs Minister A.R. Antulay.

But for the family of Assistant Sub-Inspector Balasaheb Bhonsale, it is a sequence that has hit cruelly home and meant the difference between life and death.

Bhonsale, an ex-army man, was driving the police Qualis in which ATS chief Hemant Karkare, encounter specialist Vijay Salaskar and Additional Commissioner of Police Ashok Kamte set off in chase of the terrorists who were headed for the Cama Hospital after their murderous spree at Chhatrapati Shivaji Terminus. Salaskar asked Bhonsale to move aside and took over the car. Says Bhonsale's eldest son Deepak (30), himself a policeman, 'Soon after my father handed over the wheel to Salaskar *saab,* the terrorists started firing. He told Karkare *saab* to duck and did so himself but the bullets hit them both. My father took four of them.' He says it matter-of-factly, keeping his emotions in check. But his younger brother Sachin (27) cannot. At their Naigaon residence, Sachin bursts out, 'The loss itself is difficult to bear. But constant sympathy from relatives and acquaintances make the pain unbearable. I wish they'd stop offering their sympathies.'

Balasheb's wife Sharada (53) is more resigned as she says softly, 'Anyone who aspires to be a policeman should have the ability and courage to die for the nation. I am a proud *veerpatni* (wife of a martyr).' The family now looks forward to the job Sachin hopes to get soon—he has applied for the post of a clerk in Mantralaya. Though he awaits a response, he's geared up for his new responsibilities. 'Our father took care of mother and looked after the family,' he says. 'I hope to do well in my job and do the same.' ■

'I've seen so much goodness'
Kinjal Dagli

ON NOVEMBER 26, Kunal Thakral, a 22-year-old student of the Delhi School of Economics and his classmate Shantanu Khanna had just entered Leopold Café, when two terrorists lobbed a grenade from behind them.

'About 21 pieces of shrapnel entered my leg and I was bleeding profusely. Shantanu pulled me down and dragged a table in front of us for protection,' narrates Thakral. They heard a series of gunshots and deathly screams in the minutes that followed.

The bodies falling all around them convinced them that they were going to be next, but suddenly, a lull followed and they knew the shootout had ended. 'I heard later that the two terrorists were in a hurry to reach the Taj, so they left,' he says.

Soon, the ATS arrived and a policeman put Thakral in a taxi headed for St. George Hospital. 'I was told I was on a low-priority list because I was still conscious. By that time I was unable to walk, but I decided to take a chance, and with the help of another policeman, got a taxi to take me to Bombay Hospital,' he recounts. 'The hospital didn't charge me a rupee,' he adds.

And, in an incident that has stayed with him, he remembers, he asked a complete stranger for water and was handed a Bisleri bottle. 'When I got home, the hospital in Delhi didn't charge me either. And a government official came home to drop off a compensation cheque for Rs 50,000 without any bureaucratic hassles,' he continues. The images of the shootout still haunt him. But, he says, 'I've seen so much goodness that it's easier for me to cope. I have a lot to be grateful for. I'm just thankful to be alive.' ∎

'We have to relive the nightmare'
Alifiya Khan

THE THREE KNOCKS on the door that echoed in his head for weeks have stopped. Six-year-old Yash rarely speaks of the 'bad man' dressed in black these days and is looking forward to a trip to his grandmother's house instead. One month after terrorists killed his brother in cold blood, the healing process has begun.

The Vaghela home lies in the lane adjoining Cama and Albless Hospital. On the night of November 26, as terrorists wreaked havoc, terrified residents locked their doors and almost all the lights in the lane went out. Save those in GT Hospital sweeper Thakur Budha Vaghela's house. Thakur, preoccupied with pacifying his terrified son, had not got around to turning off the lights or latching his door.

The terrorists knocked on his brother Bhavesh's door thrice before entering Thakur's house. They strode in, hurled abuses at Thakur and shot him in the stomach in front of his son. They aimed a bullet in the boy's direction as well. Fortunately, they missed.

Like Yash, Thakur's wife Karuna is slowly coming to terms with her loss. But, says Bhavesh, 'It is difficult for her to put her memories behind her when she is in the same house that her husband was murdered in.'

He complains that constant visits from the media and government officials have left them with little time or space for their grief even though he has put Yash off limits for the media. 'How can we move on when we have to constantly relive the nightmare?' he asks. I feel a pang of guilt, and consider explaining the media's position to Bhavesh. But give up the idea, given his current state of mind. Now is not the moment. ∎

II. Hidden heroes

'He didn't run away'
Vignesh Iyer

'PEOPLE NEVER USED to look at the Home Guard with the respect that they had for the police, the army or the NSG. But my brother's martyrdom has changed people's perception about the Home Guard,' says Chandrashekhar, brother of the slain Mukesh Jadhav, who died at Chhatrapati Shivaji Terminus on November 26.

Mukesh (23), a constable with the Home Guard, who was on duty near the waiting hall of CST, was shot around 9.50 p.m., but not before he had managed to save the lives of many others. 'As soon as the terrorists entered the station and started firing, Mukesh started evacuating people. Though he had no previous training in handling such situations, he did not run away from the place as many others did,' says Chandrashekhar.

The family's pride in his sacrifice is evident in the faces of Mukesh's father, 75-year-old Bikaji Jadhav, a retired sweeper with the BMC, and his mother, Sulochana, who treasure their son's Home Guard cap, badge and other belongings that they have carefully preserved.

In his 10'x15' house in the narrow lanes of Sion's Nehru Nagar locality, Mukesh's sister-in-law Sandhya says they learnt about the crisis when they turned on their television set. 'We tried to call him but he did not answer.' They kept trying, and finally a fellow Home Guard picked up the phone and told them Mukesh had been shot. They rushed to CST, from where they took him, injured but still conscious, to St. George Hospital (behind CST).

'But at the hospital, we were told we were fifth in the queue for the operation theatre,' recounts Chandrashekhar. Precious time was lost. 'The doctors informed us that had the bullets not hit his chest he could have been saved (Mukesh was shot in his chest and abdomen),' he added. This is one of the family's many regrets. The other one is that Mukesh did not live to join the army. 'Right from his childhood, his dream was to join the army. On the 26th, he had filled up a form to do so . . .' recalls Chandrashekhar. It was not to be.■

Map maker for the NSG
Kanchan Chaudhari

THE IMAGE IS stuck in memory: Black Cat commandos rappelling on to the roof of besieged Nariman House as a helicopter whirred overhead. But few know of the faceless locals who helped the NSG prepare for the offensive.

Vijay Surve, a 57-year-old political party worker and father of two who has lived in Colaba all his life, spent the better part of two days before the operation drawing up maps and estimating terrace-to-terrace distances for the crack team. And that's not all. Before he began to assist the NSG in its recce of the area, he was busy evacuating the buildings nearby—even pulling a four-month-old baby girl out of a building right next to the petrol pump that was almost blown up with grenades. 'My party office is right opposite Nariman House,' said Surve. 'Minutes after the attack began at 9.30 p.m. on November 26, a friend came running up to me saying he had heard shots fired. I rushed to Nariman House to find that a 19-year-old boy had been shot dead.' A mob had gathered and was banging on the doors of the Jewish community centre. 'I could hear the automatic gunfire and I realised this was something serious,' said Surve.

Surve decided to warn the residents of the buildings around Nariman House. It took him till the wee hours to go from door to door with his warning, but locals say he probably saved several lives. 'I had heard about the trouble in Colaba and I was rushing home,' said Edward Fernandes. 'My family was at home, right next to Nariman House, and I couldn't get in. Surve rushed in and emerged with my wife, mother and four-month-old baby.'

An old Muslim couple was not so lucky. They were shot by a stray bullet outside their front door as Surve passed his message of warning through a neighbouring building.

191

The following day, the NSG moved in. 'There are so many unauthorised structures and illegal modifications that no map can really help you manouevre in this area,' said Surve. 'But I grew up flying kites in the narrow gullies, so I didn't need a blueprint.' His hand-drawn aerial view, etched from a half-century of memories, helped the commandos finish the job.■

Courage under fire
Debasish Panigrahi

ISMAIL KHAN AND Ajmal Amir Kasab were still holding down the triggers on their AK-47s when Captain R. Tamil Selvan decided he had had enough.

The 50-something parcel contractor at CST rushed out with eight of his staff and began lifting the injured and getting them out of harm's way. 'I first heard the shots at 9.40 p.m. I had just returned from loading parcels on the Kolkata Mail. My staff was busy preparing parcels for the morning trains,' said Selvan. 'At first, I thought it was fireworks ... a send-off party for some Railways officer.'

As terrified passengers, some bleeding, began rushing into the corridors, he realised something was very wrong. But nothing could have prepared him for the gory sight outside. 'People were lying on the floor, bleeding,' he said. 'So many were dead. And about 50 metres away, I could see two men firing in opposite directions, towards the local platforms. An unexploded grenade lay a few feet away. The memories still make my blood boil.' Selvan's team began placing the wounded on the pullcarts used for transporting parcels.

'The captain got us all organised and made sure we stayed together,' said senior parcel clerk Vivek Sharma. 'He kept us focussed and moved out all the victims as quickly as possible.'

In all, they moved scores of people to nearby St. George Hospital in 20 minutes. The first ambulance arrived 25 minutes later. By then, the Captain's job was done. His courage and quick thinking earned him a felicitation from the Governor.

'But my men were with me every step of the way,' said Selvan. 'The two men were still firing and hurling grenades. Had they turned to us, none of us would have survived the AK-47 bullets.' Thirty-six of the men rescued by Selvan survived. 'But I still wake up in the middle of the night, their screams echoing in my ears,' he said.■

A hero born in golden hour
Alifiya Khan

IT'S HARD TO keep your head when all around you are losing theirs. Dr Shashi Pawar, chief of disaster cell and control room at JJ Hospital, managed to do just that on November 26, through the endless rush of the dead and injured and the news trickling in of more shooting and more attacks. He could manage to keep his calm till ATS chief Hemant Karkare's body rolled in, his face covered with a white sheet. 'It was a sinking feeling,' said Dr Pawar. 'A real shock.'

In the midst of the chaos, Pawar stopped a moment to pray. He knew it was going to be a long night. With a lump in his throat, the 32-year-old prayed for his city, and his hospital. 'Karkare's bodyguard kept repeating "The three of them are dead. The three of them are dead,"' said Dr Pawar. 'We decided to keep the news of Karkare's death to ourselves. We knew a lot of his men were out there and we didn't want to shatter their morale.'

Dr Pawar was on a bike with a friend near CST when 26/11 began. He heard one round of rapid firing, then another. The two men then passed a police barricade at Charni Road, where terrorist Ajmal Amir Kasab would be caught just moments later.

Dr Pawar rushed to the hospital and started taking stock. 'We sent a team of four doctors to St. George Hospital, the one closest to CST,' he said. 'Next, I checked the capacity at the blood bank and asked someone to coordinate.' There were just 20 doctors and 15 paramedical staff on duty. 'We started making calls and over 50 doctors and staffers arrived,' said Dr Pawar. Most of them, including Pawar, would remain on duty for the next 50 hours, till the last terrorist was finally defeated. 'Dr Pawar worked 48 hours straight and was a pillar of support to the hospital. He set up a help desk and called typists and social workers to draw up lists of the injured and dead with complete addresses, which helped relatives and the police too. His work was exemplary,' said Dr Pravin Shengare, joint director, Directorate of Medical Education and Research.■

From the force
Rachna Pratihar & Debasish Panigrahi

They were sent into battle with the most rudimentary weapons and barely any armour. Tired of being underpaid, understaffed and under attack, Mumbai's policemen want change.

Arnish Deshpande, Police Constable, Marine Drive
On the force for: 17 years
Part of rescue operations at the Trident hotel. He says: 'It was horrifying to actually see terrorists lobbing grenades. We are not afraid to sacrifice our lives for our nation, but most of us cannot function the way things are . . . forced to keep track of every bullet and cartridge and return empty shells to our superiors.'

Suresh Salunke, Head Constable, CST (GRP)
On the force for: 26 years
On duty in the outstation section. Rescued two at CST. He says: 'It was a dreadful sight . . . people screaming in pain. I wanted to attack the terrorists, but all I had was a baton. We need to strengthen our security system. We need more sophisticated weapons.'

Satish Nimbalkar, Police Naik, Azad Maidan
On the force for: 20 years
Posted at Metro cinema, where two terrorists gunned down three top police officers. He says: 'We are giving our best, but nothing is going to change until there is adequate manpower. In every police station, there is a shortage of staff. Every one of us is overworked.'

Santosh Mane, Police Constable, Marine Drive
On the force for: 12 years
Part of the rescue operations at the Trident. Worked for 72 hours straight. He says: 'The terrorists were better equipped. They had better weapons. They were well-trained. We need better equipment. We also need to be trained to handle state-of-the-art weapons.'

Vikram Nikam, Head Constable, DB Marg
On the force for: 28 years
Part of the team that arrested the only surviving terrorist Ajmal Kasab at Girgaum Chowpatty. He says: '26/11 was not just an attack, it was war against our country. To avert such an attack in the future, the government should come forward to upgrade security on every front.'

Dinesh Barad, Police Constable, DB Marg
On the force for: 10 years
On the team that battled the terrorists at the Trident hotel. He says: 'I kept thinking of all the bodies we cleared out of the hotel. All those innocent lives were lost for no reason. The police, the public and the government need to work together to keep our cities safe.'

Avinash Mahadik, Police Constable, Colaba
On the force for: 17 years
Was posted outside the Taj, armed with a baton. He says: 'I felt so helpless. I kept thinking, if only I had some weapon, I would have repaid them for daring to attack our city. We need to make sure this doesn't happen again. We need to make people aware too.'

Sanjay Patil, Police Naik, CST (GRP)
On the force for: 22 years
On duty when terror struck. He says: 'Now, some are calling us cowards. But we are not afraid—just ill-equipped. They have state-of-the-art weapons. We don't even have bulletproof jackets. Most of us are working 12-hour shifts. Who can perform well in such conditions?'

Pramod Desai, Police Constable, Gamdevi
On the force for: 5 years
On duty when a taxi blew up near the docks. He says: 'It was the most unfortunate incident I ever came across in my life. We failed to save so many innocent lives. One thing that keeps me going is the reaction of the public. They recognise our efforts.'

Ashok Pawar, Police Constable, Colaba
On the force for: 21 years
On the team that entered the Taj after the siege. He says: 'We are not cowards. We are ready to lay down our lives to protect the lives of citizens. We will work 24 hours and will not allow terrorists to strike our city again.'

Hasan Gafoor, Police Commissioner
'The Mumbai attack was unprecedented. This has necessitated certain changes and we are doing it. We have started phasing out old weaponry, improving the living conditions of the constabulary and reducing work hours. We are doing the needful in a phased manner.'

Ahmad Javed, Additional Director General of Police (Establishment)
'Policemen cater to different requirements. They are provided weapons accordingly. There is no denying the fact that better practice and facilities should be provided. The government and department have initiated several steps to upgrade equipment.'∎

The march of folly
Ayaz Amir

THE MOOD HERE is not jingoistic and there is no beating of the drums of war. But it is grim all the same with some army units being pulled out from the western marches for deployment on the eastern front and the military in a state of 'high alert'.

Mumbai has slipped into the background and the dynamic of Indo–Pak confrontation—something with which both countries are all too familiar—has taken over. Apart from the usual suspects mouthing the usual clichés about giving India a 'mouth-breaking response' (*mooh torh jawab*) few Pakistanis are comfortable with the heightened tension between the two countries or the drift towards something akin to a state of war. But the dynamic once started creates its own momentum. Thus, despite everything, tension is growing and armed forces on both sides are preparing for the worst.

Does this suit anyone, except al-Qaeda? But oblivious to the larger picture India and Pakistan are setting out on the familiar terrain of confrontation. The Americans can't be pleased and understandably are counselling restraint. But the march of folly continues.

At least this is what it looks like on this side of the border. In Pakistani eyes, and they could be wrong, chief among Indian jingoists has been Foreign Minister Pranab Mukherjee with his persistent talk about all options on the table including some kind of armed response. Pakistan army chief, General Ashfaq Kayani, was replying to him that in case of any kind of strike Pakistan's response would come in minutes. The rhetoric could have become more heated if Prime Minister Manmohan Singh had not stepped into the breach by declaring that the issue was not war but terrorism.

Whatever the sentiment on the other side, the feeling in Pakistan is that India is playing a clever game, using the moment to isolate Pakistan and build international opinion against it. There is also the feeling that India is trying to bully Pakistan, an impression heightened by the tone of Indian statements after Mumbai.

This is why President Asif Zardari and Prime Minister Yousaf Gilani have come in for sharp criticism for not standing up more robustly to Indian pressure. Their initial response to Indian accusations of Lashkar-e-Tayyeba complicity in the Mumbai attacks was considered weak and fumbling and did not go down well with public opinion. If since then there has been a change of tone from Pakistan's side—as highlighted by General Kayani's statement—it has been dictated by the necessity of standing up to perceived Indian pressure. Mercifully, there has been no rush to war in the Pakistani media with most analysts and even television anchors striking a sober note. Which is not what can be said of sections of the Indian media, especially some television channels, which give the impression that nothing short of all-out war would satisfy their craving for sensationalism.

The debate in the National Assembly on national security was also remarkable for its sobriety. The need was stressed for a firm but responsible stance towards India. There was little of the usual sabre rattling at which both Indians and Pakistanis can so easily excel.

India perhaps could do well to take a leaf out of America's book. The US has also been engaging with Pakistan and urging it to take firm action against so-called *jihadi* groups. But it has been doing so behind the scenes. The approach adopted by India—perhaps because it is new at this game—is to speak in a public manner, in a tone most Pakistanis find threatening and therefore offensive, which far from serving any useful purpose merely puts Pakistani backs up.

Few people have any doubts in their minds that the focus should be on terrorism and its sources. But what Mumbai and its aftermath have done is to shift the focus from regional terrorism onto the familiar plane of Indo–Pak confrontation. Who benefits from this? Not the US, not India, not Pakistan. But it suits al-Qaeda.

There is an urgent need to turn down the rhetoric. No one wants war but the present drift is dangerous. Both countries share a history of unwanted wars. We can do without another exercise in futility.■

Strikes up, terror down
Rahul Singh

THE NATIONAL SECURITY Guards officer, who shall go unidentified on his request, quietly left the wedding reception. He was soon headed for Mumbai, where the most daring terrorist strike in the history of India was unfolding. '26/11', as the three-day attack has come to be called, shocked the country and the world. It was our 9/11. For three days, the world watched and heard grenades explode, NSG commandos slither down a rope from a helicopter, a dead terrorist roll out of a window and rescued hotel guests walk out dazed and exhausted.

When it all ended late on November 28, 173 people were dead, mostly Indians but also a lot of foreigners. Nine of the ten terrorists—all from Pakistan—also died. The tenth is in the custody of the Mumbai Police, talking about how they did it. India had overcome one more terrorist strike. The second half of 2008 was especially eventful, logging one terrorist strike almost every month, and sometimes two. Each strike was followed by sadness that quickly gave way to anger and then helplessness.

The first of the year's terrorist strikes happened on May 13, in Jaipur, a city popular with foreign tourists. Sixty-eight people died. Indian Mujahideen, a little-known terrorist outfit, sent an email claiming responsibility. This was followed by Bangalore, Ahmedabad, Delhi, Malegaon, Imphal and Assam. Indian Mujahideen figured in most of them until they were caught and shot under what continues to be called 'controversial circumstances' in Delhi.

Malegaon turned out to be quite another story, however. Investigators of the Mumbai Anti-terrorism Squad unearthed a group of Hindu fundamentalists, which was found to have earlier done the Samjhauta Express and Ajmer Sharif blasts. They were caught. Indian Mujahideen men were caught and shot. And the Mumbai attackers were killed, all except one. India beat them back.

Bravehearts

It's hard to pick one hero in the country's fight against terror. Who was the hero of the fight in Mumbai—police officers Hemant Karkare and Ashok Kamte or Taj hotel's Karamvir Kang or the NSG officer Sandeep Unnikrishnan or the unidentified NSG men who went into buildings held by terrorists and rescued so many people? Or was it Inspector M.C. Sharma, who died in an encounter with Indian Mujahideen terrorists in Delhi? Or is it a faceless, unidentified intelligence officer working away in some windowless room to prevent terrorist strikes? Or is it the people of India, who carry on despite everything? Or is it the country itself?■

JANUARY 2009

Pak gets 26/11 proof: Top Lashkar man sings
HT Foreign Bureau

New Delhi, December 31: PAKISTAN'S INVESTIGATIONS INTO the 26/11 terror attacks have a top Lashkar-e-Tayyeba operative confessing his involvement in the Mumbai strikes, while Washington is pressing Islamabad to extradite Zaki-ur-Rehman Lakhvi, LeT operations boss, to India, two newspapers have reported.

Describing Lakhvi as the Mumbai mastermind, the *Dawn* newspaper wrote that the US had given Pakistan a taped conversation between Lakhvi and the terrorists involved in the terror hits. 'Diplomatic sources in Washington said that American audio experts had checked the tape and concluded it was genuine and that the speaker was Mr Lakhvi,' the *Dawn* said in a front-page story.

The *Wall Street Journal* meanwhile reported that Zarar Shah, one of those arrested by Pakistani authorities after the Mumbai attacks, had confessed that the Lashkar was behind the carnage.

'He [Shah] is singing,' an unnamed Pakistani security official was quoted as telling the newspaper. The admission, the newspaper said, was backed up by American intercepts of a call between Shah and the attackers at the Taj Mahal Hotel in Mumbai.

'A second person familiar with the investigation said Mr Shah told Pakistani interrogators that he was one of the key planners of the operation, and that he spoke with the attackers during the rampage to give them advice and keep them focused,' the *Journal* reported. Shah had broadly confirmed the story told by the sole terrorist to survive the attack, Mohammed Ajmal Amir Kasab, who was nabbed by the Mumbai Police. 'Mr Shah said the attackers also spent a few weeks in Karachi . . . training in urban combat to hone skills they would use in their assault.'

According to the *Dawn* story, until last week, American officials had not taken a clear stand on Lakhvi's deportation to India. The taped conversation between Lakhvi and the attackers appeared to have changed American minds. 'Officials in Islamabad, however, appeared reluctant to accept the intercepts of Lakhvi's alleged confession provided to them by American and British intelligence agencies as authentic,' the Pakistani daily said.

It said there appeared to be a serious difference of opinion between Islamabad and the Pakistani embassy in Washington over the issue. 'While Islamabad was reluctant to accept the evidence as authentic, the embassy insisted that it's authentic and that the Pakistani authorities now needed to take steps to satisfy the international community,' the *Dawn* report said.■

How the Mumbai attack played out with common Pakistanis
Kamal Siddiqi

Karachi, December 31: PAKISTAN IS A divided house. There's no single view on how Islamabad should respond to Indian demands for dismantling terrorist outfits using its territory in the wake of the November 26 terror strikes on Mumbai.

Some believe the crackdown on militant organisations is a blessing in disguise while others argue that not enough proof has been offered to justify the government's action against groups like the Jamaat-ud-Dawah, a Lashkar-e-Tayyeba front.

Muhammad Ilyas, who runs a grocery store next to the building in Karachi's Gulshan-e-Iqbal locality where the JuD had its offices, commented that he saw 'nothing wrong' with the Jamaat's activities. 'They were polite people only spreading the word of Allah, I don't see why they have been labelled terrorists,' Ilyas told *Hindustan Times*.

The right-wing Jamaat-e-Islami party recently held a conference in the city to condemn the 'unjustified attack' on the JuD. The West was targeting Islamic 'welfare organisations' helping the poor, argued Dr Meraj-ul-Huda of the JI.

There are others, however, who see it differently. Ayesha Siddiqa, a leading defence analyst, felt that the real question is not being asked in Pakistan. 'We need to ask ourselves what should we do with these militant organisations who are seen as assets by some and partially supported.' Dr Siddiqa believed that the debate in Pakistan had not focused on this issue and has been 'hijacked by a section of the media' to focus on why the government is cracking down on such groups.

Analysts said a struggle was on between the political government and an 'invisible' government. Siddiqa said the 'other side has overpowered the political government'.

That may possibly explain the somewhat confused signals of the Zardari government to international demands for action against terror groups.

But there are some who say that Pakistan is waking up to the seriousness of the situation. 'I am hopeful. I think Pakistan has reacted in a positive manner and despite all the talk of war, the message on this side has been of peace and calm,' commented former General Talat Masood. Masood was hopeful that things would improve between India and Pakistan in the coming weeks. It's a sentiment shared by Aitzaz Ahsan, one of the country's best-known lawyers and a key member of the ruling Pakistan Peoples Party.

The high-profile lawyer said that the deterioration of the relations between India and Pakistan was 'exactly what those who conducted the attacks in Mumbai wanted'.■

Outlawed by the UN, Jamaat gets new avatar
HT Foreign Bureau

New Delhi/Karachi, January 1: THE JAMAAT-UD-DAWA, OUTLAWED by the United Nations Security Council, could now be functioning under the name of Tehreek-e-Hurmat-e-Rasool (Movement to Defend the Prophet) in Pakistan, Indian officials believe.

Pointing out that Pakistan was still to ban the Jamaat, a front organisation of the Lashkar-e-Tayyeba, as required by the Security

Council, the officials said Islamabad had not complied with its international obligations.

'Effectively, it is business as usual for the JuD,' a senior official who did not want to be named said, adding that the group was also believed to be operating a new website.

In the midst of these latest claims, Pakistani officials did not confirm media reports that a US Federal Bureau of Investigation team had visited Faridkot, the home town of the lone surviving Mumbai gunman, Ajmal Amir Kasab.

On Thursday, the *Dawn* newspaper reported that a five-member FBI team, headed by William Robert, director for South Asia, had visited Faridkot.

Local officials and sources, when contacted by *Hindustan Times*, said they were unaware of the visit. The US has reportedly handed over evidence of the Mumbai attackers' links to the Lashkar in Pakistan.

Western media reports have pointed to confessions made by Zarar Shah, LeT's communications chief, confirming what Kasab has told Indian police officials in Mumbai. However, Pakistan has, so far, said nothing about where or why Shah and his boss, Zaki-ur-Rehman Lakhvi, were being detained.

Dawn, too, said the Interior Ministry did not confirm the reported visit by an FBI team to Faridkot. 'It is not in the knowledge of the Interior Ministry and the Punjab government,' Interior Secretary Syed Kamal Shah was quoted as saying.

'It is impossible for the US team to pay any visit without informing us, the Federal Intelligence Agency and the provincial Punjab government,' he said.

An FBI spokesman, Richard Kolko, when contacted by the paper, said: 'The FBI continues to assist Indian authorities with their investigation. We will work with the Indian authorities and our partners to follow leads wherever they may take us.' When asked if an FBI team had visited Faridkot, Kolko said: 'We are unable to provide details of what is being done. We refer you to Indian authorities or the US State Department for any additional information.'

In New Delhi, External Affairs Minister Pranab Mukherjee said 'tangible results' from American pressure on Pakistan to shut down terror networks in Pakistan were still awaited.■

'Kasab calm, composed; shows no fear or remorse'
Kanchan Chaudhari

Mumbai, January 1: MOHAMMED AJMAL AMIR Kasab, the lone terrorist captured alive during the 26/11 terror attacks, reportedly shows no remorse for his killing spree. Instead, the 21-year-old Pakistani national has been telling Arthur Road Jail personnel 'maine jo kiya achchha kiya (Whatever I did was good)', jail sources told *Hindustan Times* on condition of anonymity.

Kasab has been shifted to the jail for the test identification parade. Several witnesses have identified him before a special judicial magistrate. A witness, who participated in the parade on Sunday said on condition of anonymity, that it was conducted in an open hall within the jail premises. Policemen connected with the investigation were not allowed there.

Explaining the process, the witness said the parade was held before a magistrate and two panch witnesses. Kasab was lined up with six identically dressed people and the witness was called in to identify him.

'The magistrate told me that one of the people present is an accused who fired indiscriminately in the Chhatrapati Shivaji Terminus on November 26 and asked me whether I can identify him,' he said. 'I moved forward and touched and pointed towards him.'

But some witnesses were nervous, he said. 'Some of the witnesses were scared even to face the terrorist. Two of them, probably Kolis from Badhwar Park (where the ten terrorists landed and entered the city) were very scared,' he said. 'One of them somehow gathered courage and identified him.'

Kasab was composed, he said. 'The young man clad in T-shirt and trousers was dressed identically to the other people standing with him.' He was not tall but had a 'strong, well-built body', the witness said. 'Every time after the identification the magistrate would ask the terrorist his name, he would shout "Ajmal Amir Kasab".'

Kasab is being identified primarily in connection with three cases—the killings at CST, encounter at Girgaum Chowpatty and hijacking of a Skoda owned by hotelier S.R. Arasa.■

Key 26/11 planner was also behind Mumbai train blasts
Debasish Panigrahi

Mumbai, January 3: SABAUDDIN AHMAD (24), a Lashkar-e-Tayyeba operative arrested in February 2008 for an attack on an army camp in Rampur, Uttar Pradesh, has said that the terror group's chief Zaki-ur-Rehman Lakhvi masterminded the July 11, 2006, train bombings in Mumbai. The November 26, 2008, terror attack was also planned by Lakhvi, whose custody has been sought by India.

A copy of Sabauddin's 40-page confession, made while he was in the Uttar Pradesh Special Task Force's custody, is with *Hindustan Times*. Sabauddin is currently in the Mumbai Crime Branch's custody.

Sabauddin said he had flown to the United Arab Emirates from Karachi on July 1, 2006. Six days later, he flew to Dhaka and stayed at Hotel Midway on VIP Road. He heard of the train bombings on July 11, as he was trying to cross into India.

The same day, Muzammil, Sabauddin's trainer at the Lashkar camp at Baith-ul-Mujahideen in Pakistan-occupied Kashmir (PoK), asked him to return to Pakistan.

Sabauddin said he flew to Karachi, heading straight to the camp. 'I discussed the train blasts with Abu Anas [a Lashkar operative]. He told me that those responsible for the blasts had escaped to safe destinations. Lakhvi had forbidden all talk of the train blasts,' Sabauddin said in the confession.

Sabauddin, from Madhubani district in Bihar, was a good student, passing his Secondary School Certificate exams from Darbhanga with a first class in 1999. He joined Aligarh Muslim University the next year for his 10+2 in science. After the 2002 Gujarat riots, Sabauddin met one Ajmal from Gaya in Bihar, who was pursuing a BTech at AMU. Ajmal befriended him and influenced him to 'fight against the injustice meted out to Muslims'. In March 2002, Ajmal took Sabauddin to one Salim Salar in Jamalpur, Uttar Pradesh. Salar was a key Lashkar operative, sending youths to Pakistan for terror training.

Sabauddin was sent to Baith-ul-Mujahideen via Jammu and Hilkaka in the Pir Panjal range. At the camp, he was trained in arms and explosives as well as river crossing, rock climbing and border crossing. The camp was controlled by Lakhvi, he said.

After 45 days, the batch of 70 *jihadis* was taken to a training camp run by Pakistan's Inter-Services Intelligence at Marwah in Pakistani Punjab. 'There too we were given similar training for about fifty days with an emphasis on weapons use,' Sabauddin said.

In October-November 2002, the Lashkar's annual meeting was held over three days at Pattoki, 12 kilometres from Lahore. It was attended by top leaders like Abd-ur-Rehman Makki, Abd-us-Saalam Gulvi, Lakhvi and Abu Hamza.

Later, Muzammil arranged a meeting between Sabauddin and Lakhvi in Islamabad. 'Lakhvi asked me to go to the ISI and work with them as they needed a dedicated jehadi,' said Sabauddin.

Eventually, Sabauddin was taken to the Markaz-e-Tayyeba, headquarters of the Jamaat-ud-Dawa, LeT's parent body, where its chief Hafiz Sayeed stayed. Sabauddin was later taken to Lahore to meet one Colonel Kayani, an ISI staffer. 'Kayani sent me to a safe-house near Batta Chowk in Lahore,' said Sabauddin. He met Sayeed in March 2003 during prayers at Moch Darwaz mosque in Lahore.

Sabauddin said the ISI prepared his Pakistani passport, using which he flew to Kathmandu, Dhaka, Colombo and the UAE, before arriving in Bangalore to enroll in a college, as directed by Lashkar. He said he provided shelter and safe passage to Abu Hamza, who planned the attack on the Indian Institute of Science at Bangalore on December 28, 2005.

After the Rampur attack, when he was in Kathmandu, Sabauddin was asked by Muzammil to meet a man who went by the code name of 'Saquib', but whose real name was Fahim Ansari. Ansari was originally a resident of Goregaon (East) in Mumbai.

'I helped Ansari cross into India. He went to Mumbai and established himself, but did not get the weapons for suicide attacks—because the Rampur attackers had thrown away their weapons,' said Sabauddin. 'I had to get the weapons picked up and stored as one more attacker was being sent from Kashmir.' With this in mind, Sabauddin went to the hotel where Ansari was staying in Kathmandu. 'However, I was arrested there by the Nepal police.'■

FBI hands over proof to Pak: Report
Vijay Dutt

London, January 4: THE FEDERAL BUREAU of Investigation, the American agency, has given to Pakistan evidence amassed by it on involvement of elements based in that country in the Mumbai terror strikes, including on the Lashkar-e-Tayyeba handlers' warning to the attackers about the arrival of Indian commandos while watching the mayhem live on TV, *The Sunday Times* reported.

Stating that evidence is growing to prove that the Mumbai strikes were orchestrated by militants based in Pakistan, it said that Zarar Shah, a communications specialist of LeT, has admitted under interrogation in Pakistan that he advised the terrorists by phone as the attacks unfolded.

Controllers in Pakistan watched live television and warned the gunmen of the arrival of Indian commandos, the report said, citing evidence amassed by the FBI and handed over to the Pakistani government.

The FBI had decoded Skype calls over the internet that were made between the gunmen in two five-star hotels and a Jewish centre in Mumbai with their LeT controllers in Pakistan, identified as Shah, Abu Hamza and Abu Qafa, it said.

Talking in colloquial Punjabi, the controllers repeatedly told the attackers to '*Aag lagao* (Light the fire)', which has been interpreted in India as a way of maximising casualties.

During the conversation, the men were also instructed to kill all the Israelis who were held captive in the Jewish hostel, but to spare all the Muslims.

But Islamabad rejected the alleged FBI evidence. Abdullah Ghaznavi, Lashkar's spokesman, was quoted saying, 'India has failed to furnish any evidence of Lashkar-e-Tayyeba's involvement in the Mumbai attacks and America is now trying to help it out.'■

Over to Pakistan: Proof, and hope of cooperation
Amit Baruah

New Delhi, January 5: TONING DOWN WEEKS of rhetoric, India has handed over to Islamabad material directly linking the 26/11 Mumbai terror strikes to 'elements in Pakistan' in the hope that the Zardari government would track down the perpetrators.

Soon after foreign secretary Shivshankar Menon gave the material to Pakistani high commissioner Shahid Malik on Monday, India said it expected Pakistan to promptly 'undertake further investigations' into the attacks.

Interrogation details of Mohammed Ajmal Amir Kasab, the lone surviving Mumbai terrorist; details of the terrorists' communications with 'elements in Pakistan'; pictures of seized weapons, equipment and other articles as well as data retrieved from a GPS unit and satellite phones have been made available to Pakistan.

A window of opportunity has re-opened for Pakistan to cooperate with India on bringing the perpetrators of 26/11 to justice, but Islamabad, Menon said, would be judged by actions and not words.

A senior South Block official told *Hindustan Times* on the condition of anonymity that Pakistan's response had been promises to cooperate both in New Delhi and Islamabad, where Indian high commissioner Satyabrata Pal handed over the same material to Pakistani foreign secretary Salman Bashir.

Menon said Pakistan had been informed that a DNA sample of Kasab was available for verification.

The names of the terrorists killed during 26/11 have also been shared with Pakistan. Menon said India had provided the names of those on the other side of the telephone line that it could identify. Press reports have spoken of Lashkar operatives Zaki-ur-Rehman Lakhvi and Zarar Shah as being the Pakistanis speaking to the terrorists while the Mumbai carnage was on.

Menon said Pakistan should now share with India the information it had collected during its own investigation into the Mumbai attacks. He was clear that the Mumbai conspiracy had been planned in Pakistan and India wanted full details. He did not give a direct answer about whether India wanted the extradition of Pakistani suspects to New Delhi, but was clear that they must be brought to 'Indian justice'.

It is being speculated that India and Pakistan could have had quiet contacts, facilitated by a third party, that led to the material being handed over to Islamabad. Earlier, External Affairs Minister Pranab Mukherjee said: 'What happened in Mumbai was an unpardonable crime. As far as the government of Pakistan is concerned, we ask only that it implement the bilateral commitments that it has made at the highest levels to India . . .'

Officially, the Pakistan foreign office said in Islamabad that 'information material' relating to the Mumbai attacks had been received from India. By providing Pakistan with material links to 26/11, a major point raised repeatedly by Islamabad has been addressed. India has also been under pressure from key international players that it should share the Mumbai evidence with Pakistan.

What Pakistan now says
This is what Prime Minister Y.R. Gilani reportedly told US Assistant Secretary of State Richard Boucher

- The material is being 'examined by concerned authorities'
- Pakistan is willing to cooperate and have a 'joint investigation'
- Peace in the region is impossible without resolving outstanding issues

The evidence they got
Material from the interrogation of Mohammed Ajmal Kasab, the Pakistani terrorist, and from seized fishing trawler *Kuber*

- 16-inch knife inscribed with letters from the Urdu alphabet and picture of a gun on the handle
- Scarf used for namaz, with Pakistani address and phone number. It has 'Cashmilan best quality, phone 061 4516729' written on it
- A black three-quarter pant with 'South Pole, Made in Pakistan' inscribed on it
- Detergent powder marked with PAK sign
- Two packets of Nestlé Milk Pack, Nestlé Pakistan Limited
- Touchme facial cream, 'Made in Pakistan'
- Kasab's letter in his own handwriting
- Kasab's disclosure about his parents, village and training camps in Pakistan and Pakistani trainers.

Details of the terrorists' communication links with elements in Pakistan during the Mumbai attack
- Conversations transmitted using Voice Over Internet Protocol that LeT commanders Zaki-ur-Rehman Lakhvi and Muzzamil had with the terrorists at Taj Mahal hotel, Hotel Oberoi and Nariman House during the 60-hour siege. The conversations not only reveal a heavy Punjabi accent but in one of the conversations Lakhvi had given away his location which investigators have decoded.
- Recovered weapons and equipment

- AK-47 rifles and ammunition with Pakistani ordnance markings recovered from the terrorists at various spots
- Markings of Pakistani ordnance factory in Peshawar found on the 9 mm pistols recovered from the ten terrorists
- 'Arges' brand high explosive hand grenades made in Pakistan under licence from the original Austrian manufacturers, RMV Arges, recovered from the ten terrorists
- Data retrieved from recovered GPS and satellite phones
- Karachi-based landline number believed to be that of LeT operational commander Muzzamil alias Yussuf found from the Thuraya brand satellite phone recovered from fishing trawler *MV Kuber*
- Coordinates of the sea route from Karachi to Mumbai via Jhakhau, Diu and Porbandar in Gujarat, recovered from the Garmin brand Global Positioning System device found on *Kuber*.∎

Pak intellectuals warn country of isolation
Nagendar Sharma

New Delhi, January 5: PAKISTAN-BASED HUMAN RIGHTS activists, intellectuals and writers have warned their government of 'self-annihilation and isolation' in case it kept its eyes shut on the existence of terrorist outfits within the country.

'The government of Pakistan must no longer stay in a state of self-denial. It must not miss the opportunity of devising an effective strategy to overcome the menace of terrorism,' said a statement released among others by Asma Jahangir, I.A. Rehman, Ahmed Rashid and Dr Mubashir Hasan. They have also strongly condemned the Mumbai terror attacks.

Warning that the danger of an armed conflict between India and Pakistan 'still persists', the statement appealed to both the governments not to take peace for granted.

Coming down on the role played by the media in both countries, they charged it with aiding 'warmongers'.

'We regret that the media in India and Pakistan failed to present the Mumbai outrage in a proper context. Instead, they used the event to fuel hostility between the two countries,' it said.∎

This is no proof, says Pak
HT Foreign Bureau

Karachi/New Delhi, January 6: MERE INFORMATION, AND not credible evidence, had been provided by India to Pakistan on the Mumbai terror attacks, Pakistani foreign secretary Salman Bashir claimed on Tuesday as Prime Minister Manmohan Singh said that 26/11 'must' have had the support of Pakistan's 'official agencies'.

Bashir's remarks, which came a day after India passed on 'material' linking 26/11 to 'elements in Pakistan', seem to have dashed hopes of any meaningful cooperation from Islamabad in probing the attacks. Pakistan, the foreign secretary said in Islamabad, needed credible evidence to proceed with the investigation into 26/11.

In New Delhi, a tough-talking Singh launched a verbal volley at Pakistan while addressing the chief ministers' conference on internal security, blaming Islamabad and its intelligence agencies for fomenting terror in India. 'The more fragile a government, the more it tends to act in an irresponsible fashion. Pakistan's responses to our various demarches on terrorist attacks is an obvious example,' Singh said in his comments, which drew an equally high-decibel response from Islamabad.

Charging Pakistan with whipping up 'war hysteria', Singh said: 'Terrorism ... is largely sponsored from outside our country, mainly Pakistan, which has utilised terrorism as an instrument of State policy.'

In a sharp riposte, the Pakistani foreign office accused India of launching a 'propaganda offensive', which will 'ratchet up tensions' and 'destroy all prospects of serious and objective investigations' into the Mumbai attacks.

'Vilifying Pakistan . . . is unwarranted and unacceptable . . . this is a sure way to close avenues of cooperating in combating this menace [of terrorism],' Islamabad said. 'Pakistan has suffered more terror attacks than India. But we have not lost our equanimity,' the foreign office said, stressing that Pakistan was 'not a State sponsor of terrorism'.

'Our civilian and armed forces' casualties over the past year have been far more than that of India,' it said, suggesting that Pakistan was a 'bigger victim' of terrorism than India.

'The Government of Pakistan expects the Government of India to demonstrate restraint and responsibility . . . it must also take steps to de-escalate its offensive military posture against Pakistan,' the foreign office said.

A return to the war of words came amid reports of a possible visit by US Vice-President-elect Joe Biden to 'South-West Asia' in his capacity as chairman of the Senate foreign relations committee.

A South Block official in New Delhi neither confirmed nor denied the reports that Biden, who is set to visit Pakistan, would come to India too. India, meanwhile, continued its initiative to brief diplomats, with officials presenting New Delhi's case on 26/11 to the envoys of about eighty countries. Several envoys *Hindustan Times* spoke to felt that India had presented a credible case linking 26/11 to the Lashkar-e-Tayyeba and its support base in Pakistan.■

Kasab gives training details
Haidar Naqvi

Kanpur, January 6: CAPTURED MILITANT MOHAMMED Ajmal Amir Kasab has disclosed that the training programme of the 26/11 terrorists at Lashkar-e-Tayyeba camps included sessions to make them familiar with the structure and operational capabilities of Indian security and intelligence agencies. The instructors told Kasab and nine others about the strengths and weaknesses of Indian forces. The men also learnt military tactics.

In his eight-page confession—a copy of which is available with *HT*—Kasab said the assault team was given lectures twice a day and shown videos of Indian troops engaged in operation.

The security experts who interviewed Kasab said it was a military training—a capability LeT could not have unless a specialised agency was involved. 'Only the Inter-Services Intelligence has the ability and means to design such a programme, which dealt with all the aspects of an operation,' said a home ministry expert not willing to be identified. 'The militants' familiarisation with Indian forces, their style and tactics, and preparing them accordingly was not possible without the ISI.'

Kasab, who was recruited in Rawalpindi, said he first completed the Daura Sufa, a 21-day training, at Markaz-e-Tayyeba in Murdike. He was later selected for another three-week training, Daura Ama, at Manshera in Buttal village. There he was trained in handling Uzi guns, AK series rifles and Green-Os. Later they were moved to Chelabandi, where he learnt to handle rocket launchers, mortars and hand grenades from trainer Abu Mawiya.

After the training ended in September, one Zaki-ur-Rehman selected ten men for the strike scheduled on September 27. The men were divided into five teams. Kasab and Ismail Khan were Team One with the code name VTS—Victoria Terminus Station. With the help of Google Earth they were told to learn about the stretch they had been assigned. The men were to be sent on September 24, but Zaki-ur-Rehman cancelled the operation at the last moment. 'Chacha told a team member that the operation's cover had been blown,' Kasab told an interrogator. 'Later we were all told to be patient and that our time would come.' ■

Kasab is Pakistani, admits Islamabad
Kamal Siddiqi & Amit Baruah

Karachi/New Delhi, January 7: FORTY-TWO DAYS AFTER 26/11, Islamabad has confirmed that Ajmal Amir Kasab, the lone terrorist in Mumbai Police's custody, is a Pakistani national as claimed by India. A Pakistan Foreign Office spokesman said in Islamabad that initial investigations revealed that Kasab is a Pakistani national. He claimed the delay in confirming the identity was because Kasab's details were not contained in a national database maintained by the government.

At the same time, the spokesman said the identity of the nine other gunmen, described as Pakistanis by India, had not been ascertained. No decision had been taken on whether to give consular access to Kasab.

Pakistan's National Security Advisor Mohammed Ali Durrani also told the *Hindustan Times* from Islamabad that Kasab was a Pakistani national. 'In my opinion, India and Pakistan need to work together to track down those responsible for the Mumbai attacks. Pakistan wants to work with India. Cooperation is 110 per cent possible between us,' Durrani said.

Hours after he spoke to the Indian press, Durrani was sacked as NSA by PM Yousaf Raza Gilani for making irresponsible statements. Durrani, Islamabad said, had not taken all stakeholders, including the PM, into confidence before making statements to the Indian media on Kasab.

Durrani's removal is a sign that the Pakistan army–intelligence establishment and the civilian government are at loggerheads on whether to cooperate with India. The NSA, it appears, was sacked because he was one of those who believed that cooperation with India on Mumbai was the right thing to do.

Earlier in the day, Gilani said Pakistan's own investigations into Mumbai had progressed. 'We've received information of an interim nature on Indian investigations. We are prepared to take this process forward with a view to uncovering full facts, thus ensuring that the perpetrators of this heinous crime, whosoever they may be, are brought to justice,' Gilani said.

Lamenting India's negative response, Gilani added, 'We are convinced that the only effective way of dealing with the common challenge of terrorism is to develop robust cooperation encompassing all relevant departments.'

Responding to Monday's statement from Pakistan, the Ministry of External Affairs wondered how Islamabad could reject the evidence offered by India in less than 24 hours.

Spokesman Vishnu Prakash said, 'How can this rejection be credible or be based on a real examination and investigation of the evidence? This is a political rejection without any basis.'

Separately, External Affairs Minister Pranab Mukherjee has said that Pakistan had not even lodged an FIR in the Mumbai attacks. Even in the Benazir Bhutto assassination case, they had turned to the UN to investigate the case. Mukherjee told a TV channel that India would not allow the victims and perpetrators of terrorism to be hyphenated.

About turn

'Our own investigations into Mumbai [attacks] have progressed . . . We are prepared to take this process forward with a view to uncovering full facts, thus ensuring that the perpetrators of this heinous crime, whosoever they may be, are brought to justice.'

—Yousaf Raza Gilani, Pakistan Prime Minister

'We may be crazy in Pakistan, but not completely out of our minds. We know full well that terror is our enemy, not India.'

—Ahmad Shuja Pasha, ISI Director General, in an interview to *Der Spiegel*

'In my opinion, India and Pakistan need to work together to track down those responsible for the Mumbai attacks.'
—Mohammed Ali Durrani, Pak National Security Advisor, shortly before he was sacked

'The biggest foreign-policy challenge awaiting President-elect Barack Obama isn't Iraq or Afghanistan but Pakistan.'
—Stephen Hadley, US National Security Advisor, to *The Wall Street Journal*

26/11 came from Pakistan: Mulford
Tushar Srivastava

New Delhi, January 9: THE UNITED STATES will work non-stop as long as it takes to bring those behind the Mumbai attacks to book, outgoing US ambassador David C. Mulford said here on Friday.

'The United States has its own law. When American nationals are killed anywhere, we pursue those people as we are doing now. We will press ahead and we will do it non-stop as long as it takes,' Mulford said at a farewell function organised for him by the Confederation of Indian Industry.

'The Mumbai attack appeared to have come from Pakistan—monitored and managed by people in Pakistan,' he asserted. However, when asked whether the US suspected involvement of Pakistan's official agencies in 26/11, Mulford said, 'I don't think we want to take a view that we make accusations against certain parties without the usual evidences, proofs.'

Mulford said the US had an important relationship with Pakistan and would encourage a democratic government there. 'We want to see Pakistan succeed.' The war in Afghanistan, he said, had complicated that agenda.

He said that the US had suffered losses like Mumbai, and its economy, like India's, was experiencing a slowdown. So this was the time, he concurred, when friends must work together—especially in combating terrorism.

Mulford also said that he was impressed by the poll outcome in Jammu & Kashmir, adding that free and fair elections will help usher in a period of peace and normalcy in the Valley.■

Pakistani artistes hit hard by 26/11
Malvika Nanda

New Delhi, January 10: RADIO CHANNELS HAVEN'T stopped playing their tracks. But you're unlikely to see Pakistani musicians live in India anytime soon.

218

Jugaad, a forthcoming Bollywood film, had Pakistani sensation Adeel as the face and voice of its main promotional video. The ad, worth Rs 25 lakh, has been dropped. 'After 26/11, my conscience doesn't allow me to go with it,' says producer Sandeep Kapoor. 'They have targeted our lives and our economy. So we should also make a dent somewhere for them to realise the damage they are, in some ways, responsible for.'

Usually there are about a dozen big shows by Pakistani artistes between November and February. This year that number is down to zero. For many musicians across the border, India is the main source of income. Post-26/11, they are feeling the pinch.

But some are hopeful. 'The love that we receive from India is going to be lost for a while. Several concerts have been cancelled due to security reasons. But I'm willing to come to India,' says singer Shafqat Amanat Ali.

The scene in Pakistan is also gloomy. 'We've not been having any commercial concerts in Pakistan for the last two years and now we can't even go to India,' complains Goher Mumtaz of the band Jaal.

Rajeev Sogani, MD, Tips Music, says it's important to respect the public sentiment. 'There are no bookings and projects have been put on hold.' Composer Sachin Gupta, who has worked with Pakistani artists, is more firm. 'Music should be above politics,' he says. 'But our neighbours should realise that they need to respect the country many of their artists earn money from.'■

Terror takes its toll on tourism
Prasad Nichenametla

New Delhi, January 12: TOURISM IN INDIA tided over the worst months of slowdown with aplomb. But it was hit hard, as expected, by the Mumbai terror attacks.

A compilation of foreign tourist arrivals (FTAs) from the

Ministry of Tourism for December 2008 shows 5.22 lakh foreign tourists arriving in India. The figure for the corresponding period in 2007 was about 5.75 lakh. This means that in December alone, India lost about 50,000 foreign tourists—a drop of 9.2 per cent.

Tourism contributes to about 6.23 per cent of the GDP and provides direct or indirect employment to more than 50 million people in the country.

During the peak of the meltdown—in the months of September and October—tourist flow actually increased by 9.6 and 1.8 per cent over the corresponding months in 2007. Clearly, the tourists who preferred to tour the country in times of global meltdown seem to have stopped on their tracks because of 26/11.

But FTA growth, on the whole of 2008, was half of its growth rate in 2006 and 2007. FTA growth in 2008 stood at 5.6 per cent compared to 2006 and 2007 when FTA grew by 12–14 per cent. The tourism ministry, however, claims that the 5.6 percent growth in 2008 is better than the global average.

'The World Tourism Organisation has predicted a growth rate of 2–3 per cent for international tourist arrivals in the world during 2008. Therefore, the Indian scenario is much better than world scenario,' said a ministry statement.

Tourism bodies, however, do not share the government's optimism. 'At a time when we were expecting an 18–20 per cent growth, a growth of about 6 per cent is discouraging. The lack of growth is due to terrorism and slowdown,' Subhash Goyal, chairman of the ASSOCHAM Expert Committee on Tourism, said.

Union Minister for Tourism and Culture Ambika Soni had last month requested the prime minister to announce an incentive package for the sector.

- 5.22 lakh foreigners arrived in India in December, down from 5.75 lakh the same period in 2007, a 9.2% drop
- 5.37 million foreigners visited in 2008, marginally up from 5.08 million in 2007
- That's an increase of only 5.6% in contrast to the 12–14% increase in 2007 and 2006

220

- The economic slowdown didn't do much harm, with the peak meltdown months of September and October seeing foreign tourist flow increase by 9.6 and 1.8% over the same months last year
- The Tourism Ministry says the growth, though retarded, is better than the world average
- Tourism contributes to 6.23% of GDP, provides employment to 50 million-plus people.■

'India ready to snap trade, tourism ties with Pak'
HT Correspondent

New Delhi, January 13: HOME MINISTER P. CHIDAMBARAM has warned India will snap business, transport and tourist ties with Pakistan if it fails to help in the investigation into the 26/11 Mumbai terror attacks.

In an interview with *The Times*, UK, Chidambaram accused Pakistan of doing nothing to help India bring to justice the perpetrators of the attacks in which 165 people were killed.

'Zero. What have they provided? Nothing,' he said when asked what Pakistan was doing to assist the probe.

About the proposed action in case Pakistan continued to be unhelpful, he said: 'There are many, many links between India and Pakistan, and if Pakistan does not cooperate and does not help to bring the perpetrators to heel, those ties will become weaker and weaker and one day snap.'

'Why would we entertain Pakistani business people? Why would we entertain tourists in India? Why would we send tourists there . . . We need cooperation soon,' he said.

India–Pakistan trade hovers around $2 billion. It had grown from $23.74 million in 2001 to over $1 billion in 2006–07, according to the Associated Chambers of Commerce and Industry of India.

Before the 26/11 attacks, the Pakistan High Commission was issuing 350–400 visas a day to Indians. Last September, PM Manmohan Singh and Pakistan President Asif Ali Zardari signed an agreement for resumption of trade between J&K and PoK.

Speaking in the National Assembly on Tuesday, Pakistan PM Yousaf Raza Gilani said India had only submitted 'some information' and not the evidence. 'All that has been received formally from India is some information. I say information because these are not the evidence. This needs to be carefully examined,' he said.■

Pak State not behind Mumbai attacks: UK

HT Foreign Bureau

New Delhi, January 13: CONTRADICTING NEW DELHI'S stand that the Mumbai terror attacks had the support of Islamabad's official agencies, Britain has made it clear that it is not of the view that the Pakistani State had directed the attacks.

'I have said publicly that I do not believe that the attacks were directed by the Pakistani State. And I think it is important to restate that,' said British Foreign Secretary David Miliband.

Last week, PM Manmohan Singh had said that there was enough evidence to show that 'given the sophistication and military precision of the attack it must have had the support of some official agencies in Pakistan.'

Miliband arrived here on Tuesday on a four-day visit to show solidarity with India following 26/11. His next stopover will be Islamabad.

'What is relevant is the approach of the Pakistani State to the Lashkar-e-Tayyeba and the way the Pakistani State takes on the menace of the LeT,' Miliband said while addressing a joint-press conference with External Affairs Minister Pranab Mukherjee.

Earlier, the two held detailed talks where Mukherjee apprised his British counterpart of the evidence gathered in the Mumbai case.

British PM Gordon Brown, who was here in mid-December,

had said, 'We know the group responsible [for the attacks] is LeT, and they [Pakistan] have a great deal to answer for.'

'I do hope the materials provided to Pakistan, evidence given, they will act on it and they will ensure that the perpetrators of this terror act are brought to justice, and some of the fugitives violating Indian laws who have taken shelter in Pakistan will be handed over to India,' Mukherjee said.

When pointed out that the LeT's front outfit Jamaat-ud-Dawa continues to function despite the UN ban, Miliband said, 'You know there is a history of people being arrested and then not being prosecuted. In this case it is essential that those who have been arrested are brought to justice if found guilty and then properly punished. And that is an appropriate response to the evidence that has been presented.'■

PM puts TV content regulation on hold
HT Correspondent

New Delhi, January 14: IN RESPONSE TO representations made by editors of news channels disfavouring government regulation on news content, Prime Minister Manmohan Singh has put the proposed changes on hold and said 'widest consultation with stakeholders will be conducted before finalising the proposal'.

To allay fears of news channels that the government was trying to gag the media, the Prime Minister's Office on Wednesday said different point of views in the media would be taken into consideration before shaping up the changes.

Congress chief Sonia Gandhi, too, assured news channels that she will take up the matter with the PM. The I&B Ministry had earlier made it mandatory for news channels to show government footage during situations defined as 'national emergencies'.

Most news channel editors had termed the proposal as draconian and an attempt to gag the media's freedom of expression and creativity.

Denouncing any government regulation, BJP leader L.K. Advani said, 'It is imperative that a code of self-regulation be evolved, which ensures that anti-national elements are not able to take advantage of the freedom of media,' said Advani. The CPI(M), however, is for regulation through an independent body.■

Pak says it's cooperating
Kamal Siddiqi & Amit Baruah

Karachi/New Delhi, January 15: PAKISTAN SAID ON Thursday that five training camps of the Lashkar-e-Tayyeba, accused of being behind the Mumbai attacks, had been shut down and 124 people associated with its sister organisation, the Jamaat-ud-Dawa (JuD), arrested. The people nabbed included JuD leaders Hafiz Sayeed, Mufti Abdur Rehman and key operatives such as Colonel (retd) Nazir Ahmed, Amir Hamza and Zaki-ur-Rehman Lakhvi.

But Pakistan's de facto Interior Minister, Rehman Malik, said at the end of his press conference in Islamabad that 71 members of the banned groups had been detained and 124 others put under surveillance. Malik said nothing about Zarar Shah, LeT's communications' chief who, according to reports in the American press, had also been detained by Pakistan.

The Pakistani police are still to register a case related to 26/11.

Malik said the Pakistani government had launched a probe into 26/11 soon after the incident. 'The government has banned JuD publications and shut down six Dawah websites,' he said. Giving details, Malik said the government had closed 20 offices, 87 schools and several madrasas run by JuD. 'All activities of that particular organisation stand ceased,' he said.

Malik said he wanted India to allow Pakistani investigators to help in the investigation. 'In such matters we need interaction and I request my counterpart to please make the arrangements ... where our investigators can interact with each other. Interaction will bring quick results,' he said.

Pakistan also said it had formed a special team to ascertain whether the banned LeT or any other militant group was involved in the Mumbai attacks.

Meanwhile, External Affairs Minister Pranab Mukherjee nuanced the government's position that all those on Pakistani territory responsible for terrorist crimes in India be handed over to New Delhi. 'It would be ideal if they [Pakistan's government] can hand over the fugitives from India to us. If this is not possible, there should at least be a fair trial of these fugitives in Pakistan,' Mukherjee was quoted as telling a television channel.

The News, a Pakistani daily, said Lakhvi, LeT's chief operational commander, who was arrested on December 10 by the Pakistani authorities in the wake of the Mumbai attacks, was 'furious' with the JuD leadership's decision to publicly disown him in his 'hour of trial'.

Lakhvi, alias Abu Waheed Irshad Ahmad, comes from the Okara district of Punjab province. Ajmal Amir Kasab, the lone Mumbai attacker caught alive, belongs to the same area, the paper said.■

India rejects Miliband's 'unsolicited advice'

New Delhi, January 15: INDIA ON THURSDAY said it did not need unsolicited advice on internal issues like J&K from Britain. The Ministry of External Affairs seemed to be responding to an article by British Foreign Secretary David Miliband in *The Guardian* where he wrote that the 'resolution of the dispute over Kashmir would help deny extremists one of their main calls to arms'.■

Cross-border travel takes a hit
Aurangzeb Naqshbandi

New Delhi, January 15: DAYS AFTER HOME Minister P. Chidambaram talked about the possibility of snapping business and tourism ties with Pakistan, the chill in the bilateral relationship in the aftermath of the Mumbai terror attacks has already begun to tell on cross-border travel.

The numbers of applications and visas issued had come down by a third after the November 26 attacks, a Pakistan High Commission official, who didn't want to be named, told *HT*. Earlier, on an average, over 400 visas were issued every day and the numbers climbed to 500 around religious occasions. 'The number has now gone down to 100–120 visas a day,' he said.

Chidambaram had recently warned that Pakistan's failure to crack down on terror could affect relations between the two sides.

The advisory issued by the government asking Indians not to travel to Pakistan, too, had brought down the numbers of travellers, the official said. The advisory was issued after some Indians were reportedly arrested in Pakistan on charges of terrorism after the Mumbai strikes.

Both the countries do not permit tourists, but had recently allowed group tourism to liberalise visa regime. India doesn't figure in the List A of 175 countries whose nationals are issued a tourist visa for Pakistan.

Every year a large number of Sikh pilgrims visit Gurdwara Panja Sahib, Nankana Sahib, Gurdwara Dera Sahib, Rorri Sahib and Kartarpur in Pakistan. This number, too, had fallen since the 26/11 attacks, the official said.

The trade, so far, was normal, he said. It's worth around $2 billion (approximately Rs 1,000 crore). It was $235.74 million in 2001 and grew to over $1 billion in 2006–07, according to the Associated Chambers of Commerce and Industry of India. Exports from India to Pakistan grew at 60 per cent and imports at 64 per cent during 2002–07, with the balance of trade being in favour of India. Before 26/11, the two sides had set a target of $10 billion trade by 2010.∎

He took five bullets but didn't let go

Stavan Desai (Inputs from Rachna Pratihar)

Mumbai, January 16: TUKARAM OMBLE LOVED cricket, offered chocolates to children, and was the resident snake-catcher back home in his Maharashtra village.

Last November, the 53-year-old caught the big fish. As terrorists raided Mumbai in one of the biggest attacks in years, assistant sub-inspector Omble caught alive one of the attackers—Mohammad Ajmal Amir Kasab—providing India the most powerful piece of evidence in a terrorism case against Pakistani attackers. Then he went down, five bullets from the terrorists having ripped his torso.

In many ways, Omble became the first true Mumbai Police hero in a city where the icons in uniforms often come with the baggage of being 'encounter' experts. But for days, the heroism of this faceless policeman, the single act that clinched the 26/11 investigation, went completely unsung. 'Nobody told us about his heroic act,' said Omble's 25-year-old daughter Vaishali, the third of four daughters, as she sat in the family's 150-square-foot home at the Worli police quarters. 'We found out ten days after the incident.'

The faceless braveheart was not so faceless back home—in his Kedambe village in Satara district, about ten kilometres from Mahabaleshwar, where he was born in a family of rice farmers.

He was a star in Kedambe: the man who deftly caught snakes when they slithered out of their burrows in fields and from cracks in walls at homes. Then he became a bigger star—in a place with most others slogging in farmlands, scrounging for jobs or migrating to faraway cities for meagre wage work, Omble was the first policeman from the village.

'And five neighbouring villages,' added Vaishali, pursuing a Bachelor of Education course.

Omble came to Mumbai five years after he married Tara, now 48. His children were born in the city and were seeking out new ambitions—he did not insist he wanted them to join the police force. 'He said we should follow our dreams,' said Vaishali.

He was following his own dream with sincerity that is often dented in India's poorly equipped and often demoralised police force.

The family is yet to know whether the media speculation about Omble being shortlisted for the Ashok Chakra, India's highest peacetime battle honour, is true. But they wait in hope.

'We will go to Delhi to receive the award,' said Tara. 'But I am waiting for the day Kasab is punished.' ■

New hero from a village of military martyrs
Abhinav Madhwal

Ganeshpur, January 17: GAJENDRA SINGH BISHT went home to his Uttarakhand village on August 15, driving through roads emblazoned with the Indian flag. His father had died. Ten days of mourning lay ahead. When he next went home three and a half months later, he was in a coffin, having died fighting an attack on the same flag—and wrapped in one.

Bisht, a 36-year-old havildar with the National Security Guards, was killed in gunfire by terrorists who had seized the Nariman House building during the November 26 siege at Mumbai last year. He belonged to the 51 Special Action Group, a unit that slithered down ropes from a navy helicopter onto the roof of the building to kill the terrorists holed up there, holding its residents hostage.

Sixteen hundred kilometres to the north in Ganeshpur village, mesmerised villagers watched the operation on TV. A new hero was born here, where martyrdom seems to be a tradition. Four other men from here have died in combat as part of security forces.

'He was strong and agile. Everybody said he looked and behaved just the way a commando should,' said elder brother Virendra.

The five feet-six inches tall, well-built Singh was a voracious meat eater and loved reading. He was chasing a dream: he wanted to become an officer in the NSG, which handpicked him from the army. So he was learning the English language alongside to prepare for his dream.

He is survived by his wife Vinita and two children. At their home, Vinita sits quietly before a visiting journalist, declining to answer questions about her husband.

The NSG has offered her a job, which she is yet to accept.

Coming from a farming family with no source of assured income, Gajendra always wanted to join the army, which would give him economic security. Most of his classmates joined the force and he also followed, joining the Garhwal Rifles at Lansdowne in Pauri Garhwal. After some years, he was recruited into the NSG as a commando.

'He had his eyes set on the army,' Virendra recalled. 'He said he wanted to be in the army to serve at the country's borders, and be in the thick of action.■

Solve Kashmir issue, we'll shun violence: Lashkar
Arun Joshi

Jammu, January 19: PAKISTAN-BASED TERROR GROUP Lashkar-e-Tayyeba spokesman Abdullah Gaznavi has issued a statement that the LeT could shun violence if the international community took steps to hold dialogue on Kashmir's freedom. The LeT, which was considered to be responsible for the November 26 attacks in Mumbai, also sought to delink itself from any militant action in any part of India or the world—except Kashmir.

Gaznavi said in his statement issued to the Kashmiri press: 'The armed struggle was a compulsion as the world had failed to acknowledge the struggle and yearning of Kashmiris.'

However, intelligence officials who did not wish to be quoted said that it was a move by Pakistan's Inter-Services Intelligence, which controlled both the LeT and the secessionists, to convince the world that militancy was the result of the unresolved Kashmir crisis.

The sources added that the ISI had taken a cue from British foreign secretary David Milliband's recent article in *The Guardian*, linking the Kashmir issue to militancy.

But reacting to the statement, Jammu & Kashmir Chief Minister Omar Abdullah said if it was the Lashkar's honest intent, it could be an opening. 'We are always for dialogue,' he told newsmen in Jammu on Monday evening. People's Democratic Party chief Mehbooba Mufti, too, welcomed it.

While Omar takes pride in the initiative taken during the National Conference rule in July-August 2000 for talks with the Hizb-ul Mujahideen, Mehbooba capitalises on the Centre-Hurriyat Conference dialogue that began during her father Mufti Mohammed Sayeed's rule in January 2004.

The Lashkar is considered to be a foreign outfit with roots in Afghanistan and Pakistan and has close links with al-Qaeda supremo Osama bin Laden.■

Journalists worse than terrorists: Zardari
Kamal Siddiqi

Karachi, January 19: JOURNALISTS IN PAKISTAN have reacted strongly to a remark where President Asif Ali Zardari likened them to terrorists.

A report in the daily *The News* on Monday said that the Pakistani President told a delegation of businessmen from the troubled North West Frontier Province (NWFP) that 'journalists are bigger terrorists than terrorists themselves.'

Journalists are the biggest terrorists, Zardari is said to have remarked while talking about the issue of terrorism in NWFP and Federally Administered Tribal Areas (FATA).

The paper quoted businessmen as saying that the statement 'came out of the blue' and that there was 'intensity of emotion when it was made.' The paper said that the possible reason could have been the media's vociferous criticism of the Zardari-led government for its handling of the situation post the 26/11 Mumbai attacks.

'The President should remain apolitical but he is involved in the day-to-day affairs of the government,' said Arif Nizami, editor of *The Nation* newspaper, adding 'and that is why he is in the focus of the media.' Nizami adds with a laugh, 'If we are terrorising the government then we must be doing our job.'

Some journalists say it is possible that Zardari's comments could have been taken out of context. But most are upset with him. 'When politicians are unable to deliver on their promises, they retreat to a bunker-like position and believe all sorts of conspiracies,' says Talat Aslam, editor of *The News*. Many other journalists agree with his assessment.■

Obama: The regional challenges
V. Krishna

Washington, January 19: WHAT ARE THE top three issues the new administration will have to deal with in relations with India?

We asked Lisa Curtis, senior research fellow at the Heritage Foundation, a Washington think-tank. Here's what she had to say:

1. Terrorism/Pakistan
The Obama administration will have to immediately deal with the current India–Pakistan crisis created by the November terrorist attacks in Mumbai.

The US has been pressing Pakistan to take action against the Lashkar-e-Tayyeba and to bring those responsible for the attacks to justice. Pakistan, however, has focused on trying to deflect attention from itself, rather than on pursuing investigations into the attacks. It will be important for the Obama team to signal right away that it expects Pakistan to shut down the LeT altogether to avoid further attacks like those in Mumbai.

The Obama team will also have to keep up the pace of high-level visits to the region to prevent the potential for military conflict between India and Pakistan and to try to keep the lines of communication between the two countries open.

2. Afghanistan

The Obama team has already established that it will focus greater attention and resources on stabilising and securing Afghanistan.

It should coordinate closely with the Indian leadership as it reviews the strategy for Afghanistan, recognising India's stakes in the region, along with other countries in the neighbourhood.

3. Establishing India's strategic role in Asia

It will be important for Obama to signal early on that his administration is committed to building the strategic relationship between the United States and India. It is not yet clear that Obama has the same vision and force of determination to extend the partnership that we saw from Bush, especially in the way he personally pushed forward the civil nuclear deal.

Obama should somehow demonstrate that he takes the US relationship with India seriously and recognises the important role India can play in promoting stability in the broader Asian region.■

THE AFTERMATH

November 28, 2008

OUR TAKE: A nation that cannot afford to sleep

INDIA IS UNDER attack. And along with it, the idea of India is under attack. When a city like Mumbai is held hostage by marauding terrorists, with its citizens forced to cower in fear under a fog of utter helplessness, any notion that the country is secure—or will be able to re-establish its sense of security quickly and effectively—becomes a fanciful thought. This country has had its fair share of experiences with terrorism. One would have thought that our governments, law and order machinery and political establishment would be prepared to tackle and disarm these noxious forces. But the tragedy that continues to unfold in India's most vibrant, cosmopolitan city has exposed the terrible unpreparedness—and dare we say unwillingness—to fight terrorism on a war footing.

The attacks that have crippled life in Mumbai, stunned the nation and the world, have also woken up many people from the reverie that saw India as a safe house in a dangerous neighbourhood. Terrorism in the Indian mainland, either perceived as a localised menace or one coming from 'across the border', has linked itself to a global phenomenon overnight. If there was any further confirmation needed regarding the borderless nature of terror, India has got it the hard way. Regardless of the nomenclature, the Deccan Mujahideen carries all the hallmarks of the genre of terrorist networks that go under the name of al-Qaeda. This is 21st century terrorism reaching the shores of our country.

Unfortunately, Indian counter-terrorism is still in 20th century gear. Intelligence collection and intelligence coordination are two processes lying at the core of the contemporary war against terror, whether in the United States, Israel, Britain or any other targeted country. India needs to understand that and understand it quickly. It also needs to implement stringent anti-terror laws. Without these in place, India will still be fighting a contemporary war anachronistically. A department of homeland security is still shockingly a non-concept here. And to add to the general sense of flailing about is the spanner of politics. After September 11, 2001, America came together to fight a common, shape-shifting enemy. Can we as a nation that has known terrorism for far longer—and with far more wounds to show—come together to face this nation-crippling assault?

The days ahead will show whether we will be able to survive 'effortless' terrorist attacks. It will also show whether we can save the idea of India and the way we live our lives. Playing the headless chicken is no longer an option.■

The longest day
Vir Sanghvi

IN THE IMMEDIATE aftermath of 26/11, even before the postmortems begin and the excuses are offered up, three points need to be made. These are preliminary reactions but I think they will remain valid even weeks from now. First, it is utterly and completely bizarre that while we whine about the Home Ministry, the intelligence establishment gets off scot-free even as Indians are murdered on the streets. It is impossible for the police to guard every building or check every passenger. All over the world, terrorism is fought through intelligence. A good security service penetrates terrorist cells, monitors radio traffic and picks up intelligence about terrorist activity. The Bombay attacks prove that we have the worst intelligence service of any major power in the world. These attacks were meticulously planned, involved two dozen attackers, many more terrorists in back-up roles, vast quantities of arms and ammunition and, probably, crores in funding.

Yet, our intelligence services had no idea that such an attack was being planned. Clearly, intelligence is the last quality that we should associate with our spymasters. These attacks also demonstrate the hollow nature of the many claims made by various police forces to have 'broken the backs' of terrorist cells and arrested various 'terror masterminds'.

The terrorists are completely unaffected by the puny efforts of our security forces. They strike when and where they want to. And Indians die. We've had enough excuses. Heads must roll. You would have thought that by now at least one of the country's spymasters would have offered to resign. No one has. And so, dismissals become imperative. Second, we should recognise that there is a new dimension to these attacks that was missing from earlier terrorist strikes. The aim of the Bombay terrorists was to continue the global *jihad* on Indian soil. That's why they sought out American and British passport holders and that's why Israelis and Jews were among the principal targets of the violence.

Combine that shift in emphasis with the sophistication of these attacks and some conclusions become inevitable. Clearly, these terrorists were funded and, probably, armed and trained by global *jihadi* forces. These were not angry students making homemade bombs. These were world-class terrorists. That should tell us that India is now part of the global terrorist battleground. If the international *jihadi* network decides to treat us on par with Israel, England, America and other countries that are seen as enemies of its twisted version of Islam, then the Bombay attacks may only be a beginning. Worse may follow. And we have no capacity to handle the increased level of threat.

Third, L.K. Advani was right when he said that these attacks were not like the usual bombings, but he was wrong when he drew a parallel with the 1993 Bombay blasts. When we saw the television pictures of the Taj Mahal hotel in flames, it was not the 1993 blasts we thought of. It was 9/11. It sounds flip and glib to say that these attacks constitute India's 9/11. But that, in fact, is the truth. The significance of 9/11 was that it made Americans conscious of the danger they were in and aware that nothing was safe; that terrorists could destroy such powerful symbols of American prestige as the World Trade Center. In our case, 26/11 has had the same impact. By striking at the heart of prosperous and largely peaceful south Bombay, the terrorists have served notice that there is nothing they cannot do, and nowhere that they cannot reach.

Bomb blasts are painful, traumatic events. But this long drawn-out crisis is far worse in the damage it has done to the Indian psyche. The inability of the authorities to bring the situation under control in a few hours has worried and frightened Indians. With each hour that the crisis continued, we felt vulnerable, impotent and humiliated. It was as though we had lost control of our destiny. And we would never feel safe again. Guesswork in the aftermath of a tragedy is always a risky business. But I wager that when the time comes to write the history of modern India, 26/11 will be remembered as the turning point in our attitude to terror. It will be remembered as the day when we Indians came to terms with vulnerability. And, with a bit of luck, as the day when we demanded that those in charge of protecting us either did the job they were supposed to or left it to somebody more capable.

The government must realise that this is not just another terrorist strike. This one has changed all the rules, both in terms of the impact it has had on the Indian psyche and in the anger and fear that now course through our veins.

No more promises. No more speeches. It's time to act.■

India needs the political will to act against terror
Brajesh Mishra (As told to Vinod Sharma)

No more knee-jerks
In his address to the nation after the terrorist invasion that has shocked Mumbai and India, Prime Minister Manmohan Singh reiterated the need for a federal investigating agency. For its part, the BJP wants tougher laws to face up to the threat that's growing in proportion with each passing day.

As either objective cannot be realised soon enough for want of a political consensus, I would suggest urgent measures in tune with the available institutional material and human resources. But above all is the need for a political and administrative will to act—and act fast.

The Intelligence Bureau has a presence in every district of the country. Why can't it coordinate with intelligence outfits in states until the proposed federal investigating agency is in place? Equally important is the task of training the police forces and insulating them from political interference to measure up to a challenge that's quite distinct from the usual law and order duties. The police's role is pre-eminent as the terrorist groups inimical to India have, after rounds of attack on places of worship, begun aiming at 'soft targets'—especially those crucial to our economy and overall public good. One can safeguard, for instance, the army installations or the South Block. But it is very difficult to afford that kind of protective cover for railway stations, hotels and hospitals that have come under fire in Mumbai, on the pattern first witnessed in Ahmedabad.

The targeting of railways infrastructure terrorises people and pummels the economy. Similarly, if the local citizenry and foreigners have the fear of trigger-happy gunmen lurking in their backyards, what would be the fate of our tourism industry and investments we're seeking from abroad? The September 20 Marriott hotel bombing in Islamabad brought to the fore this very change in terrorist tactics. But one cannot, on the strength of this parallel, jump to the conclusion that the mayhem in Mumbai's Taj and Trident hotels is also the handiwork of those who blew up the Marriott, located in the vicinity of several high-security installations—such as the Pakistani PM's House and the Parliament complex—in Islamabad. If not from the same school of terror, the men holed up in Mumbai's landmark hotels are copycats who styled their script after Pakistan's worst terrorist attack, to deliver a more lethal blow to cosmopolitan Mumbai by engaging in wanton killings and taking foreign tourists and visitors as hostages.

Given the reach and the expanse of the challenge—not to mention the killer gangs' level of training and resolve—the fight against terror cannot be won through knee-jerk responses. It's a long-drawn battle that requires equanimity of mind, sharp reflexes and a political culture that disallows electoral objectives to take precedence over national interest.■

Bombs and bullets cannot destroy India—as long as its gates remain open

Shashi Tharoor

THERE IS A savage irony to the fact that the unfolding horror in Mumbai began with terrorists docking near the Gateway of India. The magnificent arch, built in 1911 to welcome the King-Emperor, has ever since stood as a symbol of the openness of the city. Crowds flock around it, made up of foreign tourists and local yokels; touts hawk their wares; boats bob in the waters, offering cruises out to the open sea. The teeming throngs around it daily reflect India's diversity, with Parsi gentlemen out for their evening constitutionals, Muslim women in burkas taking the sea air, Goan Catholic waiters enjoying a break from their duties at the stately Taj Mahal hotel, Hindus from every corner of the country chatting in a multitude of tongues. Today, ringed by police barricades, the Gateway of India—and gateway to India's soul—is barred, mute testimony to the latest assault on the country's pluralist democracy.

The terrorists knew exactly what they were doing. Theirs was an attack on India's financial nerve-centre and commercial capital, a city emblematic of the country's energetic thrust into the 21st century. They struck at symbols of the prosperity that was making the Indian model so attractive to the globalising world—luxury hotels, a swish cafe, an apartment house favoured by foreigners. The terrorists also sought to polarise Indian society by claiming to be acting to redress the grievances of India's Muslims. And by singling out Britons, Americans and Israelis, they demonstrated that their brand of Islamist fanaticism is anchored less in the absolutism of pure faith than in the geopolitics of hate.

Today, the platitudes flow like blood. Terrorism is unacceptable; the terrorists are cowards; the world stands united in unreserved condemnation of this latest atrocity. Commentators in America trip over themselves to pronounce this night and day of carnage India's 9/11. But India has endured many attempted 9/11s, notably a ferocious assault on its national Parliament in December 2001 that nearly led to all-out war against the assailants' presumed sponsors, Pakistan. This year alone, terrorist bombs have taken lives in Jaipur, in Ahmedabad, in Delhi, and several different places on one searing day in Assam. Jaipur is the lodestar of Indian tourism to Rajasthan; Ahmedabad is the primary city of Gujarat, the state that is a poster child for India's development; Delhi is the political capital and window to the world; Assam was logistically convenient for terrorists from across a porous border. Mumbai combined all the four elements of its precursors: a grand slam.

Indians have learned to endure the unspeakable horrors of terrorist violence ever since malign men in Pakistan concluded it was cheaper and more effective to bleed India to death than to attempt to defeat it in conventional war. Attack after attack has been proven to have been financed, equipped and guided from across the border, the most recent being the suicide-bombing of the Indian embassy in Kabul, an action publicly traced by American intelligence to Islamabad's dreaded military special-ops agency, the ISI.

The risible attempt to claim the Mumbai killings in the name of the 'Deccan Mujahideen' merely confirms that wherever the killers are from, it is not the Deccan. The Deccan lies inland from Mumbai; one does not need to sail the waters of the Arabian Sea to get to the city from there. In its meticulous planning and military precision, the assault on Mumbai bore no trace of what its promoters tried to suggest it was—a spontaneous eruption by angry young Indian Muslims. This horror was not homegrown.

The Islamist extremism nurtured by a succession of military rulers of Pakistan has now come to haunt its well-intentioned but lamentably weak civilian government. The militancy once sponsored by its predecessors now threatens to abort Pakistan's sputtering democracy and seeks to engulf India in its flames. There has never been a stronger case for firm and united action by the governments of both India and Pakistan to cauterise the cancer in their midst.

India is a land of great resilience that has learned, over arduous millenniums, to cope with tragedy. Bombs and bullets alone cannot destroy it, because Indians will pick their way through the rubble and carry on as they have done throughout history. But what can destroy India is a change in the spirit of its people, away from the pluralism and coexistence that has been our greatest strength. The prime minister's call for calm and restraint in the face of murderous rampage is vital. If these tragic events lead to the demonisation of the Muslims of India, the terrorists will have won. For India to be India, its gateway—to the multiple Indias within, and the heaving seas without—must always remain open.■

This article first appeared in The Guardian *and is reproduced by permission of the author.*

December 1, 2008

Talk is cheap, lives are not
Milind Deora

THE LAST FEW days have been devastating for every Mumbaikar. All our hearts go out to those who have lost their dear ones. I've been awake since 8 a.m. on Wednesday, barring a few hours of interrupted sleep on Thursday and Friday nights, and have witnessed the most horrific yet moving events of my life.

Immediately after the news broke, my partymen and I prevented a mob outside Nariman House from becoming an easy target for a grenade attack, had a narrow escape when a seized police Toyota Qualis vehicle hurled grenades at the car we were in, assisted shattered relatives identify bodies of their family members, and helped government hospitals mobilise resources from other hospitals that weren't as inundated with dead bodies. We must never take for granted the efforts of Mumbai's indispensable uniformed personnel: the police, the Anti-terrorism Squad, the National Security Guards, army and marine commandos, firemen and the staff of hospitals and others, especially those who are martyrs.

Unlike previous terrorist strikes in Mumbai, Wednesday's was targeted at Mumbai's well-to-do. The nature of the attack was also different from anything that the world may have ever seen. The encounters were deliberately prolonged by the terrorists to create a spectacle on television that would last for days.

Barring a few credible news channels, the electronic media began acquiring perspectives on the terror strike from the usual 'Page 3' suspects who know nothing about intelligence or policing. The stereotypical questions from such panelists included, 'Why can't India secure her borders like the US?', 'Why do Western countries have better intelligence than us?', 'Why wasn't a hostage negotiator used at the Taj and Oberoi hotels?'

Please allow me to put things in perspective. India shares her land and maritime borders with more than a handful of politically unpredictable nations, many of whom aren't too fond of India. The US and Europe don't. If America's borders are impermeable, how do illegal immigrants from Mexico enter that country? Finally, if all the might of the US, Britain, Australia, Japan and other developed nations combined hasn't been able to catch Osama bin Laden for over seven years, why do we have unrealistic expectations from India?

I'm in no way saying that we should stop expecting our state and central governments to guarantee our safety. We must remember that countries like the US benefit from effective intelligence because their global strategic partnerships allow them to share information with friendly nations. Intelligence gathering, especially when it relates to threats emanating from abroad, can't happen effectively if we work in isolation. India is working towards building important global strategic partnerships that will give our intelligence establishment access to the best information. All this will soon give us an edge when it comes to filtering through information and acting upon it decisively. However, these global partnerships would be futile unless we free our security establishments from political interference and corruption.

When I visited the Oberoi Trident hotel with its general manager and the Union Home Minister shortly after the encounter was over, the scenes were horrifying. I don't wish to divulge graphic details but I can assure you that it was clear that the terrorists weren't interested in negotiating with the government. They were cold-blooded murderers. I was very pleased to shake the hands of the NSG commandos who had fought in the encounter.

All this leads to the point that while we, Mumbai's educated middle-class, must make ourselves heard, we must also study facts before appearing in TV debates, otherwise succumbing to the anchor's sensationalism. We love to criticise Lalu Prasad, Shivraj Patil, the Maharashtra Navnirman Sena campaign, and speak liberally about how terrorism has no religion. Yet on election day, why do we vote for parties keeping our own religion in mind? Immediately after a terrorist attack, we point fingers at a particular community or country, but when those from the ATS, who died fighting for us, pointed closer to home, why did we refuse to listen to them? While one politician states that India needs a strong national anti-terror law (which already exists), another leader asks each state government to cooperate with the central government in creating a national investigating agency along the lines of America's FBI.

Do we formulate our opinions regarding which option will benefit India on facts or on uninformed chatter? Sadly, we have allowed religion and politics to enter the terrorism debate. As a result, expecting politicians to put aside their differences and work out a solution requires that we change our old ways. If we can't get over our prejudices and spruce up our own intelligence before participating in the rumours and politics of terrorism, how can we expect it from the establishment?

Mumbai, like any great city, will confront and overcome many obstacles. Hopefully, before we look for places and people to point our fingers at, we will learn to play a more constructive role.■

Clueless, defenceless
Namita Bhandare

MUMBAI IS STILL recovering from the horrific terrorist strikes that began on Wednesday night. But the hand-wringing and the sermonising have begun. Words are tossed about: 'dastardly act', 'spirit of Mumbai' and so on. But the one question we should be asking is this: what do we learn from these repeated strikes? Even as we prepare to 'stamp out' terrorism, are we even prepared for the next strike?

Speaking in New Delhi a few years ago, Rudy Giuliani, the Mayor of New York during the 9/11 attack, said something that was significant. He said there was no way anybody could have anticipated 9/11. But what New York did have in place was a blueprint to deal with other potential crises. A fire in a skyscraper? There was an evacuation plan ready. A large-scale toxin attack? There was a plan to shift and treat large numbers of citizens in hospitals. So, when 9/11 happened, New York was caught unawares. But because it had other contingency plans ready, it was able to kick these in to deal with the crisis with far more efficiency than would have otherwise been possible.

Since the serial blasts of 1993, we have faced a series of major and minor terror strikes: six this year alone. Every time there is a strike, there is a sense of déjà vu as the prime minister or home minister of the moment makes an ashen-faced appearance on TV, mouthing platitudes that mean nothing. But every time there is a strike, there is also a sense of security forces and rescue operations lurching ahead without a sense of planning. Do we, for instance, have a plan in place in case terrorists attack a hospital or a school? What about chemical warfare? Are we prepared if a group of terrorists poison our water supplies? Are we prepared for anything at all?

We had to fly commandos into Mumbai. Isn't it time the city has its own crack team? The lack of planning seems to characterise much of our disaster management. Every time there is a stampede at a religious site, we are taken completely by surprise, scrambling to manage as best we can.

After 9/11, it was feared that the US would now be an easy target for future *fidayeen* attacks. But amazingly, there has not been another terror strike on US soil. As a grim-faced George Bush vowed to wreck vengeance, we smirked at 'Cowboy' Bush. But at least this cowboy (or his speech writers) was making a serious effort to restore confidence in his people.

Contrast that with our own leaders. Even as commandos were storming the Taj, Oberoi and Nariman House, a written statement issued in the name of former PM A.B. Vajpayee asked citizens to vote for his BJP in the Delhi election. Narendra Modi, meanwhile, was offering a crore of rupees to officers who just days before were under attack from him for their investigation into the Malegaon blasts and 'Hindu' terrorism. There was no sense of urgency as the PM called for an emergency Cabinet meeting only on Thursday. And after initial reports that Leader of the Opposition L.K. Advani and the PM would travel to Mumbai together, nothing happened. They went to Mumbai on separate aeroplanes. How much that one gesture of being united in the face of a common enemy would have conveyed. Instead, a desperate city in search of heroes clapped and cheered the army and the National Security Guards commandos as they went about their brave job. They were the true heroes of the moment. In a crisis, people need two things: a plan to effectively counter it (or even better, to prevent it), and strong and resolute leaders. Our real tragedy is that we seem to have neither.■

Bound by sorrows
Mohsin Hamid

IN THE RUSH to blame Pakistan for the attack in Mumbai, a dangerous mistake is being made. The impulse to implicate Pakistan is understandable, given past examples of Pakistani and Indian intelligence agencies working to destabilise the historical enemy across the border. But it is too soon to know who is behind the attacks. The desire of some in India to ascribe guilt to Pakistan before the evidence is in is an attempt to avoid introspection. India and Pakistan are more alike than politicians tend to acknowledge. The triumphal narrative of India as an incredible success, and the defeatist narrative of Pakistan as an impending disaster are both only half true. For much of this young century, Pakistan has enjoyed economic growth rates not far behind those of India. India, like Pakistan, is home to many simmering insurgencies. Had recent protests in Kashmir occurred in a former Soviet Republic, they would have been hailed by the world as a new Orange Revolution. Both Pakistan and India are plagued by extremism. Both have in their six decades of independence dramatically failed their poor. The reason to look at the similarities between India and Pakistan is not to drag India down, but to point out that the countries are in this together. Their fights against extremism cannot be separated by national borders into convenient compartments, marked 'domestic' and 'foreign'. The destruction of the Islamabad Marriott foreshadowed the attacks on the Oberoi and the Taj, and the pitched gun-battle between extremists and government forces in south Mumbai has eerie echoes of last year's bloody and prolonged stand-off at Islamabad's Red Mosque. Just as Delhi has seen bombings this year, so has Lahore. Just as rogue elements of Pakistan's armed forces have been accused of supporting terrorists, so has a lieutenant colonel in the Indian army. India and Pakistan are not the same, but the parallels are remarkable. Continuing to ignore this serves only to divide two countries that could benefit greatly from greater unity. When terrorism strikes, divisive anger is a natural response. Wisdom, however, lies in realising that we of India and Pakistan are united by our shared sorrow.■

Courtesy: *The Guardian*

December 14, 2008

The medium is the mess
Vir Sanghvi

BEWARE OF THOSE whose anger you fan. Because one day, that same anger will be directed at you. If that's not an epigram, it should be—as the TV news channels are now discovering.

Within the electronic media, there's a considerable degree of self-satisfaction over the coverage of the Bombay attacks. The intense criticism that the TV channels have come under in the aftermath of the attacks is sought to be ascribed to irrational public hysteria.

I do not dispute that some of the criticism is overblown, unjustified and unfair. In times of crisis, people tend to lash out wildly at anybody they associate with that crisis. In the case of the Bombay attacks, it began as rage against politicians, was transformed into hatred of Pakistan and has now mutated into anger against the media.

But two points need to be kept in mind. First of all, TV channels encouraged and fanned irrational public anger and hatred, giving airtime to everybody—small-time film stars, midgets on the fringes of journalism, party kings and party queens, advertising know-it-alls, etc—to rave and rant against politicians, democracy, the Indian State, civilian authority, Pakistan and god alone knows what else. Now that this hatred has turned on them, can they really complain?

Second, many of the criticisms are justified and valid. Unless the media stop patting themselves on their backs and accept that they made many mistakes, things are not going to get better in the next crisis.

One problem with much of the TV coverage—and the principal reason why people are so angry—was the complete misjudgement of tone. At times of national crisis, we don't need hysterical reporters telling us how bad things are. We can see the pictures for ourselves. Too many journos failed to realise this, inflicting their own sorrow on us and needlessly emphasising the emotional dimension of the crisis. We didn't need that. We needed calm authority and a sense that even as the horror of the crisis unfolded, the rest of India was still functioning normally. Anchors also misjudged the national mood. They either spoke to relatives of the hostages or listened only to Bombay trash celebrities and believed wrongly that this was the mood of the national audience. But it wasn't our mood at all. India was united during that tragedy. We were all Bombayites for those three days. But we were not all sipping champagne in Simi Grewal's suite at the Four Seasons and worrying about the danger posed to our facelifts by the slumdwellers below our windows. The rest of India retained its perspective and its rationality even if Page 3 people did not.

No matter what the media may say now, there is no doubt that security considerations rarely entered into their programming calculations or affected their news judgement. Was it right to show the commandos being lowered on to Nariman House in real time? Should TV channels have revealed that many guests had taken shelter at the Chambers at the Taj? These are just two instances but in both cases lives were lost. The NSG believes that one of its commandos died in the Nariman House assault at least partly because the terrorists knew he was coming. And we know now that terrorists went to the Chambers and opened fire after they heard that guests were hiding there.

It's not good enough to say, as the TV channels are saying now: we simply did what we were told. The defence offered by the channels is as follows: 'The authorities never told us what not to show or where not to go. How were we to know any better?' This is a dangerous argument because it suggests that the media are incapable of any kind of self-regulation and unable to think beyond the next shot unless they are instructed what to do. This is an invitation for censorship or external regulation.

For all the lectures that TV pundits give politicians every night, telling them how to run the country, it is clear that a) they turn into small children at the slightest signs of a crisis, bleating helplessly 'But nobody told us what to do' and b) they have no emergency protocols and no lists of dos and don'ts for disaster coverage.

But the government is also to be blamed. It's all very well for the Information and Broadcasting Ministry to issue advisories now and call meetings of TV channels. But where was the ministry when the crisis was raging? What was it doing then?

I accept that the events of the first night took everyone by surprise. But the crisis went on for three days. Why was nobody issuing instructions or evolving guidelines? Why bother to send an advisory about repeats of footage when you could have intervened when the footage was actually going out live?

Briefings during the crisis were rare and followed no particular pattern. Most bizarre of all was the role of the Indian navy—and it is no surprise that the government has asked for explanations. I think all of us owe a debt of gratitude to the navy's commandos for their role on the first night when they were briefly involved (for a few hours) in the action at the Taj till the NSG arrived and took over. But the naval commandos would have come off better if the naval high command had not decided to turn their brief intervention into the centrepiece of a PR campaign. Senior officers gave TV interviews while the operation was still on, proudly displaying evidence for the cameras without considering the security ramifications. In a monumental error of judgement, the commandos—who are supposed to be a shadowy secretive force—then gave a press conference, also while the operation was still continuing and NSG officers were laying down their lives. Worse still, they gave details of what they had found at the Taj. And even worse, some of these details were wrong. For instance, they claimed to have found Malaysian ID cards on the terrorists—quickly amended to Mauritius ID cards—when in fact the one card they had found was subsequently traced to a guest at the hotel.

Too many agencies talked too much and in different voices. Three things are clear. The first is that the suggestion made by *Hindustan Times* a week ago about delayed coverage has not been seriously challenged or disputed by anyone. We had said that one way of avoiding security breaches was to ensure that all live coverage went out after a delay (this could be as little as 10 minutes and as much as 20). That way, terrorists would not get information in real time and authorities could intervene to stop the telecast of anything that might compromise the operation. It's time to implement this suggestion. Second, we desperately need a unified command structure when such crises occur. I accept that the police need to call in help, from the army, the navy, the NSG, the CRPF, etc. But all these agencies cannot operate in isolation. There needs to be one boss; one man who calls the shots while everybody else listens. Third, we need a PR protocol. There must always be somebody in a position of authority on the spot who decides where to draw the line; what can be shown and what can't; how far away the press must be from the action; how to prevent released hostages from being mobbed by TV reporters; how to punish and stop channels that air interviews with terrorists or give false news such as the claims of fresh firing at VT station. This person or agency must also be in charge of briefing the media. Three briefings a day are normal in these situations and could easily have been arranged during the Bombay siege.

If you don't give information to the media, then they will get it from other sources: talkative policemen, relatives of hostages, publicity-hungry naval officers, etc. And nearly always, this information will either be wrong or will compromise security.

We are all agreed on some things. Politicians must learn to be accountable. The intelligence apparatus must be overhauled. Our reaction times must be quicker. Our forces should get the arms and facilities they need. To that list, add one more: the TV channels must never repeat the mistakes of the siege of Bombay.■

Of Asif, Ali and Zardari

Manas Chakravarty

FIRST OF ALL, they're very unclear who exactly is a terrorist. Do we mean militants or freedom fighters or *jihadis* or extremists or those people whom Asif Ali Zardari says are 'non-State actors'? That's made even more complicated by the fact that these guys keep changing their names so that the Lashkar-e-Tayyeba becomes the Jamaat-ud-Dawa, or the Harkat-ul-Something becomes the Jaish-e-Something-Entirely-Different. Besides, they also have Sunni fanatics, al-Qaeda operatives, Taliban militia, all adding to the confusion.

We could argue that all of them need to be put down immediately. Ah, but who's going to do it? As Zardari has said, they have non-State actors in Pakistan. They also have State actors, non-State non-actors and State non-actors. Zardari is obviously a State non-actor. What they don't seem to have are those who act on behalf of the State.

But that depends on which State we are talking about. The army, for instance, is a State within a State. The ISI is a State within the Army State within the State of Pakistan. And this ISI State also apparently includes 'rogue elements'. To make it easy for you, I have made an illustrative but by no means exhaustive list of the various groups in Pakistan. Here it is: pro-State, pro-army; pro-State, anti-army; pro-non-State, pro-non-army; pro-State, anti-ISI; pro-army, anti-ISI (this is reportedly an oxymoron); pro-State, pro-army, pro-ISI, anti-rogue elements in the ISI (these are reportedly morons); progenerals, anti-retired generals; pro-retired cricketer, anti-retired general etc.

I'm uncertain whether the picture is clear now, but at least you have some idea of how complicated things really are in Pakistan.

What's more, nobody is quite sure which of these factions runs the country. In short, if you need to hand over a list of demands the first thing to do is make about 500 photocopies and give it to each of those groups. That's because very often the State's left hand has no inkling what its right hand is up to. For instance, when A.Q. Khan exploded that nuclear bomb, the Pakistan government had no idea what he was doing. Why, even A.Q. Khan says he hadn't a clue. 'I had put my clothes in the washing machine, quite forgetting about the lump of uranium in my trouser pocket and then I went to the market to buy some veggies. Imagine my surprise when, on my way back, I saw this little mushroom cloud over my bungalow,' he told this reporter. He then went on to explain that the uranium must have reacted with the heavy water in the washing machine (he always uses heavy water for washing, it's good for stains) and inadvertently produced a nuclear explosion. The point of this story is to emphasise just how difficult it is for anyone to know who is doing what in Pakistan.

Rumours have also reached me that this muddle about non-State actors and State actors has gone to such lengths that people are no longer pro-Asif Ali Zardari. Instead, some of them are pro-Asif but anti-Zardari, others are pro-Ali but anti-Asif and so on. This can, of course, happen only in Pakistan. As for Zardari himself, he has now split into three distinct personalities—Asif, Ali and Zardari—so that if you ask him about that list of terrorists he can claim you never gave it to him at all because you handed it to Asif but the guy who's before you now is Ali.

So if you see the president of Pakistan sitting quietly at his desk, don't for a moment assume the poor man is lonely and depressed. For all you know, he may be having a wild party with Asif and Ali.■

———————————————

December 17, 2008

Breaking news, not views
Seema Goswami

AS THE MEDIA brouhaha about the television coverage of the Mumbai attacks rages, it's time to stop being defensive and to try and understand just why people are so upset. The words used— in social discourse, on the internet and in the print media—to describe the coverage are telling. Over the top, sensationalist, exploitative and melodramatic—these are just some of the adjectives being thrown about.

But the fury of the response and the venom of the attacks suggest that this is not a one-off thing. This resentment over the way TV channels cover events has been building for a while. The 26/11 attacks were just a catalyst for people to express long-standing grievances. At the root of this anger lurks the resentment of the viewing public about the assumption of journalists that their opinions are the only ones that matter. Just as offensive is their presumption in inserting their own views into the narrative of whatever story they happen to be covering. What is under attack here is the constant contamination of the news by the views of those who disseminate it on television. As the cliché goes, comment may be free but facts are sacred. And when it comes to the news space, they need to be kept apart. The problem with TV is that there is a constant blurring of the lines so that one never quite knows where the news ends and the views begin. God knows the print media has its own problems and it often gets things wrong. But where it scores is that the dividing line between opinion and fact is always very clear. Opinion belongs on the edit and op-ed page—and in the feature and style sections. The news appears on all the other pages, uncontaminated by the views of those reporting it.

Yes, newspaper columnists can be as self-indulgent and self-obsessed as TV reporters (and I'm guilty as charged for my weekly column in *Brunch*), but on the whole they restrict themselves to the spaces reserved for the venting of opinion.

In TV that is hardly ever the case. Newscasters start editorialising in the middle of a news broadcast, anchors of panel discussions are more interested in holding forth than eliciting the opinions of their guests, and interviewers routinely interrupt their subjects in mid-sentence only to insert their own agendas. And that's what viewers resent the most: being told how to feel or how to think. We are not imbeciles sitting at home that you have to tell us over and over again that an event is a national tragedy. We can work it out for ourselves.

Is it really surprising then that the viewing public has finally snapped and said: Don't tell us how to feel about things. Don't even tell us how *you* feel about things. Just give us the facts and let us make up our own minds. But while it is easy to knock TV journalists, let's not forget that some of these problems are inherent in the medium itself. In the print media, when you sit down at a computer terminal to write your story, you are already one step removed from the event. And that in itself lends some distance and hence, some perspective to your report. Television journalists don't have that luxury. The nature of their job demands that they report from the thick of things in real time. And when there are flames billowing behind you, grenades exploding, bullets being fired, feelings running high, it is difficult to step back from the event so that you can report it dispassionately. But it is easy to start to think that you are part of the story. It is easy to con yourself into believing that it's all happening to you rather than around you. It is easy to fall into the trap of thinking that your emotions, your reactions matter—that your pain, your anger, your anguish are part of the narrative.

Only they're not. Your job is to tell the story, not become the story. More important, it's your job to tell the story as an objective observer in a manner devoid of hyperbole. The event is big enough; you don't need to magnify it through needless hysteria.

As the post-mortems on the TV coverage of 26/11 get under

way, one thing is clear. What people resent most is getting the news through the prism of someone else's emotions.

A reporter is supposed to be the filter, not the funnel, between the news and the viewer. A filter helps keep all the extraneous clutter out so that you can concentrate on the essential details of the story. A funnel on the other hand just pushes everything through without bothering about the contents too much.

All of us in the media—both print and TV—need to treat the news as a sacred space inviolable by opinion. And just as we exhort the government to keep Church and State apart, we need to draw a line between news and views—and make sure that we never violate it. The message from the public is loud and clear. And we journalists ignore it at our own peril.■

December 20, 2008

Loony tunes
Barkha Dutt

IF THERE IS anything more tragic than India's Muslims having to vouch for their nationalism in the aftermath of every terrorist strike, it is the insane utterances of some of their self-appointed saviours. By the time this goes to print, A.R. Antulay's resignation as Minority Affairs minister would have most likely been accepted by the prime minister. (If it hasn't, it should be.) But the damage would have been done.

Antulay's reckless suggestion that a wider conspiracy claimed the life of police officer Hemant Karkare has played right into the hands of fellow loonies on the other side of the border who claim that 'Hindu Zionists' plotted the attacks in Bombay. His demands for an independent probe to examine whether the Malegaon investigations may have cost Karkare his life only embarrass India and give Islamabad the wriggle room it is seeking. And worst of all, his comments will only reinforce the nonsense spouted by the small radical fringe within the community. The young conspiracy theorists who come to television talk shows holding posters blaming the CIA/Mossad for the terror attacks will now feel emboldened to manufacture more imaginary enemies. This is not the first time that Antulay has been in the news for all the wrong reasons. Whether it was his complicity in a major corruption scam involving cement licences or his grandstanding promises on bringing the Kohinoor back to India, the former Maharashtra chief minister has long had a reputation for being a bit of a loose cannon. But his statements this time go well beyond regular political fallibilities.

The worry is not so much whether the world will now view the Bombay outrage in a different light. Independent American intelligence points to the same conclusion as the official Indian position on the role of groups like the Lashkar-e-Tayyeba. The Russians have spoken about clear links between underworld gangster Dawood Ibrahim and the attacks. And Pakistan's own newspapers have run hard-hitting stories from inside Kasab's village with confessional accounts from his parents on their terrorist son.

The embarrassment of a Union minister speaking out of sync aside, India doesn't really need to worry about any serious diplomatic fall-out. The real damage of Antulay's remarks is within and on home turf. With one careless 30-second sound byte he has caricatured the response of the Indian Muslim. He has spawned a pool of other headline hunters who are falling over themselves to issue press releases in agreement. Former IFS officer Syed Shahabuddin is among those who congratulated Antulay for 'speaking the unspeakable'. A section of the Urdu press is now arguing that demanding an investigation into the death of an officer probing Hindu radical groups is entirely legitimate.

Online polls apparently show that their readers agree. Some Muslim intellectuals have argued that the minister's remarks have played into an already existing panic among ordinary Muslims and should not be confused with prejudice. They say that fearful minorities who view the police with suspicion saw Karkare as a hero and his abrupt end left them stunned and even more scared.

But frankly all of these rationalisations are just self-destructive and perpetuate the worst sort of stereotypes about us as a people. At a time when India should have stood united, Antulay's remarks have pushed the debate along an unfortunate Hindu–Muslim faultline. His comments are designed to pull at our religious equilibrium. And as a Muslim politician he has committed that all-too-familiar crime yet again: he is hellbent on keeping his people locked into ghettos (some real, some imaginary) of victimhood. But why are we all so surprised? Before ten men with guns struck Bombay we saw the blatant politicisation of the terror debate in how both the Batla House encounter and the Malegaon blasts probe were debated by the Congress and the BJP. Both parties made faulty assumptions about votebanks as they constantly calibrated their public positions. Antulay's remarks are just an extension of the same brand of cynical politics. And those of his cabinet colleagues who are unwilling to take a clear position on his remarks are just as culpable.

If there is one lesson we should have learnt in these past two weeks, it is that the process of law—and not politicians—has to settle investigations, however contentious and sensitive they may be. Yes, there may be a genuine cause of mistrust between the people and India's police force. But the answer to that simply cannot be that political agendas are used to set the course for police action. For Antulay to suggest by innuendo that Karkare's own men may have led him to his death is outrageous and unacceptable. Scurrilous allegations cannot be confused with the need for genuine police reform. That a Union minister would dare to do that is frightening.

Antulay's real betrayal is that he has let down his own people. Yet again, the Indian Muslim has been pushed into a corner of clarifications. Mercifully, groups like Javed Akhtar's Muslims for Secular Democracy have broken the lazy assumptions of a Muslim monolith by demanding Antulay's resignation and dismissing his remarks as 'ridiculous nonsense'. But is it fair that at a time of national crisis a minister and Member of Parliament should push his own community on the defensive? Does he not owe them better than to stereotype them in the worst possible manner? A.R. Antulay owes an apology: to the Congress, to his community and to the country. He can no longer continue as minister. And if he does, it's a good reason to wear black bands in protest again. Because remember, it is controversies like this one that undo our secularism. Antulay must go.■

MISA, TADA, POTA, Hakuna Matata!
Pratik Kanjilal

Draconian (adj.) Brutal, atrocious, bloody-minded. Derived from the Latin *draco*—dragon.

AFTER THE MUMBAI attack, we got it right for once. India was clearly the wronged party. The Pakistanis had made fools of themselves, trying to deny responsibility for non-State actors. But then our own non-State thespian, Minorities Minister A.R. Antulay, walked into Parliament and insinuated a home-hatched conspiracy to kill Hemant Karkare. No wonder his government has declared him a lone operator and everyone else wants his head.

Antulay may have diplomatically embarrassed his government and breached parliamentary norms, but he has also reflected the national mood of uncertainty and suspicion. A spate of terror attacks has left behind too many unanswered questions. The institutions which should have the answers seem compromised or incapable. And when we see even the horror of Mumbai turned into political capital, willing suspension of belief seems like a reasonable response and conspiracy theories acquire the air of valid public discourse. Now, the Congress has joined the BJP and fallen for the soft option of a hard law. It may prolong the reign of terror by cornering marginalised communities and cancel out the benefits of the proposed federal agency, which represents a real step forward. Its only benefit is political—the public will be assured that something has been done, without bothering their heads about what precisely has been done.

Draconian laws have been in force periodically for 60 years, since when Sardar Patel passed the Madras Suppression of Disturbances Act (1948) to put down the Telengana rising, though he found it repugnant to the ideals of newly-free India. The Armed Forces Special Powers Act, only a decade younger, has prolonged regional conflicts for half a century. Such laws are conjured up after the State neglects to engage politically with local issues and aspirations. Even our worst insurgencies have political roots and could have been nipped in the bud by political initiatives. But we have always let them fester, then invoked the holy cow of national security and drummed up a new law giving security forces special powers to put them down savagely. Four states are now seeking Central approval for new draconian laws to lengthen an already endless list—MISA, TADA, POTO, POTA, MCOCA, goddammit whatsitsname . . . Tapora, Bambaiyya Batata, Hakuna Matata, Brakkadakkadadada! Sorry, a momentary lapse of reason. The onomatopoeia at the end is clearly Sgt Rock of Easy Company opening fire on the Viet Cong. I'm getting as intemperate as Antulay. My mind is dangerously fragile after considering half a century of draconian laws that have not increased our security an iota. If I have to learn the acronym of one more useless band-aid law, it will crack like an eggshell. Reader, I hope your mind is in better shape.■

December 23, 2008

Bridge the troubled waters
Arun Prakash

THE 'BLAME-GAME' THAT reared its ugly head in the aftermath of the 26/11 Mumbai terror attacks instantly reminded me of the fervent appeals of three successive chiefs of the Research and Analysis Wing to the naval headquarters to loan them naval officers for analysis of maritime intelligence. They were seriously concerned that they did not have the necessary expertise available to draw the right conclusions from the mass of information the agency collected from open, human and technical sources. And very correctly they approached the navy. Lack of maritime intelligence has also been the navy's bane for years. So we understood the handicap the R&AW worked with and felt that it was the navy's duty to help. As the chief of personnel, I recalled having personally selected some officers for deputation to the R&AW. But to my consternation, I learnt within a few months that most wanted to return to the navy.

The naval officers deputed to the R&AW did not wish to continue with their deputation because when they were assigned their desks in the Cabinet Secretariat they found to their dismay that they had been placed under officers who were many years their junior in terms of service. Having taken this stoically, they then found that they were deprived of things like telephones, stenographers and transport because the 'status' assigned to them did not entitle them to these utilities. The R&AW authorities were sympathetic, but pleaded that they were not in a position to alter the equivalences apparently 'laid down' by a Kafkaesque Department of Personnel.

This is symptomatic of a larger malaise: the lack of coordination between organs of the Government of India, that also contributed to the recent Mumbai fiasco. This should not come as a surprise. The GoI is so laissez faire in its approach that it won't intervene to eliminate interagency inequity that can result in crippling dysfunctionality. If you progressively marginalise, downgrade and degrade your own armed forces, you are undermining the security of the State. At the risk of exaggerating, I would venture to state that this is exactly what the Sixth Central Pay Commission (CPC) seems to have achieved. Today, there is a distinct impression that the CPC has erred grievously on many issues relating to the armed forces. They were not represented in the Commission and its recommendations have spread confusion and consternation. One of the most serious consequences is the sudden and arbitrary alteration of relativities between the armed forces and their civilian counterparts, to the detriment of the former. The resulting change in relationships between the armed forces and para-militaries has grave operational implications that do not seem to have been understood at all at the political level.

Ex-servicemen, too, are confounded to see the number of anomalies thrown up by the CPC. Take one example: no one understands by what logic a lieutenant-general, a major-general and a brigadier are going to be paid exactly the same pension, while a colonel (with half the service) will receive just Rs 100 less. The government has again rejected the 'one rank one pension' demand. But not even a feeble attempt has been made to bridge the gap between today's and yesterday's pensioners of the same rank. There is also a distinct impression that the CPC recommendations have been changed by the bureaucracy without due authorisation from the political level.

The most logical way to avoid this confusion and the sense of grievance among the armed forces and ex-servicemen would have been to place a service representative, if not in the CPC, in the review committee. This would have avoided controversy, speculation and unhappiness. A few retired service chiefs, including myself, had written to the prime minister to accord this concession. But the appeal remains unanswered. Spreading unhappiness among the nation's armed forces or demoralising them and the 2–3 million-strong ex-servicemen community does not serve anyone's interest. Should someone in authority not sit up and take notice?■

Opportunity knocks down
Ajit Doval

PEOPLE WANT CHANGE. There have been two dozen major terrorist incidents in the last four years that have left over 900 dead. Against this backdrop, the audacity of the Mumbai carnage has generated unprecedented national fury. Anger was compounded by the US's ABC News quoting intelligence sources that warnings shared with Indian agencies were specific: '. . . from the sea against the hotels and business centres in Mumbai'. From street corners to drawing rooms, there are angry outbursts against the polity, systems, laws, State apparatuses and intentions and capabilities of those entrusted with the task of national security.

Change we must. But anger is probably the worst stimulant for the change required. There is another tragic side to the story. In India, governments agree to 'change' only when bled or pressurised beyond their political endurance. The government making laws to fight terrorism, which are a near repeat of the Prevention of Terrorism Act (POTA) that it repealed on coming to power four years ago, is illustrative. Do we always need 'Mumbais' to trigger the change? There is an outcry to keep politicians out. In a democracy, if they have to be excluded from countering a threat that challenges our civil society, we first have to abandon democracy. Tackling Pakistan, enacting the right laws, running the government and insulating the populace from *jihadi* influence are all part of a political process. In a democracy, elected representatives have to do all this. It is the politician's indifference and low prioritisation of terrorism that is the problem—not his over-indulgence. While terrorism should figure high on India's political agenda, it is the execution of counter-terrorism policies and apparatuses that should be depoliticised. Today, it is the other way round. The Supreme Court's judgements on depoliticising the police and its repeated demands for compliance have been ignored by politicians both at the Centre and in the states. This is illustrative of where the problem lies. Terrorism cannot be fought unless the police are reformed. This can't take place unless the police force is depoliticised.

Terrorists have to be fought both in the defensive and offensive modes. While in the defensive mode, we have to protect our people and interests; in the offensive mode, we have to neutralise and deter our enemies. Operating exclusively in the defensive mode is like playing football with one goal post where you only take the hits. This way, the defending team can never win. Fourth generation warfare against an invisible enemy can't be won unless the costs are made unbearably high for the perpetrators and supporters of terror. A credible covert capacity, the use of which can be controlled and calibrated, will be an effective deterrent. Unilaterally lowering the deterrence threshold—like the declaration in Havana on September 15, 2006, that Pakistan was a 'terrorist victim State' and not a 'terrorist-sponsoring State'—only reduces the pressure on the enemy and emboldens it. Whatever the government's considered policy might be, it is bad counter-terrorist strategy to give them assurance of impunity. The nation needs to build deterrent covert capabilities against terrorism.

In the defensive mode, strong anti-terror laws—substantive and procedural—are necessary. It is gratifying that the government has almost re-enacted POTA. However, in the proposed new law, inadmissibility of disclosures made before the police remains a lacuna. How can the police get evidence of the planning, preparation and logistics that lie beyond their reach and jurisdiction? Making admissions even before senior police officers inadmissible will only help the terrorists. How can a society unwilling to trust its police against a foreign terrorist expect a policeman to lay down his life to protect it?

A seamless integration of the three functions that go in fighting terrorists—developing operation-grade intelligence, coercive action to pre-empt or prevent terrorist actions and investigation—is required. One of the reasons why terrorists are able to display greater surprise, speed and success in their operations, despite low human and material resources, is that each terrorist group synergises all the functions that go into perpetrating a terrorist act. A unified national response will check the menace of passing the buck that has cost the nation for so long. The creation of a National Investigating Agency, though a move forward, will prove to be inadequate unless all counter-terrorist intelligence tasks are placed under a unified command-and-control system. An investigating agency, at best, may get a few more convictions in the courts. But a 'war against terrorism' cannot be won in the courts. What we need is a National Counter-Terrorist Agency with stand-alone capacities to fight terrorism. For empowerment of the state police, states should be encouraged to enact laws to control activities of organised criminals, counterfeiters, gun-runners, drug syndicates, etc. who have collaborative linkages with terrorists. It is regrettable that the Centre has not accorded its concurrence to many anti-terror state legislations like those in Gujarat and Madhya Pradesh for years, even as such a law exists in Maharashtra.

It matters to a nation what happens to it. But what is more important is how it responds to it. Today a national consensus can be the driving force for bringing about many changes that are long overdue. Let us turn a calamity into an opportunity and force a change in our antiquated security set-up and make it a state-of-the art instrument that serves the nation.■

December 26, 2008

Something's got to give
Rajdeep Sardesai

ONE OF THE more joyous moments of fatherhood was taking my son, then all of nine years, to watch an India–Pakistan one-day match in Lahore in 2004. Our Pakistani friends had rolled out the traditional Punjabi hospitality: from the waiting limousine at the airport to the best pavilion seats, we were treated as honoured guests. In a sea of competing blue and green, my son was caught up in the excitement of the occasion. Through the day, he had been furiously waving the Tricolour. In the last overs, as it became clear that India was winning, some visibly frustrated Pakistani supporters handed over a Pakistani flag to my son. The offer was promptly accepted, and on our way home he had two flags in his hand: the Tricolour and its Pakistani equivalent.

Call it the innocence of a nine-year-old, but the Indo–Pak equation has always had a romantic edge. No relationship has been as schizophrenic as that between the two subcontinental neighbours. Where else can you have a heated argument on Kashmir one moment, and then proceed to draw up an all-time best Indo–Pak cricket eleven the very next? How does one explain travelling to the headquarters of the Lashkar during the day, and sitting in the evening in the hotel lobby listening to a pianist play a Lata-Rafi melody?

The dualism was starkly driven home when I was interviewing then Prime Minister Nawaz Sharif in the midst of the Kargil war in 1999. The interview saw a few sharp, testy exchanges over just who was responsible for the war. With the camera off, Sharif was back to being his gregarious self. As we ate a several course feast in the luxurious prime ministerial gardens overlooking the Margalla hills, the tone was anything but bellicose. Instead, Sharif proceeded to reminisce on his favourite Hindi film star, Rajendra Kumar. '*Waah, kya* actor *tha*!' (perhaps the only time anyone has recognised 'Jubilee' Kumar's acting capabilities). The conversation then drifted to Sharif's other great obsession, cricket, and he appeared awestruck by Tendulkar's batting. Finally, while leaving, I mentioned that I hadn't eaten better kebabs. Sharif, the foodie, smiled, 'Not as good as the ones I once ate in Purani Dilli. And the *gajar halwa* was something else!' Perhaps, the food and conversation was only meant to soften an Indian journalist in a time of war, but the affection has always felt just as real as the enmity over the years. Has 26/11 changed that? Are we now as a people less inclined to give our Pakistani counterparts the benefit of doubt, less prepared to distinguish between the Pakistani State and its civil society, less willing to get carried away by nostalgia and shared interests?

At one level, the end of the *jhappi-pappi* culture in the Indo–Pak relationship is to be welcomed. Candlelight at Wagah and the sound of guns along the Line of Control were always colliding images that discomfited those whose minds were less cluttered by sentimentalism. Geography and generational change had perhaps something to do with contrasting attitudes. For those who had been affected by Partition, the love–hate relationship with the 'other side' was connected with their collective memories of childhood. But for those who lived south of the Vindhyas, with no real connect with Pakistan, the obsessive relationship always seemed a little incongruous. The romantics were looking for a *Veer Zara* equation; while the extremists on both sides were keen for a *Gadar*-like confrontation.

The more mature approach lies somewhere in-between, based on a more pragmatic and less emotional assessment of the relationship. Take cricketing ties for example. In the afterglow of that heady 2004 series when chants of 'Balaji *zara dheere chalo!*' were heard across Pakistani stadiums, the romantics believed that there had been a tectonic shift in attitudes, with the average Pakistani ready to embrace the idea of India. The truth is that cricket has its limitations beyond the boundary. Cricket matches cannot be a substitute for statecraft, an Indian cricketer being cheered by a Pakistani crowd does not mean that the terror infrastructure has been dismantled. It is too much in the first place to have ever expected our cricketers to achieve what politicians on both sides of the border cannot: a permanent peace. You cannot, for example, have a situation where cricket is expected to compensate for our failures to work out a meaningful joint mechanism against terror. It is no use for Pakistan to claim that it, too, is a victim of terror, and then use that as an excuse not to act against Masood Azhar or Dawood Ibrahim. What 26/11 has done is driven home the double-standards of a feeble Pakistani State to the average Indian citizen: how can you play 'normal' cricket with a country which is living through an 'abnormal' situation by denying the links between a section of its State apparatus and terror groups?

And yet, it is difficult to accept the extreme view that all Indo–Pak sporting and cultural contacts be abandoned as a demonstrable measure of our anger post-26/11. The idea that the social isolation of Pakistan could have the same effect as that of the ostracism of South Africa during the apartheid years is misplaced.

The campaign against apartheid worked because it was a global effort. Moreover, apartheid was institutionalised by the South African government while Islamabad retains the fiction of terror being a 'non-State' act. Importantly, the only hope for a stable Pakistan lies in the strengthening of its civil society as was seen during the anti-Musharraf lawyers' protest. We haven't seen the same kind of nationwide movement against the *jihadis* yet.

The challenge then is to strike the right balance. We must hold the stick of sanctions—economic, sporting and cultural—if Pakistan refuses to cooperate with the 26/11 investigation but also offer the carrot of even greater interaction if there is concrete proof that Islamabad is acting against the *jihadis*. Above all, we must all live in hope that sanity will ultimately prevail. My now teenaged son certainly does: he still has the Pakistani flag in his room.■

December 27, 2008

Why war isn't an option
Barkha Dutt

I JUST GOT an email from a friend in Pakistan. He had written just five words: do something; stop this war. War? I wrote back arguing that there was no war to run scared from and that the illusion of an imminent catastrophe had been manufactured on the other side. Our dialogue collapsed in a dead-end, which may work well for TV talk but not in real life. Most Pakistanis I have been speaking to in the last one month are convinced that the Indians are coming. And most Indians, with the inarticulateness that comes with rage, want the government to 'do something'. We just aren't sure what that 'something' can or should be.

We are frustrated and angry that even a month after the Bombay attacks, there is no tangible shift in the way Islamabad is responding. If anything, things have only got worse. Even the

UN-pushed crackdown on the Jamaat-ud-Dawa (the ideological launchpad and political front of the Lashkar-e-Tayyeba) has turned out to be cosmetic. And Masood Azhar—the terrorist who walked free in exchange for the safety of the IC-814 passengers—has vanished, after being declared under house arrest. The flip-flops are brazen enough to destroy diplomacy. And yet, the truth—painful as it may be to families who have suffered directly in the Bombay attacks—is this: war is not an option; it is neither practical nor desirable.

First, there are the commonsensical reasons to rule it out. A military conflict will not manage to eliminate the seeds of terrorism that are sown deep into the subsoil of Pakistan's strategic architecture. Washington cannot be treated as the automatic deterrent to nuclear conflict; the stakes are too high, the game too risky. A civilian establishment that does not trust its own institutions to investigate the assassination of Benazir Bhutto (the centrepiece of the PPP's election campaign was the promise of a UN probe) will hardly be able to control rogue players with a mind of their own, in case of a war. Even surgical strikes (bound to escalate into a full-blown conflict) don't have ready targets to plan with. Terror camps can be swiftly dismantled and resurrected at new locations once the conflict is over. A military conflict does not even guarantee that the Indian forces can come home with Dawood Ibrahim, Hafiz Sayeed or Masood Azhar. So, what would we really achieve by risking the lives of our soldiers? But for those who dismiss all this as arguments made by the fainthearted, there's a more compelling reason not to consider war: India would be playing straight into the hands of Pakistan's military regime. Talk to Pakistani commentators and they agree that a war with India strengthens the Pakistan army like nothing else has or could in the past year. Some even suggest that precision air strikes by India will present a near-perfect scenario for the Pakistan military. Islamabad will retaliate without immediately risking the fatalities of on-ground conflict; Washington will jump in within days and the military will be back in the centrestage of public approval. This in a country where just a few months ago, General Pervez Musharraf was pushed out unceremoniously and the army was blamed for everything from the rise of the Taliban to the price of onions.

Bhutto's tragic assassination (blamed by her own people on elements in the security establishment) was meant to usher in a political revolution. Exactly a year back, in December, I remember sitting in the Bhutto House at Larkana, and feeling goosebumps when Bilawal Bhutto announced in a trembling voice that 'democracy' would be the 'best revenge' for his mother's murder. But we have seen that democracy being whittled down systematically. Many in Pakistan believe that sections of the ISI and the army have moved in with quiet but brutal aggression because President Asif Ali Zardari was moving too quickly in peace talks with India. The offer of a no-first-use of N-weapons, the consent to start border trade across the Line of Control, the attempts to reign in the ISI and the willingness (at least on paper) to investigate its role in the Kabul bombings—none of this made Zardari popular with his own security establishment. And frankly, in the last month it has become clear that neither Zardari nor Nawaz Sharif is the author of this script any longer. The refusal to send the ISI chief to India, pushing Sharif to retract his statement on Pakistani involvement in the Bombay attacks, and now the artificial war hysteria created by moving troops and flying air force jets over residential areas—all have the imprint of a larger plan—one that goes well beyond the terrorist strikes in Bombay.

By whipping up the impression of imminent war, Islamabad's security establishment is hoping to catapult itself back into the role of saviour. It isn't my argument that India should be overly concerned about the inner failings of Pakistan's experiment with democracy. Our decisions should be guided by self-interest. And so we must ask, does India want to strengthen the very section of the Pakistani power structure that it sees as innately hostile to us?

Yes, the domestic mood remains one of 'enough is enough'. And contrary to the rather over-imaginative understanding of some TV-bashers that this was an exhortation to war, it's a simple, effective phrase (first used passionately by Shobhaa Dé) to capture the mood of a country that is no longer willing to accept a system that lets us down and fails to protect us. But before we demand quick-fix solutions on moving against Pakistan, let us ask ourselves this: are we helping India? India must now look for an unconventional solution that lies somewhere between war and peace.■

December 28, 2008

Round one to Pakistan
Vir Sanghvi

ARE YOU AS surprised as I am by the war hysteria that suddenly seems to have become the defining feature of India–Pakistan ties? In the aftermath of 26/11, many of us took pride in the maturity of the Indian reaction. Even though we knew quite quickly that the attacks were the work of terrorists based in Pakistan, Indians refused to give in to the knee-jerk response to retaliate. We had telephone intercepts that demonstrated that the Pakistan-based Lashkar-e-Tayyeba was behind the attacks. Phones recovered from the dead terrorists offered proof of regular calls to Pakistan. And Ajmal Kasab, the one terrorist to be captured alive, soon confessed to his Pakistani origins. There were two ways we could have responded to this mountain of evidence. The first was to say that this proved that Pakistan was involved and to then launch surgical strikes on terrorist training camps in Pakistan. The second was to buy Asif Zardari's claim that while the terrorists may have had Pakistani origins, they had no State sponsorship. In fact, said Zardari, the same terrorists were the ones who had killed his wife and launched attacks within Pakistan.

I reckoned we had been reasonable in choosing the second path. We rejected the war option and, somewhat surprisingly, Indian public opinion did not demand a retaliatory strike. Instead, most of us trusted Zardari, or at least gave him the benefit of doubt, believing that he was sincere when he talked about wanting peace with India and appreciating his offer not to launch a first nuclear strike made at the *HT* Summit. Plus, we had faith in America. Many foreign policy experts told us that America was on our side; that Pakistan was so indebted to America that it could not afford to offend Washington; and that diplomatic pressure from the likes of Condoleezza Rice would ensure that Pakistan cracked down on the groups that had organised the Bombay attacks.

One month after those terrible incidents, two things have happened. The first is that Pakistan has gone back on its early willingness to help India get the perpetrators of the terror strikes. An offer to send the ISI chief to India was hurriedly withdrawn and the current position of the Zardari government appears to be that there is no evidence at all of any Pakistan involvement in the attacks. Even Ajmal Kasab, whose Pakistani origins have been unearthed by Pakistan's own media is sought to be denied his rights as a Pakistani citizen. We do not know who he is, says Islamabad, and we don't believe that he is a Pakistani. The second development is that while we have congratulated ourselves on our restraint, Pakistan has built up the war hysteria on its own anyhow. Each day the Pakistani people are told how an Indian attack will be repulsed. More troops have been moved to the border with India. Pakistan air force aircraft fly sorties over major Pakistani cities. And Pakistani ministers accuse India of needlessly targeting Pakistan.

In effect, therefore, we have the worst of all worlds. We avoided threatening war in the hope that the Pakistani government would cooperate in the investigation. But all offers of cooperation have been withdrawn and far from helping us, Islamabad is dedicating its energies towards claiming that India is lying about Pakistani involvement. Further, the very war hysteria we hoped to avoid by counting on Zardari has been created anyway—not by us, but by Pakistan. In effect, we've been forced into a situation where we can expect no cooperation from the Pakistan government while simultaneously defending ourselves against charges of seeking to invade Pakistan and forcing war on the region.

How could things have gone so wrong?

I am now coming round to the view that they've only gone wrong for us. They've gone very right for Pakistan. Islamabad has got exactly what it needs, and what it always wanted.

Consider the situation that Pakistan found itself in a few months ago. The US was ready to commit more troops to Afghanistan and pressure was growing on Pakistan to clear its Pashtun areas of Taliban and al-Qaeda elements. The Americans believed that Osama bin Laden was probably hiding in those areas. Thus far, Pakistan had been able to go along with American ambitions for the region but it was now reaching the point of no-return. First of all, the Taliban are an ISI creation. Pakistan was one of the few countries in the world to recognise the Taliban government in Afghanistan. So it has no desire to entirely crush the Taliban, either in Afghanistan or in its own tribal areas.

Secondly, the Pakistani army is about three-fourths Punjabi and one fourth Pashtun. This means that it will happily kill Baluchs, Mohajirs and Sindhis but that the soldiers have no stomach for fighting Pashtuns. Already, there have been an unprecedented number of desertions from the army.

Thirdly, even if Pakistan did want to impose order on the tribal areas, the reality is that the region is ungovernable and has been semi-autonomous even during the British Raj. And finally, there's the Obama factor. The President-elect has been threatening to get tough with Pakistan and even launch US strikes on its soil.

Faced with this combination of unfavourable circumstances, what could Pakistan do?

Well, here's one scenario. It is no secret that elements in the army and the ISI have links with extremist organisations. Why not urge one of these organisations to strike at the heart of the Indian State? India would react by threatening military action. Pakistan would then claim that it was under threat, would shift troops from the tribal areas to the Indian border and tell America that it was unable to be its ally in the war against terror because its own security was under threat from India. No war would result, of course, because the Americans would not let two nuclear States go to war. But as tensions mounted, Pakistan would say to Washington that the time had come for a more permanent solution to its problems on the eastern border. It could only take the politically unpopular step of acting against the Pashtuns and the Taliban if it could show its people that Pakistan had got something in return. And what would that something be? Well, what about a Kashmir settlement? Why didn't the US appoint a special envoy and force India to negotiate some kind of joint sovereignty? That way, the Pakistani masses would believe that the US had Pakistan's interests at heart and would support a war in the tribal areas. Two things could go wrong with this scenario. One, the Americans could refuse to play ball. In which case Pakistan could sulk and refuse to continue the operation in the tribal areas claiming that its genuine grievances were being ignored. Which suits Pakistan, anyway.

Or, India could refuse to take the bait and would shy away from threatening war—rendering the whole scenario inoperative. If the second happened, Pakistan would claim that India had threatened it anyway. Perhaps a menacing phone call from Pranab Mukherjee could be manufactured. Perhaps there could be so much hype that a war hysteria was created regardless of the absence of provocation.

If you think that this scenario is far-fetched, then consider what's happening today. The operation in the tribal areas has stalled. The Taliban have sworn to back the Pakistan army against India. Troops have been moved to the Indian border. The incoming Obama administration is talking about appointing a special envoy for India and Pakistan.

And forget about acting against those who organised the Bombay attacks. Pakistan isn't even willing to hand over Dawood Ibrahim or Masood Azhar. Moreover, Washington seems largely content with this state of affairs. I don't want to sound like a pessimist or a war-monger—especially since I have always applauded New

Delhi's moderation and restraint—but it is beginning to seem to me that Pakistan has out-manoeuvered both India and America. We won't get cooperation or justice. And we may have to battle American demands for negotiations over Kashmir.

Where does that leave Asif Zardari? Where he always was: a smarmy, crooked irrelevance in a country run by the army.

And where does that leave India–Pakistan relations? Well, where they've always been. In a dangerous place.

And India must confront an enemy it can never trust.■

December 31, 2008

Words are all we have
Brahma Chellaney

ON THE NINTH anniversary of India's Kandahar capitulation, it is evident that its costs continue to multiply. That cave-in set in motion a seemingly inexorable dual process—making India an easy prey for transnational terrorists, and the further softening of the Indian republic. Today, India has the dubious global distinction of suffering the largest number of terrorism-related casualties. Yet, far from waging its own war on terror, it is more interested in collecting evidence on Pakistan's complicity while obsessively craving international sympathy as a victim.

Such a masochist approach raises troubling questions. Are there no limits to India's patience in the face of increasingly provocative transnational terrorism? How much further can India be assaulted and terrorised before it finally concludes enough is enough? Or is it that the more terrorism it suffers, the greater becomes its capacity to absorb strikes? The Parliament attack was supposed to be India's 9/11. Now it is the Mumbai assaults. That is, before a new set of terrorists again expose the Indian leadership's cravenness. Strategically, India's imperative not to brook the latest terrorist assaults but to respond effectively parallels America's post-9/11 attitude. Non-stop live television coverage of the 67-hour strikes has created not only an upsurge of patriotic revulsion and national unity, but also a propitious international setting for Indian counteraction. The providential capture of one *fidayeen* attacker alive helped unravel the Pakistani-scripted plot. Yet, having offshored India's Pakistan policy, the ageing leadership is throwing away a golden opportunity that won't repeat itself. The December 12 Parliament resolution on terrorism thus will go the way the Parliament resolutions of 1962 and 1994 on Chinese and Pakistani territorial aggression did—as mere words. The latest resolution, in any case, is long on rhetoric. The terrorists and their patrons certainly will not be taken in by words that palpably ring hollow by spelling out no action, yet smugly declare India will be 'victorious in its fight against the barbaric menace of terrorism'.

All talk and no action bleeds India. Punitive military action, of course, is at the top rung of the strategic ladder—a daunting choice tied to good timing so that the adversary is taken unawares and snow-blocked Himalayan mountain-passes bar China from opening another front. But Prime Minister Manmohan Singh thus far has not taken the smallest of small steps against the terrorists' haven, Pakistan. By shying away from invoking the mildest diplomatic or economic sanctions as a token expression of India's outrage, he has capped India's response at impotent fury. Instead, Singh bafflingly expects—and indeed urges—the international community to deal 'sternly and effectively with the epicentre of terrorism'.

Israel's heavy response to however small a provocation and India's non-response to frontal attacks on its security and honour make these countries polar-opposites. Still, as the international response to Mumbai and Gaza illustrates, it is the meek that get counselled while the intrepid wage action unhindered. While Atal Bihari Vajpayee took India on a rollercoaster ride with an ever-shifting policy on Pakistan and terror, under Singh the chickens have come home to roost. Vajpayee's blunders—of which Kandahar

276

remains a bleeding shame—have been more than matched by Singh's bungles, including his surprise action on the fifth anniversary of 9/11 in declaring the sponsor of terror, Pakistan, as a victim of terror like India. To consummate that policy somersault, he established a still-existing joint anti-terror mechanism—a case of unforgettable naïveté, akin to the police setting up joint investigations with the mafia. The advent of *fidayeen* attacks happened under Vajpayee. The manner Vajpayee fought the Kargil War—entirely on Indian territory, on the enemy's terms—emboldened the invading State to launch *fidayeen* terrorism no sooner than that conflict had started winding down. Kargil was followed by Kandahar, after which terrorism morphed from hit-and-run strikes to daring assaults on military camps, major religious sites and national emblems of power. But under Singh, suicide attacks have qualitatively escalated to such an extent that India has come under a terrorist siege.

Singh now has a person of his choice in place of the home minister who was eased out as a scapegoat. Singh expects P. Chidambaram to bring down terrorism. The new incumbent has told Parliament: 'We have to take hard decisions.' But so far nothing much has happened. Let's be clear: Had India's leaders not ignored institutionalised policymaking in favour of an ad hoc, personality-driven approach, not repeated the very mistakes of their predecessors and not insisted on learning on the job, the terrorism problem would not have become so acute. In the manner a fish rots from the head down, the rot in India is at the leadership level.

Just the way Pakistan goes through the motions of cracking down on its terror groups, New Delhi responds to each terrorist strike in a perfunctory or mechanical way, without commitment or resolve. And just as Pakistan has a track record of easing up on its terror groups when the spotlight is off, India's leaders go back to business as usual no sooner than a terrorist attack has begun to fade from public attention. While Pakistan is guilty of sponsoring terror, India's leadership is guilty of encouraging terror and making the country an easy prey. Make no mistake: If Pakistan is to dismantle its State-reared terror complex, India's leaders will have to first dismantle their terror-emboldening outlook.■

Courting the devil
Harsh Mander

AS THE FLAMES of war are being fanned in both India and Pakistan, fortunately there are sane voices of restraint against the futility of sacrificing precious young lives in both countries. Also, since military pressure on terrorists operating along the border with Afghanistan would ease as troops engage the Indian armed forces, nothing will be gained in the battle against international terror. There could be heavy civilian casualties, although there is no conflict between the people of the two lands. In times of global economic crisis, the economies on both sides of the border will flounder, inflaming prices, and extinguishing food and jobs.

But this orchestra of war and hate has muffled an important debate which concerns the major defence of the Pakistani establishment, as voiced by President Zardari, to the effect that the State has no responsibility—legal, moral or practical—for the violence perpetrated by what he describes as 'non-State actors'. This means that even if non-State individuals and organisations based in Pakistan plan and execute acts of terror, within its borders or outside, the Pakistan government cannot be held responsible. Arguments like these have enabled these organisations to operate with impunity, given the assurance that they will go unpunished for their transgressions. The issue gets murkier when allegedly non-State organisations implement the illegal, unconstitutional and violent political agendas of the State. Blurring the already thin lines between the State and non-State are elements within the State which openly or tacitly support these organisations—whether logistically, morally or politically.

States must accept responsibility for the crimes of hate and violence perpetrated by non-State organisations. In a salutary ruling following the 2002 Gujarat carnage, the National Human

Rights Commission Chairperson Justice Verma had held that States were vicariously but directly responsible for crimes that organisations outside the State commit, if the State does not do enough to rein in, control and punish them. In practice, however, most communal riots tend to be more in the nature of pogroms, where non-State organisations commit hate crimes with impunity, given a sympathetic political command, police, magistracy and judiciary, which often shares their ideology of hate. States often use non-State actors as their front-line forces, without spilling the more costly blood of their men in uniform. Examples in India are militant renegades, such as the surrendered militants in Kashmir, the *ikwanis*; or in insurgent north-eastern regions, like the surrendered ULFA. Armed by the State, answerable to no law or code, they loot and kill civilian populations in conflict zones without fear of punishment. Vigilante armies like the Salwa Judum have been set up by the state in Chhattisgarh to provide dispensable foot soldiers in the battle against Maoist insurgency. But those who play with fire will one day burn in it, like the Taliban has turned against Pakistan in alliance with extremist religious fringe groups which have miniscule support, but are holding the country to ransom. But this is not a time for war, because a war will only strengthen and embolden the forces of hate and terror and engender enormous human suffering. Instead, it is a time to tell our governments unambiguously that they can no longer protect and foster those who live by the gun, by hate and terror. It is a time to refuse to accept the thin and dishonest defence of government helplessness before the crimes of non-State actors.■

Terrorist
Mahesh Bhatt

AS A TIRED hunter lay sleeping one night, just before the first light of dawn seeped into the sky, he was woken with a start. He peered outside through a crack in the wall and saw a huge beast on the top

279

of a hillock close by. Frightened out of his wits, he reached for his gun
and courageously stepped out to kill the beast before the beast killed
him. As he inched through the mist and the foliage, he discovered that
the beast was after all not a beast, but a wild bear. Uncocking his
gun, he went a bit further, and as the mist cleared some more, he
discovered that it was not a bear after all, but a man. Thinking the
man to be a bandit, he put his finger on the trigger, ready to kill him.
Just then, the morning light hit the man, and he discovered that the
man was not a bandit, but it was his twin brother!

I had barely settled down in my chair in the dimly lit room, which
was chequered with a patch of strong sunlight filtering through a
single window, when two calm looking cops walked in leading a
smallish made young man in his early twenties who was not even
handcuffed. He did not have a beard, nor did he have any scars,
nor did he have a bloodthirsty look in his eyes. In fact he looked
like guy just out of college. Could this man really be a terrorist I
thought? The tall, well built super cop who had arranged for this
informal and unofficial meeting between us and this terrorist,
looked at me and smiled, as if he could read my mind. He had
reason to smile, because I had always disbelieved the police's claims
of nabbing the real culprits of the various bomb blasts which had
ripped our cities apart. He had taken this initiative to dispel our
doubts. He signalled to the boy to sit down. The other two cops
sat down next to the terrorist, maintaining a vigil.

There was a moment of heavy, palpable silence, in which the
eyes of the terrorist met my own. They showed no trace of
remorse. In fact, the being in there, behind those eyes, seemed to
be ready to face the consequences of his actions. There was
something naked in that look. A brief moment of stillness enveloped
the room. A strong current of emotion surged across from him to
me, and me to him, both colliding somewhere in the middle, in
suspended animation. That stillness had more power in it than
anything with motion. And then the sharp sound of a horn blaring
from the Mumbai city traffic below tore through the silence of the
room in a surge of violent sound. As the sound died down, the

super cop turned to the terrorist and said in a low, very calm voice, 'Tell them everything from the very beginning. Tell them why you did what you did.'

A strange brightness shone in his eyes, and a sick smile played about his lips as he began to speak. One could feel at the very onset that he felt he was God's warrior, a young *jihadi* from the group which called itself the Indian Mujahideen. I wondered who had been able to brainwash this gentle looking English speaking, well educated young man, who had a pay cheque which upwardly mobile Indians aspire towards, and a bright future in a multinational media company; into believing that the divine forces themselves had chosen him to implement its terrifying call to militant piety. I realized that these are the people, unlike the lumpen elements who were enlisted by the underworld for a few bucks in the 1993 Mumbai blasts, who have blown up women and children in marketplaces and in local trains, who have gunned down worshippers in mosques, temples and churches, and are highly motivated all over the world. What power compels them to do so?

As I sat and listened to his chilling account, which he almost narrated with nostalgia, step by step, spotlighting the savage attacks against the Muslim community in Gujarat which had prompted him to combat terror with terror, I realized that I was face to face with a defining moment in the history of our time. This surely was the human race collapsing in on itself at the end of a long and slow process of rot which had eaten into its own sores, like a gangrene spreading all over itself. Why did we let it go so far? How did this happen to us? It would be too easy to lay the blame at the feet of a handful of evil men.

But the truth is that the nation had chosen not to look at the birth of this monster born out of despair which in turn festered and turned into anger and hatred, finally growing into an angry beast out of all control. What were we doing when it raised its ugly head in other parts of the country like Assam, Nagaland and Kashmir, and when its leaders chose to look away and deny justice to the victims after the carnage in Gujarat? Nothing. We were like the proverbial man who shuts off the light when there is a poisonous serpent in the room and pretends that it does not exist. Are we not guilty of doing the same?

And that has come back to haunt us.

It is not the misdeeds of a few evil men, but the silence of the millions of very good men which ultimately leads to the disintegration of a civil society. Looking at that boy, I realized that it was inevitable that our land of sages and seers is moving towards its death march and no power can reverse it, unless the saviour within this brutalized heart could be awakened.

When he finished giving us a detailed account of his participation in various bomb blasts, one of the members of the group with me asked him a simple question. 'Do you think the Muslim community whom you are doing all this for, is better off after these attacks, or have you left them more naked and vulnerable than ever, in a nation that is always on the brink, and in which people like us are doing so much to combat in terms of preventing communal violence?' The young man paused and said, 'you have to combat terror with terror. Force is the only way to end tyranny against my people,' he concluded with chilling conviction.

'Yes, I know that it is not in the "love thy neighbour as thyself" creed, but in the realization that if you strike your enemy you too will be destroyed, that there will be enduring peace. But whom have you really succeeded in terrorising after all? Have your bomb blasts hurt those who actually orchestrated the attacks against your community? Or have they given those very people a few more reasons to use against your community, for whom you pretend great love? Because ultimately you only shed the blood of the innocent and not the guilty, and contributed to the grist of the mills of the fundamentalists . . .' I asked him. 'The body count says that you killed children and women and poor men. And in doing so, jeopardized the lives of so many others. Because those were not just numbers. They were lives, and had dreams and others dependent on them . . .' I added, unable to contain the anguish that I felt.

The human heart is after all a mirror. The pain that I felt was for a moment reflected in his eyes, I could see that. For the first time since I was there, I felt that he suddenly looked frail. And then what he said surprised us. 'I was mislead into believing that this was the way to solve the problem. But I was wrong.'

An anguished silence seeped into the room. Then after a while I said, 'I meet a lot of young people and give a lot of talks . . . what is it that I should tell them. What is the message that you would like me to carry to them?' Everybody looked at him then, waiting expectantly for his response. He paused, in a Pinteresque fashion. Then he looked at me with those young, doomed eyes and spoke as if he was pulling out the words from deep within himself. 'Tell them that the path that I took to fight for the cause of the people was wrong. If anybody out there is angry and hurt and has been wronged and he chooses to set it right, he should do it from within the system. That is the only way.'

As I walked out of there, after thanking the super cop for giving me a real taste of the times that we live in, the sound of the *azaan* from the nearby mosque resonated in the air. I was reminded of what a passionate young Muslim cleric had once told me as we waited in the streets of New Delhi for the motorcade of General Pervez Musharraff, the then President of Pakistan, to pass. 'Our Prophet in one of his *Hadith* said *Help your brother, whether he is a victim or a tyrant.*'

'What is that supposed to mean?' I had asked. 'How can you possibly help a tyrant?'

'A tyrant is also your brother; to free him from his tyranny is also the duty of a true believer. That is the only way to bring enduring peace,' he added, interpreting the words of the Prophet.

The answer I guess lies in that. Only in the terrorist's redemption can there be enduring peace.∎

This previously unpublished article was written by Mahesh Bhatt in the immediate aftermath of 26/11.